THE INSTITUTE OF POLITICS PUBLICATIONS
WILLIAMS COLLEGE, WILLIAMSTOWN, MASS.

UNITING EUROPE

UNITING EUROPE

THE TREND OF INTERNATIONAL
COÖPERATION SINCE THE WAR

BY

WILLIAM E. RAPPARD

MEMBER OF THE PERMANENT MANDATES COMMISSION OF THE LEAGUE OF
NATIONS; SWISS DELEGATE TO THE ASSEMBLY OF THE LEAGUE OF
NATIONS; DIRECTOR OF THE POST-GRADUATE INSTITUTE
OF INTERNATIONAL STUDIES; PROFESSOR AT THE
UNIVERSITY OF GENEVA

WITH A PREFACE BY
EDWARD M. HOUSE

NEW HAVEN
PUBLISHED FOR THE INSTITUTE OF POLITICS
BY THE YALE UNIVERSITY PRESS
LONDON · HUMPHREY MILFORD · OXFORD UNIVERSITY PRESS
MCMXXX

PREFACE

At the close of the Great War Paris became the meeting ground for the leaders of all the nations. Each country sought its foremost statesmen, soldiers, scientists, scholars, industrialists, and financiers and called them into active consultation. Never in one small compass has there been such a gathering of the great and near great from the ends of the earth.

Among those representing Switzerland was Professor William E. Rappard, an unassuming scholar of modest mien whose influence was soon felt in the many conferences held and to be held affecting his state. Later his activities took on a wider range, and many questions of post-war reconstruction came within his purview. He had a background which peculiarly fitted him for these tasks, and he brought to the problems given him for solution a rare equipment of long and painstaking scholarly training.

Inevitably, such a man was drafted by the League of Nations to help in the work of bringing order out of chaos and in maintaining world peace. This gave him an unusual opportunity of ascertaining the conditions, the needs and the aspirations of post-war Europe. That he made full use of this opportunity his lectures at Williamstown bear eloquent testimony. These have now been placed in book form as a permanent record, and will be indispensable to those who would know the intimate facts about this period. Being in this position of advantage to ascertain the facts Professor Rappard's exceptional mental equipment enabled him to evaluate their bearing, and his scientific training guarantees an objective presentation.

In the flood of books, good, bad, and indifferent, that have been written of the Great War and its aftermath, *Uniting Europe* ranks among the best. It is of especial concern for Americans as it shows how inextricably our interests are interwoven with those of other nations.

It would seem that Woodrow Wilson's desire to make the world safe for democracy has largely come true, for while not all the victorious nations in the War were republics, yet all the vanquished were monarchies and with but two exceptions these have become republics. If the Central Powers had won, the drift would have been the other way, for it would have been felt that in time of war peril, democracies could not compete in defensive efficiency with autocracies. Professor Rappard shows quite clearly how greatly Woodrow Wilson aided in bringing about the dissolution of the monarchies in both Germany and Austria-Hungary. In Germany it was his differentiation between the war lords and the people themselves. In Austria-Hungary it was the demand for self-determination. Count Andrassy, the last Foreign Minister of the Dual Empire, has said: "The propaganda of Wilson was a more destructive weapon against us than many army corps."

Professor Rappard, who is not only an historian but a philosopher of historic phenomena, believes that the present dictatorships are temporary.

On the economic and industrial side we are told

that three states, Germany, the United Kingdom, and the United States dominate the commercial relations of Europe. Together they supply and absorb a large part of the total imports and exports of Europe.

Professor Rappard is at his best when he studies questions relating to the legal organization of international peace. The weak but law-abiding small states lead all others in the desire for peace. Among the World Powers next in order come Germany and the United States. An examination of recent treaties of guaranty and mutual assistance leads to the conclusion that they are intended to enhance national security not so much by directly diminishing the danger of war as by reducing the chances of defeat in case of war.

There can be found no more valuable epitome of the formation and working of the League of Nations than in this book, "Little by little a technique of voluntary intergovernmental coöperation is being devised and perfected. . . ." American readers will be gratified to learn that "Today . . . no government . . . is taking a more active, a more helpful part in the labors of all conferences, committees and subcommittees summoned to Geneva than the American Government."

While the League endeavors to promote general prosperity and welfare by international coöperation, its main function is and always must be the prevention of war. The list of international disputes handled and for the most part peacefully settled by the League is extremely long. These are given in detail.

After reading this remarkable book no one with

an open mind can doubt that the League is fulfilling the expectations of its sponsors. Already it has grown to be the safety valve of Europe, and its beneficent influence has become as wide as the world itself.

EDWARD M. HOUSE.

New York,
   November 29, 1929.

CONTENTS

PREFACE BY EDWARD M. HOUSE   vii

INTRODUCTION   xiii

PART I. THE STATES OF EUROPE: THE AGENTS OF IN-
  TERNATIONAL COÖPERATION   1

Chapter I. The Post-War Political Evolution of
    Europe   3
    I. The Principle of Self-Determination and the
        Multiplication of Independent States   3
   II. The Spread of Republican Institutions   5
  III. The Crisis of Democracy and the Rise of
        Dictatorships   36
   IV. International Repercussions   48

Chapter II. The Post-War Economic Evolution of
    Europe   56
    I. Population   60
   II. Production   76
  III. Trade   93
   IV. Conclusion   103

PART II. THE METHODS AND RESULTS OF COÖPERATION   105

Chapter III. Coöperation outside the Framework
    of the League of Nations   107
    I. The Execution of the Peace Treaties   112
   II. The Promotion of Prosperity   131
  III. The Promotion of International Security   148

Chapter IV. Coöperation inside the Framework of
    the League of Nations   188
    I. The Changing Structure of the League   188
        1. The Members of the League   189
        2. The Council   196

3. The Assembly   205
4. The Secretariat   211
5. The Advisory Commissions   221
6. The International Labor Organization   223
7. The Permanent Court of International
Justice   224
8. The Seat of the League   229

Chapter V. Coöperation inside the Framework of
the League of Nations (*Concluded*)   245
II. The Changing Activities of the League   245
1. The Execution of the Peace Treaties   247
2. The Promotion of Prosperity and
Welfare   260
3. The Promotion of Peace and Security   272

Conclusion   300

Index   303

INTRODUCTION

THE task set European lecturers at Williamstown is assuredly almost as difficult as it is fascinating. The subjects they are expected to discuss must be of international and of contemporaneous interest. The treatment should be both novel and sound.

Now the number of international topics of contemporaneous interest is necessarily limited. Moreover, most of the world's keenest minds are constantly watching, and many of its most active pens are, from day to day, describing the flow of current events. We are warned, furthermore, that the books and articles thus published are, as soon as available, read and noted by every member of these vigilant and tireless Williamstown audiences. How, under these circumstances, one can be expected to appear original without being purely imaginative, or how one can hope to be truthful without seeming trite, it is truly difficult to conceive.

Four years ago, I was privileged to deliver from this awe-inspiring platform, a series of lectures which, I was pleasantly surprised to learn, were deemed to have fallen not too far below the requirements of our hosts and the standards set by many illustrious predecessors. This good fortune, due to an exceptional circumstance, was quite unmerited.

Having just left the Secretariat of the League of Nations, after more than four years of close cooperation with that remarkable body, I was then in a position to present a picture of the Geneva organization which I was told was novel, and which I still believe was, and is, fundamentally sound.[1] The League of Nations can be, and is, discussed by three types of witnesses. There are first those who, being officially connected with it and therefore intimately acquainted with its inner workings, know, but cannot speak freely. Then there are those, far more numerous, whom nothing—neither their enthusiasm, nor their hostile prejudices, nor any insight into the real facts of the case—limits in the spontaneous expression of their opinion. They speak freely enough, but do not know. Finally, there is a little group of favored individuals who, having been in a position to know, have then been removed to one in which they find themselves free to speak. Four years ago I happened to be a member of this privileged group, and that circumstance alone explains whatever interest my lectures may have aroused. That I deserve no credit for it, is clear from the fact that I am powerless to reproduce the circumstances which accounted for this interest.

To speak at Williamstown once is, for the reasons just stated, inevitably a venture. To speak there twice is obviously to court disaster. And it is doubtless no mere accident that very few should heretofore have been rash enough to attempt it.

That is what I wisely said to myself and irrefutably explained to President Garfield at my fireside in Geneva last January. Having made it quite clear that it was out of the question for me to accept his renewed, highly flattering and alluring, but most ominous invitation, I was led on a few hours later

[1] These lectures were published by the Yale University Press, under the title of *International Relations as Viewed from Geneva* (New Haven, 1925).

to discuss the program of the present course of lectures. Let those who have never been subjected to the subtle charms of President Garfield's diplomacy blame my frailty of purpose, and those who, having never tasted of the delights of Williamstown, have never been exposed to the temptation of reviving its cherished recollections, scorn my weakness. I fully realize that I deserve no mercy, but I feel still more strongly that I badly need it. My plea is, therefore, that all sympathy be not denied a penitent sinner who would be inexorably doomed if he could appeal only to your sense of justice.

The subject President Garfield and I finally agreed that I should attempt to present was "The Trend of International Coöperation in Europe since the War." It might more journalistically and less academically be entitled "Changing Europe."

My purpose is to show in outline the main alterations, political and economic, which the Old World has undergone since the end of the War. That unfortunate continent, viewed from America, must somewhat resemble the country to which, eighty years ago, the Czar Nicholas the First referred as "the sick man." The European patient is certainly the most faithful client of the political clinic of Williamstown. Year after year, one or another of his diseased organs are taken under the microscope of critical analysis and under the knife of intellectual surgery, so that Americans may well be surprised at his persistent survival! It is not my intention to try my hand at a new local operation. Rather would I like to view the recent course of the European malady as a whole, a course which, in spite of more than one disquieting symptom, may, I believe, be correctly described as a slow, irregular, but still a gradual convalescence.

Such a synthetic examination is, of course, not likely to lead to any startling revelations. It may, however, suggest a conception of the evolution of Europe, both sounder for the past and more hopeful for the future than the detailed study of any of its particular ailments.

Europe is a geographical expression, but distinctly not a sociological unit. In spite of its relatively small size and of its very ancient history, its component parts have much less in common than have those of America, or even of Pan-America, if I may be allowed to use the only apparently available term of the American language to include those states of America which Americans from the United States invariably exclude when they speak of America. Not only have the component parts of Europe less in common among themselves than states of this double continent, but many of them have far more in common with America than with the rest of Europe. This is true whether we base our comparison on language, on religion, on law and political institutions, on economic structure, on foreign trade, or even on that subtlest and perhaps most significant of all criteria, the state of mind. To exemplify but the last, I will say that a citizen of Geneva, Switzerland, feels more at home in Williamstown, that is—how shall I put it?—within exhorting, admonishing, rebuking, or frowning distance of Boston, than he would, not only in Dublin or Warsaw, but even in many respects, in Paris.

My point in emphasizing this characteristic of Europe is to justify the method of treatment I pro-

pose to adopt. To study that heterogeneous continent is and can be but to study its component parts
and their international relations. Accordingly, I
propose to devote the first part of these lectures to
an examination of the political and economic evolution of the various European states, and to consider
in the latter their growing coöperation without and
within the framework of the League of Nations.

PART I

THE STATES OF EUROPE: THE AGENTS OF
INTERNATIONAL COÖPERATION

CHAPTER I

THE POST-WAR POLITICAL EVOLUTION OF EUROPE

I

The Principle of Self-Determination and the Multiplication of Independent States.

THE most striking political change that has come over Europe in the course of the last fifteen years is clearly shown by a comparison of pre-war and post-war maps. It is the greatly increased number of sovereign and independent states.

If we disregard such minute principalities and republics as Liechtenstein, Monaco, San Marino, and Andorra, there were twenty-one separate political units in Europe in 1914. Today there are twenty-seven—twenty-eight if we include, as we should for most purposes, the Irish Free State, and thirty if we add the Free City of Danzig and the Saar Basin.

This change, due to the political emancipation of hitherto subject nationalities and to the consequent dismemberment of empires, is particularly significant for one who would study the trend of international coöperation. The progress of civilization in the realm of production, distribution, and consumption of wealth, no less than in that of the arts and sciences, makes for more and closer intercourse between individuals and collectivities. Now if, as has been the case in Europe in the course of the last years, political change apparently runs counter to the progress of civilization, there is bound to be a

clash. It would seem that as a result, one of two
things must happen: either the progress of civilization is impeded, or political evolution is checked.
That general progress has in many ways been retarded through the political decentralization of the
continent of Europe—a continent hardly larger than
the United States and Alaska combined—cannot be
denied. But that it has not been forced back, nor
even completely arrested, is due, among other causes,
to the new development of international relations.

The intensity of these relations, other things being
equal, stands, of course, in direct ratio to the number
of states, and in inverse ratio to their size. This is
admirably shown, for instance, as concerns international trade, by a map inserted in the second volume
of the invaluable *United States Commerce Year
Book* for 1928. The countries of the world are there
presented, covered with red dots and triangles, representing each $100,000,000 worth of exports and
imports respectively. Whereas the plains of Siberia
and the center of Africa are almost immaculate, and
while South America is slightly and the United
States rather heavily besprinkled, the whole continent of Europe is shown as one red blot. This is
due, not, of course, to the superior production of
wealth, but, in spite of a much inferior production,
to a relatively still smaller average size of the national producing units. The smaller the state, the
lesser its economic independence, and the greater its
foreign trade.

Now, as a matter of fact, and as we shall see later,
the multiplication and the consequent shrinking of
states on the continent of Europe have not, as might
have been expected, yet given rise to a correspond-

ingly increased volume of international trade between them.

This is due to the impoverishment of Europe, and
to the morbid and rather pathetic desire for economic self-sufficiency which has inspired European
statesmanship since the War. Nevertheless, the multiplication of states always and everywhere enhances
the importance of international coöperation as a
condition of human progress. In Europe, in spite of
the recrudescence of nationalism, which is one of the
most alarming characteristics of the aftermath of
the Great War, and perhaps the most serious re-
tarding factor, international coöperation has increased to an astonishing extent in the political, if
not yet in the economic field.

II

The Spread of Republican Institutions.

The second great political change that has come
over Europe in the course of the last fifteen years
is the spread of republican institutions.

Of the pre-war European states, three alone—
that is, less than 15 per cent—were republics. Today
thirteen out of twenty-seven—that is, nearly 50 per
cent—have adopted the republican form of government. These figures, striking as they are, give but a
very incomplete idea of the importance of this
change.

If, in 1914, a politically minded inhabitant of
Mars had visited us and indulged in what, to his
amusement, he found called a world tour, he would
undoubtedly have reported back to his home planet

that the inhabitants of this backward globe were of
two types. There were those who inhabited what for
some strange reason they called the Old World, and
who were ruled by kings and emperors. And then
there were those who, in order to escape the domina-
tion of monarchs whom they formerly considered
obnoxious and whom they had since come to look
upon as merely absurd, useless, and expensive,
although picturesque, like most other things of the
Old World, crossed the seas, and having killed off the
native inhabitants of the lands they found beyond,
there established what they called free republics.

If, before setting out on his tour, our visitor had
been so well advised as to undergo the careful
training which is that of graduate students in approved American universities, he would not have
failed to note three slight exceptions to this general
observation. France, he would have remarked, although situated in Europe, called herself a republic.
As her citizens, however, seemed rather fond of titles
and decorations, as the best dressed and the most
distinguished looking among them proudly called
themselves royalists, and as the others were always
quarreling over who was to be the head of what they
called the Third Republic (the third in a little over
a century), he would have refrained from attaching
too great an importance to this exception. Portugal
was not a large country, and her kings, having been
led to spend several years in America some time
earlier, had probably, he would have concluded,
become infected with foreign republican notions.
As for Switzerland, our intelligent guest would
readily have understood that no throne could safely
be set up in a country so small and so mountainous,

whose inhabitants were, furthermore, too rough and
too ill bred to make possible courtiers.

Having thus satisfactorily disposed of these three
slight exceptions, the visitor from Mars would, in
1914, have been confirmed in his view that Europe
was as monarchical as America was republican. If, on
his return home, anyone had doubted the validity and
the significance of this brilliant generalization, he
would have quoted to his fellow Martians several
pages from the original Monroe Doctrine, to which,
during his travels in Europe as well as in America,
he had often heard allusions made, and which, having
been a graduate student at an approved university,
he had actually read. The mere mention of this famous Doctrine would doubtless, even on the planet
Mars, have sufficed to silence all opposition and to
suppress all further discussion.

In the brief space of fifteen years, Europe has become Americanized in this, as in no other respect,
which is saying a great deal. Not only, as we have
noted, are nearly half the states of Europe organized
as republics, even if we count neither Hungary nor
the Irish Free State as such; not only are more than
three-fifths of all Europeans citizens of republics,
but the form of more or less absolute monarchical
government which was characteristic of central,
eastern, and southern Europe before the War, has
absolutely disappeared. Dictatorships have arisen,
as we shall see presently, in the remaining monarchies as well as in the new republics, but in no
case except in Albania and Yugoslavia is the monarch the dictator, and neither of these *régimes* in any
way resembles pre-war Kaiserism or Czarism.

Why this great change? What is its true signifi-

cance? What we may call the republicanization of
Europe during and since the War, is, of course, much
more than a mere sequence. It is in most cases a
direct effect, and in the others a somewhat less immediate, but still a certain result of the great con-
flagration.

Let us briefly consider first the well-known facts,
and then their very obvious explanation. There are
today ten, and there were a year ago, before the
proclamation of the new kingdom of Albania, eleven
more republics than in 1914. Of these eleven, nine
emerged from the tomb of the three defunct empires
of Germany, Austria-Hungary, and Russia. In the
two others, Albania and Greece, monarchs had abdicated or had been deposed since 1914. Albania had
been abandoned by her prince in 1914 and overrun
during the War. Greece, although nominally victorious in 1918 in spite of her king who had abdicated,
was, under the already badly shaken rule of his second son, decisively beaten by Turkey in 1923 and
adopted a republican constitution in 1924. Furthermore, in semi-European Turkey, the republic was
established by a victorious general who had re-
trieved the defeat of the deposed Sultan.

The mere recital of these facts suggests the nature
of their principal cause.

Although not all the victors of the Great War
were republics, all the vanquished were monarchies,
and all, with but two exceptions, became republics.
Moreover, the two exceptions—Hungary, a kingdom
without a king, and Bulgaria, whose monarch barely
saved his crown by transmitting it to his son in the
presence of an almost triumphant republican government in October, 1918—tend to confirm the rule more

than to disprove it. The new republics of Europe were as clearly the children of defeat as the French Republic had been fifty years before. As in 1870 and 1871, so in 1914 and 1918: a war, largely dynastic in its origin, proved the downfall of the monarchs whose prestige it had been undertaken to enhance or to defend. In all the eleven cases mentioned, the military factor suffices, surely, to explain the undoing of the established monarchs.

Does it alone also explain the rise of the republics?[1] If we consider, as we obviously must, military defeat to have been the mother of these new republics, we have still to ask ourselves who the father was. In other words, what was the constructive principle that animated the peoples and their statesmen when they set out to substitute a new form of government for that which they had discarded under the stress of invasion and revolution?

Prima facie, it is clear that the principle was not in all cases the same. In Petrograd and Berlin and to a large extent in Vienna and Budapest, the Russian, German, and Austro-Hungarian monarchies were overthrown because they were monarchies. In Prague, Warsaw, and Helsingfors, and in the Baltic

[1] In his remarkable lectures on *The Republican Tradition in Europe* (London, 1911), p. 278, Mr. H. A. L. Fisher, one of the most liberal of British publicists, writing three years before the War, noted "the decline of republican feeling in Europe" and added: "It is now a very general belief that the cause of European peace is assisted by the social and family ties which subsist between the monarchs of Europe." In so far as Mr. Fisher was right in thus establishing or recognizing a connection between the pacific and the monarchical ideals prevailing in pre-war Europe, it is clear that the outbreak of the War in itself, must have tended to promote the spread of republicanism.

capitals they were overthrown because they were Austrian, German, and Russian. The revolts and the antagonisms which caused the downfall of the old *régimes,* were everywhere somewhat different, but the result was apparently everywhere the same, a result absolutely contrary to the dominant traditions of Europe. It is surprising that a political phenomenon, at once so general and so strange, should not have been more discriminatingly investigated and more widely discussed.

It cannot be our task here to inquire into the detailed circumstances which led to the triumph of the republican idea in each of the eleven European states where it prevailed during or after the War. It is worth while, however, to mention each case separately, and briefly to examine the most important.

Historically, the first of the European monarchies to turn republican during the War was Russia. Everything pertaining to that tragic event, which it is impossible even to date with precision, is extraordinary. In no European country was there less of anything resembling a republican tradition than in the Empire of the Czars. In none of the European revolutions was the establishment of the republic less expressly demanded by those who guided its course, than in that which led to the abdication of Nicholas II. Not only were the majority of those to whom it fell to govern Russia on the morrow of this abdication confirmed and professed monarchists, but even the leading members of the Petrograd Soviet, who represented the radical revolutionary element surrounding the cradle of the new state, did no more than to disparage "all acts defining in ad-

vance the form of the future Russian government.'"[2]
And in no country, at no time, was there such a con-
sensus of opinion as in the early spring of 1917 in
Russia that the monarch must go. The workmen in
the factories, the peasants on the land, the soldiers
at the front, felt it no more keenly than the *bourgeoisie*, the most conservative member of the most conservative Fourth Duma, the generals in command of
the armies, and indeed, almost all the members of the
royal family.

On March 12, 1917, the revolution breaks out in
Petrograd. A provisional government is formed by
the Duma in unofficial session. On March 15, Nicholas
II abdicates in favor of his brother, the Grand Duke
Michael, who at the urgent request of the majority
of the royalist Provisional Government on March 16,
follows suit by signing this curious document:[3]

Inspired, in common with the whole people, by the belief
that the welfare of our country must be set above everything else, I have taken the firm decision to assume the
supreme power only if and when our great people, having
elected by universal suffrage a Constituent Assembly to determine the form of government and lay down the fundamental law of the new Russian State, invest me with such
power.

Calling upon them the blessing of God, I therefore request all the citizens of the Russian Empire to submit to
the Provisional Government, established and invested with
full authority by the Duma, until such time as the Constituent Assembly, elected within the shortest possible time
by universal, direct, equal, and secret suffrage, shall mani-

[2] Alexander F. Kerensky, *The Catastrophe* (New York, 1927),
p. 24.
[3] *Ibid.,* p. 71.

fest the will of the people by deciding upon the new form
of government.

(Signed) MICHAEL ALEXANDROVITCH

Petrograd, March 16, 1917.

The Constituent Assembly, to which reference is
here made, was elected only at the close of the year,
after Lenin had already established his dictatorship. It met in January, 1918. As the "will of the
people," manifested "by universal, direct, equal,
and secret suffrage" proved to be that of so-called
"class enemies of the workers and peasants," the
Assembly was promptly dissolved.

In the meanwhile, there is no doubt that Russia
had become a republic, but when and how it is impossible to assert with assurance. Professor Graham
in his excellent work on *New Governments of
Eastern Europe,*[4] noting that the Manifesto of the
Provisional Government to the People of Russia, of
March 19, 1917, was addressed "to the people as
citizens and not as subjects," concludes that "by
implication the monarchical *régime* was discarded"
from the first.[5]

But Sir George Buchanan tells us[6] that on his referring to Russia as a republic later on, Miliukov,
then Minister of Foreign Affairs, had caught him
up "saying that it was only a Provisional Government pending the decision of the future Constituent
Assembly." On the other hand, Mr. Miliukov himself, comparing the Russian with the French Revo-

[4] London, 1928.

[5] Graham, *op. cit.*, pp. 41, 571.

[6] Sir George Buchanan, *My Mission to Russia and Other
Diplomatic Memories*. 2 vols. (Boston, 1923), II, 71.

lution in his book on *Russia's Collapse,* published in 1925,[7] writes:

There was no fight for or against the monarchy. The Czar had immediately abdicated, and his successor refused to ascend the throne before the decision of the Constituent Assembly. . . . Those political groups which were professedly royalists, remained silent and took no part in the movement. All parties including the Conservatives, who were active in the political arena, had in reality or only formally, become republican.

In any case, Kerensky felt it advisable formally to proclaim the republic on September 14, 1917, after the crushing of the Kornilov revolt.[8]

If ever in the course of history, individual and even collective will was here annihilated by the crushing force of overpowering circumstances. This is well shown by one who might, more than most, have laid claim to a directing part in the establishment of the new *régime.* In an extraordinary page of his almost autobiographical book, *The Catastrophe,* Alexander Kerensky writes of these first revolutionary days:

It was an extraordinary time, an inspired time, a time of bold daring and great suffering. It was a time unique in the pages of history. All the small daily preoccupations of private life and all party interests vanished from our consciousness. One common devotion and anxiety united us. We had one common inspiration—Russia! Russia in peril, struggling through blood and chaos, Russia betrayed by the old regime, Russia a prey to the blind, raging, hungry mob.

[7] Paul Miliukov, *Russlands Zusammenbruch* (Berlin, 1925), I, 26.

[8] Graham, *op. cit.,* pp. 68, 590.

Between these two gulfs—on the one hand the decaying, tottering government and, on the other, the anarchic sweep of the people in revolt—a new light appeared. Russia became conscious of a new purpose, a new will. Inside the old walls of the Tauride Palace this devotion to the state and the nation burst forth in clear form, expressed in a tremendous effort and determination to save the country from anarchy and to shape the life of the people along new lines of law, freedom and social justice.

Representatives of nearly all classes rallied around the Duma in those first days of the Revolution. In those first days of the Revolution the Duma became the symbol of the state and the nation. By a determined, united effort a new authority and the rudiments of a new national structure were set up. I saw new forms of government shaped by men who the day before would have turned in horror from what they did that day with their own hands. They did it because something inexplicable, mysterious, miraculous had happened—that which we are accustomed to call revolution. This something lit up the souls of men with a purifying fire and filled them with love and readiness for boundless self-sacrifice.

We forgot everything that was merely personal, all that was a matter of class or caste, and became for the moment simply men conscious of our common humanity. It was a moment when every man came into touch with what is universal and eternally human. It was most exhilarating to see about me these men, so transformed, working together with sublime devotion for the common good. Historians, sociologists and theorists of all kinds will describe learnedly and wisely the events of March 12, 1917, in Russia, in Petrograd, in the Tauride Palace. They will find scientific, historical (and very prosaic) explanations to account for the performance of every actor in the first scene of this great tragedy of death and rebirth. They may label the drama and the actors in any way they please, but they will have said nothing that is essential if they forget to say that

the Revolution was a miracle, an act of creation performed
by the will of humanity, an epic sweep towards the eternal
and universal ideal.

A few pages further on, Kerensky, who in the
Provisional Government represented the tendency
most opposed to that of Miliukov, also emphasizes
the fact that the revolution was not the work of any
one party or class, but of the whole people:[9]

It was not physical force, still less the organized force of
the revolutionary democracy or of any party, which over-
threw the autocracy and the dynasty. The revolutionary
democracy appeared as an organized force only when the
first stage of the Revolution was over. This is an indispu-
table fact which history will establish beyond contradiction.

I assert emphatically that no one class can claim to be
the author of the great Russian Revolution, nor arrogate
to itself alone the honor of bringing about that upheaval.
The Russian proletariat (especially the proletariat of Petrograd) is peculiarly unjustified in making this claim. On
March eleventh, the day before the crash, the so-called Information Bureau of the Parties of the Left (i.e., the
Social-Revolutionaries, Social-Democrats, Bolsheviks, Popu-
list-Socialists and Labor party) held its regular meeting
between 6 and 7 p. m. in my apartment. At that meeting
men who a few days later became the most uncompromising
revolutionaries asserted emphatically that the revolutionary movement was losing strength; that the workers
were quite passive in their attitude towards the demonstrations of the soldiers; that these demonstrations were
unorganized and without purpose or direction; that it was
impossible to look for a revolution of any kind in the near
future, and that we should concentrate our efforts on propaganda alone as a means of preparing a serious revolu-

[9] Kerensky, *op. cit.*, p. 6.

tionary movement later on. Such was the attitude and the opinion of the spokesmen of the most extreme revolutionary elements only the day before the outbreak of the Revolution.

This first triumph of the republican idea in Europe after 1914 was significant much less as a result, than as a precedent. It showed the goal to which absolutism necessarily tends sooner or later when it is oppressive, incompetent, and corrupt and to which it leads very soon in war when it is unsuccessful on the battlefield. But as this first Russian Republic of 1917 was without a foreign model, and indeed without a national or any other constitution, so it was without any immediate contagious influence abroad.

As we shall see presently, the gale which a year and a half later was to uproot the two other imperial thrones in Berlin and Vienna, was to blow not from the East, but from across the seas to the West —not from Petrograd but from Washington. The colors under which the republican idea was to triumph in Berlin and Vienna, as well as in all the minor capitals, were not the red flag of Moscow, but the Stars and Stripes of America.

The story of this victory, in so far as Germany is concerned, is clearly, although unwittingly told by Prince Max von Baden, the last Imperial Chancellor, in his *Memoirs*.[10]

[10] Prinz Max von Baden, *Erinnerungen und Dokumente* (Stuttgart, 1927). The emergence of the German Republic can be clearly and most instructively studied, thanks to the very numerous autobiographical publications of the principal actors on the political stage. Of these the most enlightening are, perhaps, besides the above: General Erich Ludendorff, *Meine Kriegserinnerungen* (Berlin, 1919); Friedrich von Payer, *Von Beth-*

Toward the end of August, 1918, when it became clear that the tide had turned definitely against the Central Powers, Prince Max wrote to Emperor William II, to offer his services as head of a new government. Prince Max, who was himself the heir presumptive to the crown of the Grand Duchy of Baden, was not what in other times and places would have been called a liberal statesman. He declares in his *Memoirs* that he was then still opposed to the establishment of a parliamentary *régime,* that is, of a truly constitutional monarchy.[11] But he was a South German and not a Prussian, and at home as well as abroad, enjoyed the reputation of being free from reactionary and narrowly nationalistic prejudices. In his aforementioned letter to the Kaiser, he wrote:

The appointment of a new government would hardly bring peace; but it would make the war easier for Germany and more difficult for her enemies. . . . This is the last chance for the monarchical idea in the world. In the East it has already miserably collapsed, and in the democracies of the West, all possibilities have long ago disappeared for the free decisions of a leading personality. . . . That is not so in Germany. The monarchical tradition is still so well entrenched in popular opinion that a saving act of the Emperor would be gratefully welcomed by the people.[12]

mann-Holweg bis Ebert (Frankfort-on-Main, 1923); Philipp Scheidemann, *Der Zusammenbruch* (Berlin, 1919); Admiral von Tirpitz, *Erinnerungen* (Leipzig, 1919). A good and clear popular account in English, with an excellent bibliography of the subject, is H. J. Daniels, *The Rise of the German Republic* (London, 1927).

[11] Max von Baden, *op. cit.,* p. 298, ". . .das parlementarische Regime, dem ich gerade vorbeugen wollte."

[12] *Ibid.,* p. 315.

The Kaiser replied in a friendly tone on September 11, 1918, but declared that the time was not yet ripe for a new government. Shortly afterward, however, Austria and Bulgaria began to sue for peace, and on September 29, the decisive panic took place in the German military headquarters. General Ludendorff decided that an armistice had become necessary, and Prince Max was called upon to head the government that was to engage in the negotiations with Washington on the basis of President Wilson's Fourteen Points.

Even before the final draft of the note of October 3, 1918, which was six weeks later to lead to the signing of the Armistice, had been agreed upon, it was generally realized in Berlin that it might cost Emperor William II his crown. The Kaiser himself had, in private conversation, asked what would happen if President Wilson were, in reply to the note, to demand his abdication. Max Warburg, who was looked upon as a specialist on American affairs, had immediately declared: "Wilson . . . will demand a German Republic."[13] The new chancellor was so worried about this danger that, after allowing the first German note to be sent to Washington, and before receiving a reply, he submitted his scruples to the judgment of colleagues at a cabinet meeting. Scheidemann, who represented the majority of Socialists in Prince Max's Cabinet, declared that the situation was serious, especially in the city of Berlin, but added, "I take it that we will never be confronted with such a demand." Erzberger, the Catholic leader, opposed this optimistic view, but held that the establishment of a republic would imply the dis-

[13] Max von Baden, *op. cit.*, p. 344.

memberment of Germany, the southern states being strictly monarchical (*streng monarchisch*). Prince Max, not content with these declarations, thereupon turning to Scheidemann, whose loyalty to the Crown was the least certain, asked, "What would be the attitude of the German people if Washington pressed for the establishment of a republic as a condition prior to the conclusion of peace?" Scheidemann replied, "If we were confronted with the alternative 'War or down with the Hohenzollerns,' the people would choose peace even at this price. Personally," he added, "I shall oppose this view, and we may be successful, because such an insolent (*unverschämt*) demand would doubtless be accompanied by other demands still more insolent."

After recalling this discussion in his *Memoirs*, Prince Max adds:

None of the parties represented in my cabinet would have proposed abdication if Wilson had not deliberately carried the fight about the person of the Emperor into Germany. At this time, the only suggestions of abdication came from the extreme Right and from some convinced monarchists on the Left, such as Max Weber and Naumann, who particularly resented the idea that the Emperor of Germany should have asked President Wilson for an Armistice.[14]

It cannot be my purpose here to pursue the demonstration of a fact as certain as it is generally admitted. At the end of October, 1918, after four years of unsuccessful war, Germany was still overwhelmingly monarchical. But the seed of republicanism, sown and then carefully nurtured by President Wilson in

[14] *Ibid.*, pp. 376 *et seq.*

his successive notes, was to bring about a decisive change. It is not easy exactly to date this change, but it unmistakably took place between this moment and July 31, 1919, when the republican constitution of Weimar was adopted by a majority of 362 votes against 75. The National Constituent Assembly had been elected on January 19, 1919, by over thirty million German citizens, on the basis of free, secret, universal suffrage. The above majority is larger than the total number of Majority Socialist, Center, and Democratic deputies would account for, and it does not include the score of Independent Socialists, who voted with the Nationalist party, not because they shared the latter's monarchical views, but because they were in favor of a more radical republic. There can therefore be no doubt that, even when relieved of the immediate pressure of the enemy on the frontiers, the German people had clearly shown their preference for the republic.

A profound change in public opinion thus took place between October, 1918 and July, 1919; that this change was due primarily not to defeat only, but also to the persistent propaganda of the Wilsonian gospel, may be clearly shown by the recital of the following few additional facts.

On October 9, 1918, the first note of the State Department was received in Berlin. To the query it contained as to who was in effect responsible for Germany's policy, Prince Max could, on October 14, truthfully reply that his government enjoyed the confidence of the Reichstag, that is, of the German people. Writing privately to his cousin, the Grand Duke of Baden, on the following day, Prince Max declared:

I still hope to save the Kaiser and the Hohenzollerns.
. . . For Baden there is only one hope of salvation. The
Crown must seek to rest firmly upon the people. Our old
institutions have not failed us. But the general catastrophe
will in Baden as elsewhere, expose the Crown to a terrible
danger. The old belief in authority is gone.

The second American note, received in Berlin on
October 16, in which all the emphasis is placed on
the dualism of the German people and their arbitrary rulers, increased the tension. At a cabinet
meeting held on the same day, Minister Haussmann,
reporting on the state of public opinion, declared
that Wilson's note had produced the effect of a bomb-
shell. All of Berlin was discussing the question of
the Kaiser. Haussmann added: "We should carefully ask ourselves whether Wilson demands abdication, or would be content with a constitutional
monarchy."[15] Scheidemann believed the latter. The
German reply of October 21, avoiding the question
of the Crown, sought to explain and justify the
democratic evolution which had bridged over the
differences between the Government and the people.
For Ludendorff, who proposed to resume offensive
operations on the front, the note was too weak. But
for the parties of the extreme Left, it was too evasive
of the main issue. At the Reichstag, on October 23,
Haase, the leader of the Independent Socialists, up
till then an almost negligible party, defiantly declared: "All further shedding of blood is pointless.
All around us republics are being established, and
crowns are rolling on the pavement. . . . And you
wish Germany alone, surrounded by republics, to

[15] Max von Baden, *op. cit.*, p. 415.

maintain a crown-wearer, or the wearers of many crowns and crownlets?''

Even the Majority Socialists, who in spite of their theoretically professed republicanism, were at bottom almost unanimously in favor of saving the monarchy, began to see that the Kaiser would have to go, were he to save his dynasty.

Wilson's third note of October 23, with its final allusions to "military rulers and monarchical autocrats," led to Ludendorff's dismissal on October 26 and to the adoption two days later of a constitutional amendment establishing the principle of parliamentary responsibility. Before the German reply was sent, Emperor Charles of Austria had informed his German ally that he was obliged to sue for a separate peace, adding: "Internal order and the monarchical principle are exposed to the gravest danger if we do not succeed in ending the War immediately."[16]

By now even Prince Max had recognized the necessity of obtaining the abdication of him whose throne he could no longer hope otherwise to save. He sent written suggestions and various emissaries to the Kaiser, but could not, as heir to a crown himself, bring himself personally to urge His Majesty to make this supreme sacrifice. But William II, relying on the loyalty of the Army, remained deaf to all advice and to all warnings.

Soon, however, it became doubtful whether even an abdication could save the throne. On November 2, the German ambassador in Vienna, reporting on the revolution which had there swept away the throne, mentioned the possibility of an Austro-Ger-

[16] Max von Baden, *op. cit.,* p. 508.

man union; but, he added, the *Anschluss* movement
was checked by international considerations. "It
was believed," he wrote, "that German Austria
would be in a better position for the peace negotiations if it gave itself a form of government which
corresponded to President Wilson's ideas.[17]

In spite of all this pressure from without, and of
these ·innumerable indications as to the inevitable
course of events, not only did the Kaiser refuse to
act, but even German public opinion still hesitated
to do more than to demand a change of sovereign.
Ebert himself, the future chancellor and president,
although a convinced republican, would still on
November 7, have accepted the second son of the
Emperor as regent, pending the meeting of a national assembly. David, another moderate socialist,
when asked at this date about the summoning of
such an assembly, declared:

Elections would at present seriously embarrass our party.
As professed republicans, we should have to work for a republic. But most of us would prefer a democratic monarchy. If Germany were to become a republic, we should
be in the awkward position of having to face a monarchical opposition.[18]

Even on the following day when angry mobs in the
streets of Berlin were already demanding the abdication of the Emperor, and when Prince Max, unable
to obtain it under the threat of the majority of the

[17] *Ibid.*, p. 563.
[18] *Ibid.*, p. 600. The picture of the socialist state of mind as
presented by Scheidemann, it is true, is not quite the same as
that drawn by Prince Max, but it is not essentially different.
Cf. Scheidemann, *Der Zusammenbruch* (Berlin, 1921), pp. 197 *et
seq.*

Socialist party, had sent in his resignation as chancellor, Landsberg, one of the leaders of the latter party, officially made the following most significant declaration:

We do not dream of introducing the republic. Although republicans, we are above all democrats, and as such we refuse to impose the opinion of a minority on the majority of the German people.[19]

It was only after the Emperor had learned of the abdication of other German sovereigns, after he had been convinced at general headquarters of the Army's refusal to follow him to Berlin as he had proposed, and after the socialist Ebert had succeeded Prince Max to the chancellorship on November 9, that, having abdicated as head of the Empire but not as King of Prussia, he finally fled ingloriously over the Dutch border—it was only then that the end of the German monarchy became apparent.

Bismarck had once remarked that if a later German generation ever became republican, it would be "not for lack of royalists, but for lack of kings."[20] Such was truly to be the case. It was the flight of kings that caused the panic among their countless followers. The belief in the divine right of the sovereign—a mystical faith in a rationalistic age and country—could not survive the naked fact that, in an hour of extreme national peril, the Hohenzollern family relied on motor cars rather than on Providence for the safety of their lives, if not of their crowns.

[19] Max von Baden, *op. cit.*, p. 619.
[20] Quoted by W. Mommsen, *Wie die deutsche Republik geboren wurde* in A. Erkelenz, *Zehn Jahre deutsche Republik* (Berlin, 1928).

It was thus that under the pressure of a crushing defeat and only in the hope of escaping its most cruel consequences, the disillusioned German people reluctantly entered upon their republican destiny. President Wilson, disavowed by his own nation, was recognized as the foremost leader of opinion by another when on January 19, 1919, the German people elected a national assembly whose majority, as we have seen, was pledged to enact a republican constitution.

There is not, I believe, in the history of the world, another example of successful international propaganda on such a scale. Of course, such propaganda would have been impossible in times of peace or in the event of a German victory. But war and defeat alone do not suffice to explain the downfall of the German monarchy. Resting on the traditions of centuries and on the instinctive conviction of an almost unanimous people, it had withstood many wars and several defeats when it fell suddenly at the close of 1918 under the blows of an eloquence strange to German ears. How, under these circumstances, the last German Emperor has found it possible to declare in his most recent book that the Revolution of 1848 was ultimately responsible for the downfall of the Prussian monarchy in 1918 can be explained only, as most of his other stupendous errors, by his unbelievable imperviousness to fact.[21]

In September, 1919, several months after the Weimar Constitution had been put into operation, there appeared in Germany a book of *Memoirs*. Not

[21] William II, *Meine Vorfahren* (Berlin, 1929), "Die Märztage von 1848 pflanzten den Todeskeim für die preussische Monarchie."

remarkable either in form or in substance, it was read perhaps more widely than any other, because it bore the signature of the greatest of those faithful servants of the Kaiser and of the Fatherland whose loyalty to the latter had not been shaken by the disappearance of the former. At the end of this book the author, having recalled the monarchical confession of faith of the Prussian minister of war of 1811, adds:

At present, a deluge of wild political passion and resounding phrases has swept away all our former political conceptions, and apparently destroyed all our sacred traditions. But this deluge will not last forever. Then, out of the ever-moving sea of national life, will again emerge the rock to which the hopes of our fathers had once clung, and on which the future of our country was founded, thanks to our might, nearly half a century ago! *das deutsche Kaisertum!*[22]

Some years later Field Marshal Hindenburg who in these words proclaimed his undying faith in the German monarchy, indissolubly bound up with his hopes for the German future, was elected President of the German Republic. Could anything more forcibly show the strange nature of this German Republic, or more clearly attest its foreign origin?

The same impression was borne in upon me some months ago when, coming out of the lane of Prussian kings in the Tiergarten in Berlin and strolling about in front of the Reichstag amongst the statues of former German generals, I suddenly noticed that the square around the Siegessäule was now called "Platz der Republik." It was as if an American

[22] General Feld Marschall von Hindenburg, *Aus Meinem Leben* (Leipzig, 1927), p. 405.

should hear the White House referred to as "The Imperial Castle"!

These remarks are not intended to convey any doubts about the future of the German Republic, but merely to explain its origin. In view of its stormy birth, which would certainly not have been possible without the forceps of foreign inflence, it is, on the contrary, surprising to note its present apparent health and strength. All the Germans whom I have consulted on the subject, including many inconsolable and impenitent royalists, are of the opinion that the republic has come to stay, if not forever, at least for a long time. The simultaneous breakdown, without exception, of Germany's pluralistic monarchy in Berlin and in all the provincial capitals, the ignominious disappearance and, curiously enough, also the rapid remarriage of William II, the lack of popularity of his son, and the absence of any other likely pretender—such are the main reasons usually given for the sudden and decided conversion of the German people to republican democracy.

Russia and Prussia had been, ever since the Napoleonic era, the two main columns of the temple of monarchical absolutism in Europe. When they collapsed, it was clear to all that the religion itself was doomed. That it could find no lasting protection in Vienna was especially obvious. The Austro-Hungarian throne, already in 1914 the least stable of the three great imperial thrones in Europe, was also the one which subsequent events had done most to shake.

More immediately responsible for the War than either the Romanovs or the Hohenzollerns, less certain of the loyalty of large bodies of their subjects, more directly challenged by the battle cry of "self-determination" which Washington kept dinning in their ears and in those of their peoples, the Hapsburgs could not hope to survive their younger and more powerful imperial colleagues.

The Emperor Charles, keenly conscious of all that threatened his historic throne, forfeited the confidence of his last supporters in trying *in extremis,* to save it. Austria-Hungary had professedly attacked Serbia in 1914 in order to preserve her own territorial integrity and to combat the disaffection of her southern Slav subjects. Ever since the beginning of the War, the Czech and Slovak cousins of the latter had begun to conspire for their independence. Only the fear of Russia and repeated promises of Polish autonomy had prevented the Poles of Galicia from following their example. When, in tardy deference to the principle of self-determination, the Emperor Charles, on October 16, 1918, proclaimed his intention of federalizing his whole empire, he thereby menaced the rule and lost the confidence of his most faithful Hungarian subjects. And when it became obvious that he was seeking to make peace without his German ally, his most faithful Austrian subjects likewise forsook him.

On October 31, 1918, Count Karolyi, although not yet at the time by conviction a republican, and although formally called into office by his king, in fact found himself at the head of the revolutionary government of an independent Hungarian republic.[23] Already on the day before, a provisional national assembly in Vienna had proclaimed the republic in

[23] M. Karolyi, *Gegen eine ganze Welt* (Munich, 1924), pp. 465 *et seq.,* 498 *et seq.*

Austria, although Emperor Charles withheld his expected abdication until November 11.

The revolution which overtook the Hapsburgs under the pressure of foreign invasion and of domestic famine had a twofold character. It was both national and republican, but it was preëminently national and only accidentally republican. This, as we shall see presently, was obviously so in Prague. It was less obviously but none the less certainly so also in Budapest and in Vienna. The Magyars, who had always been overwhelmingly royalistic, accepted the republic only when they realized that the policy of the Crown was tending to sacrifice their national interests to those of their Slovak and Rumanian subjects. And the German-Austrian *bourgeoisie,* once they felt their privileged position in the Empire gone forever, submitted to the republic that was being set up by the working classes, only when they saw that Germany herself was becoming republican. As long as the republic appeared as an obstacle to the *Anschluss* they were, for national as well as for traditional reasons, monarchical. As soon, however, as the republican idea, ceasing to be a screen, became a link between Vienna and Berlin, they accepted it for national reasons and in spite of their royalist traditions.[24]

The Wilsonian origin of the Austrian and Hungarian republics is less manifest, because less immediate, than that of the German. But it is not less certain. The doctrine of self-determination could not but disrupt the archaic empire of the Hapsburgs, and the Emperor, fully conscious thereof, could not

[24] On this interesting point see, for instance, Otto Bauer, *Die oesterreichische Revolution* (Vienna, 1923), p. 102 *et passim.*

and did not survive the dissolution of his empire. As Count Julius Andrassy, the Hungarian statesman, who was the last foreign minister of the Dual Monarchy, writes in his war memoirs:

. . . The propaganda of Wilson was a more destructive weapon against us than many army corps. . . . It was not difficult to anticipate that, if we determined to reorganize the monarchy upon a new basis at the time of our defeat, the monarchy would inevitably collapse.[25]

In this rapid survey of the rise of republicanism in post-war Europe, the Austro-Hungarian revolution forms the natural transition from the Russian and German experiences, which we have outlined above, to those of the new states of Europe, about which we shall say a word in closing this section.

That the status of Poland, partitioned among three of the belligerents, should change as a result of the World War, was probable from the outset. That the ancient kingdom of Bohemia might rise again from its grave had been the dream of Czech patriots ever since 1914 and before. That Finland, Esthonia, Latvia, and Lithuania would regain some form of autonomy or even of independence, seemed probable from the time of the two Russian revolutions of 1917. But that any of these countries would come to be sovereign republics as the result of the War was even to their own national patriots an unexpected development.

Nations once free who have lost but hope to regain their freedom naturally feed their hopes on their past traditions. Now none of these six peoples

[25] Count J. Andrassy, *Diplomacy and the War* (London, 1921) pp. 251, 255.

had any republican traditions whatever. It is therefore not surprising that, while aspiring to national
resurrection as an ideal, they should not in the least
have draped their dreams in republican garb.

President Masaryk of Czechoslovakia tells us in
his memoirs that at the beginning of the War, his
fellow countrymen were overwhelmingly monarchical. Most of those who strove for national freedom
hoped to see a Russian grand duke on the throne of
their liberated country. Masaryk, although himself
a republican by personal conviction, would have preferred a candidate from one of the ruling houses of
western Europe.[26] Even after the Russian revolution had shattered the confidence of Czechoslovakian
patriots in the Romanov dynasty, and until the very
end of the War, the prevailing sentiment in Bohemia remained monarchical. Although Masaryk and
Benes, the former somewhat under American and
the latter more under French influence, were active
in favor of the republican ideal, which was also officially that of the Czech socialists, Doctor Kramar
and General Stefanik, the two other leaders of the
national movement, were, with the bulk of the people,
royalistically inclined. As late as October, 1918,
there was talk in Prague of the Duke of Connaught
or of some Russian or Italian candidate for the
newly-to-be-erected throne. The republican principle was agreed upon only at Geneva on October 31,
1918, and publicly proclaimed in Prague on November 5, 1918.[27] The desire to win the confidence of the

[26] T. G. Masaryk, *Die Weltrevolution* (Berlin, 1925), pp. 14,
15.

[27] *Ibid.*, pp. 139, 411 *et seq.* See also Ed. Benes, *Souvenirs de
Guerre et de Révolution* (Paris, 1929), II, 393 *et seq.*

United States and of France, who in the eyes of the
Czech patriots were the major allies, seems to have
turned the scales against the monarchy.

As for Poland, from 1914 until 1918, about all possible forms of government except the republic
seemed to have been considered, not only in Petrograd, Berlin, and Vienna, but even in Warsaw. According to strategical fluctuations, the Czar, a Russian grand duke, the Emperor of Austria, the King
of Prussia, or some other Austrian or German or
even Polish prince seemed to be the most favored
candidate to the throne of Poland, whose frontiers
were naturally as uncertain as her political destiny.
When Russia, Austria, and Germany had all in turn
succumbed to revolution and defeat, Poland found
herself not only free, but almost automatically a
republic. Not only was she emancipated from her
former masters, but all the various candidates to
the throne as well as all the prominent Poles who
had coöperated with them to the end, were definitely
out of the running.

On October 22, 1918, Josef Swierzynski, a former
member of the Russian Duma who had never despaired of the Allied cause nor associated himself
with the temporary German and Austrian victors,
set up a cabinet. He excluded therefrom all so-
called "activists," that is, those who, under the protection of the Central Powers, had been active in
favor of some monarchical solution. Swierzynski
furthermore promised as soon as possible to summon a constitutional diet to be elected by equal, direct, secret, universal, and proportional suffrage.
Thus, equally opposed to the conflicting influences
of eastern bolshevism and to western reactionary

monarchism, he favored a middle course which could
but head toward a democratic republic. That goal
was to be reached ultimately, but neither under
Swierzynski's leadership nor along the paths he had
proposed.

On November 7, 1918, Daszynski, a socialist leader
from Galicia, set up at Lublin a so-called People's
Republic. But shortly both he and Swierzynski gave
way to Pilsudski, another Galician socialist who, at
the beginning of the War, had formed a Polish legion
under Austrian protection, but whom the Germans,
suspicious of his intentions, had interned in July,
1917. Long before any constitution was adopted,
freed from the fortress of Magdeburg and returning
to Warsaw as a popular hero, he had been welcomed
as Chief of State, and as such had called upon Ignace
Paderewski to form the first Polish ministry.

All parties of Polish patriots, more interested in
securing their country's political existence and in
favorably impressing the Allies, on whose good will
so much depended, than in framing a constitution,
rallied around this first ministry. On December 20,
1918, a declaration signed by the Supreme People's
Council of Posen, and by no less than thirteen Polish political parties, was addressed through the
Polish National Committee in Paris to the governments of all the Allied states.[28]

This declaration contains no mention of the form
of government which Poland then intended to adopt,
but only the somewhat grandiloquent statement of
her territorial ambitions. The fact, although hardly

[28] This declaration as well as much other relevant material is
reprinted in Graham's *Governments of Eastern Europe,* pp. 773
et seq.

surprising, given the nature of the document and its date, is still characteristic of the renascent, romantic, and nationalistic Polish people. That this people was destined finally to submit to a republican form of government seemed very probable, inasmuch as no foreign sovereign could be tolerated and as no national candidate was available. But there was certainly no enthusiasm for the republican ideal, nor any haste to adopt a republican constitution.

The authors of the provisional law of February 20, 1919, stressing the rights and the duties of the so-called Chief of State, recognizing the Diet as "the sovereign power and the supreme legislative authority of the Polish State," refrained from defining this state. Such a definition is to be found only in the constitution finally adopted on March 17, 1921, whose Article I reads: "The Polish State is a Republic."

Considering as a whole the course of events which led to the adoption of this constitution and which followed, one cannot escape the impression that the republic in Poland is a negative rather than a positive *régime*. Poland today is a state without a king, but ruled and governed by a man more truly powerful than any of the surviving kings of Europe.

The evolution of Finland and of the other three Baltic states, although different in many details, is at bottom essentially the same.

The first Russian revolution created a movement in favor of national autonomy, if not of national independence, under free institutions. The triumph of bolshevism in Petrograd led to violent struggles in what were fast tending to become the four border states. Under the German occupation which followed and which put down the local soviets and the Red Guards, the influence of the conservative and reactionary elements of the populations was strengthened. Monarchical ideas prevailed and German princes were invited to occupy the various thrones. With the downfall of Germany, several of whose princes, including the Kaiser himself, had shown great interest and indeed mutual jealousy over these thrones in the course of 1918, the republic appeared as the only truly national and democratic solution, and was promptly adopted as such.

Thus the new Europe became republican. Under no possible interpretation of history can this post-war emergence of republican institutions be explained by the triumph of the republican ideal. Nowhere was any widespread enthusiasm for the political sovereignty of the people to be found, such as preceded and accompanied the genesis of the American and of the French republics in the eighteenth and nineteenth centuries. Military reverses, the material and moral consequences of war and defeat for the vanquished, the natural desire of radical change thus engendered, and the hopes of national resurrection raised among the subject peoples, combined with a widespread contempt for the incompetence and weakness of the crowned rulers and the absence of any monarchical ambitions among the new leaders —such are the foundations on which the new republics of Europe were built.

Except in Russia where a *sui generis* constitution was set up as the indirect result of a spontaneous national revolution, the models adopted for the new constitutions were as foreign to the people who adopted them as was the general inspiration of the republican movement as a whole. The inspiration was essentially American, and the constitutional models preëminently French, with some American and some Swiss additions and modifications.

It is not our intention to study the new European constitutions, which have been very thoroughly and ably analyzed by many authors.[29] Our purpose was merely to stress the extent and the nature of the republicanization of Europe which as a political phenomenon does not seem to have attracted the attention it deserves, and to outline the general historical circumstances which led up to it. The significance and the probable consequences of this phenomenon for the future of international coöperation, we shall have occasion to consider below.

III

The Crisis of Democracy and the Rise of Dictatorships.

After the multiplication of independent states and the spread of republican institutions, the third and last political fact to which we wish to call attention is the so-called crisis of democracy and the rise of dictatorships in Europe.

This last fact, by far the most spectacular, has given rise to the most comments, although it may well be doubted whether it is at bottom as far-

[29] For instance, by Professor Graham in his two above-mentioned volumes on *New Governments in Western and Central Europe;* by Professors Delpech and Laferrière in their new editions of Dareste's *Constitutions modernes;* by Professor Mirkine-Guetzevitch in his *Constitutions de l'Europe nouvelle.*

reaching and as fertile in lasting consequences as is sometimes assumed.

It may at first glance seem surprising that one should be led to speak of the crisis of democracy in post-war Europe, when and where we have just noted the spread of republican institutions. But there is, of course, no necessary contradiction between the two. As President Masaryk has written:

There may be, and there often is a fundamental difference between a republic and a democracy—the republic is the form, the democracy is the substance. The form, the written constitution, does not always guarantee the substance.[30]

As a matter of fact, if by a democracy we mean a *régime* in which the people, that is, the majority have their way politically—and that is since the times of Herodotus a generally accepted definition—there are today no more democratic governments than the British or Belgian monarchies. And on the other hand, there are and always have been oligarchical, aristocratic, and even dictatorial republics.

Furthermore, if we examine contemporaneous Europe a little more closely than do those publicists who point to the rise of dictatorships as the crucial symptom of the crisis of democracy, we will be bound to make another distinction. That there are dictatorships in contemporaneous Europe is an undoubted fact. And that democracy is undergoing a crisis, in Europe as elsewhere, no one will deny. Indeed, no one has admitted it more candidly or shown it more clearly than that great apostle of democracy who spoke from this platform in 1921,

[30] T. G. Masaryk, *op. cit.*, p. 510.

Lord Bryce. But to declare that the European dictatorships are symptoms of this crisis is to assume
that democracy prevailed yesterday where they
triumph today, an assumption as groundless as it is
fallacious.

In those parts of Europe where democracies can
be said fairly to have been established, i.e., Great
Britain, France, Belgium, Switzerland, Holland, and
the Scandinavian countries, not only are there no
dictatorships, but dictatorships would be as unlikely
and as unwelcome as, say, effective prohibition in
New York or militant atheism in Tennessee.

On the other hand, if we examine the countries in
which political liberties have been suspended or
suppressed, we shall be led to certain quite definite
conclusions.

Before doing so, we may be allowed to state explicitly that we are not in the least actuated by the
desire to make a case for or against any given form
of political organization. We shall, on the contrary,
rely only on the evidence of obviously undeniable
facts. And we trust that in dealing with this highly
delicate subject, we may avoid offending any national susceptibilities.

The countries in which more or less full-fledged
dictatorships have been set up in Europe since the
War, and in which they prevail today are, setting
them in their geographical order from west to east:
Portugal, Spain, Italy, Yugoslavia, Albania, Hungary, Poland, Lithuania, and the Soviet Union.

The first conclusion to be drawn from this enumeration is a negative one. Dictatorships can clearly
not be correlated either with geographical position,
population, area, newness of statehood, or with any

particular form of constitutional government. Of the nine states under dictatorships, some are large and some are small. Some are densely and others sparsely populated. Two dictatorships prevail in countries whose frontiers were not changed since the War, at least four in states which may be said to have retained their former political identity, five in monarchies, and four in republics.

In all nine cases, however, dictatorships can be correlated directly or indirectly with war and its social, financial, and political consequences. The problems of government in post-war Europe are infinitely more varied and more difficult than they were in pre-war days, when the traditional constitutional theories and practices had been adopted and worked out. It was because in some countries these theories and practices, as applied by the available personnel, appeared ill adapted to the solution of the new problems, that dictatorships arose. This is so well known that it needs no further elaboration.

Furthermore, dictatorships are very clearly correlated also, and this has not to my knowledge ever been pointed out before, with the economic structure of the countries involved.

If we arrange the states of Europe in the order of relative importance of the proportion of the gainfully employed population which is engaged in agriculture, we shall have the following table:[31]

[31] These figures are taken from the *United States Commerce Yearbook*, 1928, Vol. II, Foreign Countries, and from *Die Wirtschaft des Auslandes* 1920-1927, Bearbeitet im Statistischen Reichsamt (Berlin, 1928).

Order	Country	Per cent
1	U.S.S.R.	82.4
2	Bulgaria	82.4
3	Yugoslavia	ca. 80.
4	Rumania	79.5
5	Lithuania	76.8
6	Poland	75.9
7	Spain	ca. 70.
8	Greece	70.
9	Finland	68.9
10	Ireland	ca. 63.
11	Latvia	61.
12	Esthonia	59.
13	Hungary	58.2
14	Portugal	57.5
15	Italy	56.1
16	France	41.5
17	Czechoslovakia	40.3
18	Sweden	38.7
19	Luxemburg	37.8
20	Norway	36.8
21	Denmark	34.8
22	Germany	30.5
23	Switzerland	25.9
24	Netherlands	23.6
25	Belgium	19.1
26	Great Britain	7.1

Statisticians will be unanimous in questioning these figures, as to their absolute accuracy and as to their international comparability. No one will deny, however, that they are more than sufficiently reliable in both of these respects fully to justify the statement that dictatorships have been established in Europe since the War only in countries still predominantly agricultural. The omission of Albania from the above table, due to the entire absence of any even approximate statistics, does certainly not weaken or limit the scope of this generalization. That interesting but very backward country is probably the most strictly agricultural state in Europe.

How is the above table to be interpreted? Surely not to the effect that agriculture is the economic synonym for political dictatorship. Nothing would warrant, and the figures shown would disprove rather than confirm, such a simple conclusion. But they do point to a certain correlation between the two terms. The true inference is less that peasants love tyranny and favor dictators, than that political liberty may by and large be considered to be essentially a product of urban life and of all that city-dwelling implies, in terms of social instability and in possibilities of individual enlightenment and of collective organization.

If the chief aim of government is to maintain public order, while allowing the greatest possible measure of individual freedom compatible with it, there is bound to be everywhere a certain conflict between order and freedom. Now, in this conflict of ideals it may, I believe, be held that, in Europe at least, the ideal of order is more stressed in the country and that of freedom in the city. That is shown, for instance, by the fact that rural populations are more often and more generally conservative than urban communities. On the other hand, history teaches that a large measure of political freedom is compatible with the reign of order only at a given stage of social evolution, which is rarely attained under predominantly agricultural conditions. European dictatorships have as a rule been

established in rural countries which, having bor-
rowed political and parliamentary institutions from
their more advanced industrial neighbors, found
them ill adapted to their post-war needs. As it was
obviously impossible, and perhaps not deemed desirable to hasten the course of social evolution so as to
adapt the state of the people to the exigencies of
liberal institutions, national interest demanded that
the institutions be adapted to the state of the people.
This involved the necessity of a political reaction
which is hardly conceivable except under dictatorial
conditions.

Such is, as I see it, the general explanation of the
rise of all the new European dictatorships except
one. Whether established by former socialists as in
Italy and Poland, by military men as in Spain and
Portugal, or by leading rulers and statesmen as in
Hungary, Yugoslavia, Albania, and Lithuania, in
spite of all the considerable local differences, these
dictatorships have much in common. Their professed aim is always the protection of national
interests and the promotion of national ambitions
declared to be threatened by internal disorder,
license, incompetence, political dishonesty, as well as
by external hostility. And their methods, the substitution of executive decision for parliamentary discussion, are always more or less frankly and drastically
illiberal and undemocratic. The general tendency of
all these dictatorships is reactionary, in that they
tend to suppress or limit the rights and liberties of
the people, which it has been the boast of the last 150
years to proclaim and establish. But they may also
lay claim to being progressive, and they may even
justify that claim in so far as they succeed in actually

enhancing the efficiency of government and thereby improving at least the material conditions of life in their respective countries.

Although the Russian dictatorship presents in its spirit and methods many curious analogies with those established in other parts of Europe, it is in essence in a class by itself. Its program is social, not national; its tendencies revolutionary, not reactionary; its aim not the maintenance and establishment of political order, but the creation of a new social order. Therefore, in contrast to the other dictatorships, it is supported by the towns and not by the country. However, as all dictatorships, that of the proletariat would be difficult to conceive in an advanced urban community. There the number, culture, and influence would be too great of those who, valuing individual freedom above all other civic goods, were prepared and able to defend their rights against even the most masterful, the most ruthless, or the most patriotic autocrat.

Political cynics have often pointed, not without satisfaction, to the fact that one of the most important results of a war professedly waged to make the world safe for democracy, has been to suppress democracy and to favor the establishment of dictatorships. At the risk of differing with political cynics and of spoiling their self-complacency—always a doubly perilous undertaking—I must, as already indicated above, point out that this is a fallacy. What the War has destroyed is not democracy, neither its spirit and its ideals which have on the contrary been strengthened, nor its institutions, there where they really functioned. What the War has done away with in several countries, whose economic and social structure was not yet such that the people could be ripe for the responsibilities of democracy, is a superficial appearance and a popular delusion. And the present dictatorships may well be a blessing in disguise for democracy itself, both in dispelling from within the confusion which the nineteenth century undoubtedly created between true democracy and pseudo-democratic institutions, and in challenging the former from without. It is only if democracy should fail to meet this challenge that its doom would be sealed.

This the future alone can decide, but can be relied on to decide conclusively. It is obvious that, in this competitive world, the law of the survival of the fittest applies as well to political forms as to biological species.

Although it may seem idle, it is always tempting and sometimes suggestive to speculate about the future. For my part, I cannot but look upon the present European dictatorships as most interesting, as perhaps wholesome and necessary, but always as essentially temporary phenomena. My main reasons for this view are twofold.

In the first place, permanent dictatorship implies either an immortal dictator or an infallible method of choosing his successor. Now dictators, although usually young on assuming power, are not immortal. They are, in fact, for obvious reasons, rather less so than ordinary mortals.

On the other hand, the problem of succession has never been satisfactorily solved, even by the most brilliant dictators of history. The hereditary principle could perpetuate a dictatorship only if it could be relied upon to bestow upon the sons of dictators both the very exceptional personal gifts and the very extraordinary political circumstances, thanks to the combination of which their fathers were able to create their own position. Such an achievement could not be expected except by the intervention of Providence. And it is not at a time when Europe, as we have seen, has unanimously dismissed all its former kings by divine right, that it is likely to bow to the authority of dictators by divine right.

The choice of successors by their predecessors, or by bodies set up by the latter, is not more promising. It is a noticeable fact that even the strongest dictators, in fact especially the strongest, seldom tolerate strong personalities about them. This being so, and as admittedly it takes an uncommonly strong personality to be a successful dictator, it is difficult to conceive how he is by dictatorial choice to be selected.

If finally the people are to select their own dictator—a method to which none of the present incumbents owe their position—the result would in fact be a democratic republic and certainly not anything resembling the *régime* we are discussing. Nations may at certain crises in their development, need dictators. They hardly ever desire them.That is why even those autocrats who most insistently claim that they faithfully represent their peoples' real preference, are careful never to expose their authority to the test of a free and sincere popular election.

Besides this internal and technical reason which leads me to doubt the possibilities of permanent dictatorships in the modern world, there is another historic reason which as I see it is of a more general and more decisive nature still.

It is surely not an accident that, as we have noted, the dictatorships of Europe should all have been established in predominantly rural and agricultural countries. Now the world in general and Europe in particular are from generation to generation, and almost from year to year, becoming less rural and less agricultural. With the growth of urban civilization and all that it brings with it in the way of progressive public instruction, developed critical faculties, enhanced love of freedom, and intolerance of intolerance, the areas on which dictatorships can flourish seem destined to become narrower and narrower. Except during temporary crises such as wars and revolutions or threats of war and revolution, when even the most enlightened and most independent recognize and submit to the necessity of authoritarian leadership and of political restrictions, democracy in Europe will, I believe, definitely and generally triumph over dictatorship.

This view implies neither satisfaction with democratic government as at present constituted, nor blindness to the dangers to which it is exposed and to which it may give rise. These dangers I see far less in the assaults of dictatorships from without, than in the internal difficulties of legislation and administration. The complications of government, both domestic and international, are, with the progress of wealth, of economic technique, and of non-political organization, increasing at a rate that is truly alarming. In the race between the art of statesmanship on the one hand, and the social forces which the state is called upon to control on the other, the latter often seem to outstrip the former. While voters, parties, parliaments, and governments are debating such matters as the budget, the tariff, national defense, and state insurance, society is being revolutionized by factors much more important and quite beyond the control of voters, parties, parliaments, and governments. New technical discoveries and inventions are being made; new tastes and fashions are springing up; new secret and often international agreements are being concluded between politically irresponsible financiers and industrialists, which, by changing the course of trade and modifying the price level, by creating unemployment here, and by accumulating wealth there, affect the well-being of the individual and the future of the race much more vitally than any decisions governments may make.

That, as I see it, is the real reason for what is often alluded to as the crisis of democracy even in the most advanced countries and those least threatened by dictatorships. Doubtless the state has never been, and can never be entirely supreme. Attempts brutally to subject all manifestations of social activity to its rule, such as the world has witnessed in the Soviet Union since 1918, must either fail of their purpose, or result in general ruin. But as the power of man over nature is increasing on a constantly shrinking, ever more densely populated globe, social control is becoming more necessary, and social control through the state more difficult.

The problems thus arising are not peculiar to one continent alone. But they are particularly acute in Europe, on account of the density of its population— a density roughly twice as great as that of Asia and ten times as great as that of America—and on account of the multiplicity of its so-called sovereign and independent states. That is also why, in Europe, international coöperation, which is but one form of political control of social forces, is exceptionally important for the well-being of its peoples and for the peace of the world.

IV

International Repercussions.

Before examining this coöperation as it has been developing since the war, and before casting a glance at the changing economic structure of the continent whose recent political evolution we have sought to characterize, let us briefly consider the international repercussions of this evolution.

We have already noted the main consequences of the emancipation of formerly subject nationalities and of the multiplication of independent political entities to which this emancipation has given rise. We have seen that as the number of sovereign states increases on a given territory, and as the population grows, the importance of coöperation between them is inevitably enhanced.

The obvious truth of this generalization has been clearly illustrated by recent developments in Europe. In no period of the known history of this continent have there been so many conferences, agreements, conventions, and treaties intended to regulate the international relations of its constituent parts, as there have been in the brief space of the last ten years. This change has been so striking that, even if we knew nothing of the other causes to which it is to be attributed, we could not explain it merely by the constitution of seven or eight new states. The

fact is that the World War directly and indirectly
created many new wants and needs which cannot be
satisfied except by international coöperation. Some
of them, such as the adjustments called for by new
frontiers, are doubtless of a temporary character.
Most of them, however, being the result of a more
keenly felt solidarity, are more likely to prove permanent. The fear of a renewal of war and the
desire to combat its possible causes by pacific agreement have raised to the international plane many
problems which were formerly considered to be of
purely domestic concern.

The most important political problem of this
nature is that of the treatment of racial and linguistic minorities. This may appear surprising in view
of the reduction in the numbers of minority populations which has resulted from the resurrection, as
independent nations, of nationalities which had for
centuries been deprived of their political freedom.
This resurrection itself, the internationalization of
the problem, was essentially due to the triumph of
the principle of self-determination, which was
America's greatest contribution to the ideals for
which the World War was fought and won. This
principle, while explaining the political resurrection
of the Poles, the Czechs, the Finns, and all the other
suppressed peoples, triumphed so completely that
where it was not or could not be strictly applied in
the drafting of the post-war frontiers of Europe, it
gave rise to new international guaranties; and these
in turn have given rise to new occasions for international discussion and coöperation.

Thus the first of the three great changes we have
noted—the multiplication of sovereign states—has

intensified and widened the scope of the internationalization of Europe. The two other changes—the rise of republicanism and the emergence of dictatorships—have contributed to modify its methods.

Before proceeding to make any further observations on this interesting but very difficult topic, it is well to be reminded of some general considerations.

The domestic *régime* of a state is, of course, but one of the various factors that determine its foreign policy. Internal political conditions are usually of less importance in international relations than geographical position, demographical evolution, historical traditions, and economic development. As the philosophically minded historian has no experimental laboratory at his disposal in which he could, by processes of isolation, study the effects of each of the several causes of the phenomena he is considering, his conclusions will necessarily be tentative, and somewhat conjectural.

When he seeks to assess the influence on European international affairs of the spread of republican institutions and of the rise of dictatorships, his statements cannot therefore be dogmatic without being fraudulent. As he would be no less guilty were he purely imaginative, the best he can hope is to be cautiously plausible and sanely suggestive.

Trusting that I may be inspired by these remarks, which I believe to be as sound as they are undoubtedly trite, I would venture the following impressions, based both on the psychology of republicanism and of dictatorship, and on the appearances of recent European history.

The autocrat, especially if he must rely for his

authority on his popularity with the most active, restless, and articulate of his followers, is apt to appeal constantly, insistently, and passionately to national pride. His foreign policy is therefore apt to be nationalistic and dynamic in spirit. Whether he will it or not, it is also always in danger of becoming bellicose because nothing so violently stirs up the sentiment of nationality and so effectively silences the murmurings and criticism of internal opposition as the prospect of war, unless it be the reality of war.

As for his methods, the autocrat will naturally prefer to deal with foreign powers one by one rather than to meet them collectively, and he will prefer secret negotiations to "open covenants openly arrived at." Why? Because an autocrat naturally desires and often needs sudden and spectacular triumphs, and naturally loathes and often fears long-drawn-out public discussions, necessarily ending in compromise and mutual concession. Secret negotiations with individual powers, especially if they be weaker, may give rise to real diplomatic victories. When truly successful, such negotiations may with impunity be heralded abroad as masterpieces of Machiavellian skill if no time is lost over final signatures and ratification. And powerful autocrats may both practice themselves and impose on their partners great expedition in these matters. When only partly successful, such negotiations may be presented as minor triumphs and when unsuccessful, entirely hushed up.

None of these possibilities exist when a considerable number of national delegations meet around a table to settle important matters of general interest.

Multilateral negotiations, never secret and prover-
bially slow, cannot give rise to dramatic national
victories. If in the course of the debate, one of the
negotiating parties is so fortunate as to secure more
than its due share of concessions, it must be very
discreet about its successes for fear of preventing
ratification by the other parties and thereby de-
priving itself of the fruits of its diplomatic victory.

It would be possible further to elaborate these
statements and easy to cite several instances in recent European history, particularly Italian, Span-
ish, and Russian, to illustrate them. I have said
enough, however, to show the very strong natural
ties which associate internal absolutism with the
traditional spirit and methods of the so-called old
diplomacy. This spirit and these methods were those
of monarchical absolutism from the end of the
Middle Ages; they were those of Louis XIV and of
Frederick the Great as well as of almost all the pre-
war chancellories of Europe, and especially of Berlin, Vienna, and St. Petersburg. With appreciably
less elegant patience and somewhat more boastful
oratory they have been adopted and practiced by the
plebeian dictators of Europe, as they had been for
centuries before by their dynastic predecessors. This
spirit and these methods are, of course, the very
opposite of that new diplomacy which, although not
created by the World War, has been much more
freely practiced since than before, not only at
Geneva, but also at Washington, Locarno, and
Havana, for instance. Here the aim was general, not
merely national interest, and the method, public
discussion and compromise, not secret intrigue and
bullying.

"But," one may object, "granting that there is some slight causal relation between political absolutism and the old diplomacy, granting that autocracy—monarchical or dictatorial—prefers clandestine to open diplomacy as a means, and spectacular victory to undramatic compromise as an end, is that not equally true of democracy? Are elected presidents or parliamentary prime and foreign ministers not at least equally dependent on their popularity for their political existence, and therefore equally tempted in their general policy to subordinate foreign to domestic affairs, and in their foreign policy, the common welfare of mankind to the national pride and interest of their respective constituencies?"

No one who has carefully studied the history of democracy, no one who has been in a position closely to observe its workings in the field of international affairs, can deny that there is much truth in the views underlying this query. And still, I believe that there is an appreciable difference between democracy and autocracy in this respect.

The constituency of a democratic leader is the people as a whole. It is not, as that of past monarchs, the army and the bureaucracy, not, as that of most modern dictators, a group of particularly restless and noisy patriots. What the people as a whole, that is, those who respond to the roll call of universal suffrage and their representatives, demand of their chiefs in the conduct of foreign affairs is not so much national prestige and glory as international security and welfare. In every parliament the extreme Right, where dictators usually find their most ardent, if not always their earliest supporters, is confronted with and usually outnumbered by moderate, progressive, and radical parties, which are almost everywhere less nationalistically inclined. Furthermore, the democratic leader is apt to be much less his own master than is an autocrat, in point of historic fact as well as by definition. Being dependent on the support of many others, and often of a great variety of others, he is both less tempted and less able to resort to secrecy, and more attracted by methods which permit of a continuous appeal to public opinion. He is, of course, not systematically averse to discreet negotiations and to bilateral agreements, nor always reluctant to indulge in intrigue and bluff. On the whole, however, he often finds the methods of the new, that is, of open, public, and multilateral diplomacy better suited to his own political tastes and interests than the autocrat.

Whatever the truth or error of these somewhat abstract considerations, whose only purpose is to explain the correlation between internal and external policy, one thing is certain: such a correlation is undeniable in the recent experience of Europe. The statesmen who have most persistently and most successfully practiced the new diplomacy, whether it be within or without the framework of the League of Nations, have, without a single exception, been representatives of democratic states. Such names as the following prove it more convincingly than the most thorough, scientific demonstration: Léon Bourgeois, Herriot, Briand, MacDonald, Cecil, Balfour, Chamberlain, Stresemann, Hymans, Vandervelde, Benes, Branting, Nansen, Motta.

And on the other hand, the aloofness from the public councils of the world of the new European dictators, and often their undisguised hostility to the new spirit and to the new methods of international intercourse, may well serve as a counterproof. It is surely not a mere coincidence, to quote but one example, that the only two European states which—although members of the Council of the League of Nations—have never been represented thereon by their prime or foreign ministers, are Italy and Spain.

We have seen above that perhaps the most significant incident in the recent political history of Europe has been the unprecedented spread of republican institutions. Although all the new republics are constitutionally based on the principle of popular sovereignty as expressed by universal, free, and secret suffrage, they are not all in fact democracies. It is certain, however, that taken as a whole they are far more liberal than the autocratic empires from which they sprang. And it is at least probable that, even where subjected to dictatorships upon whose rule we cannot look as permanent, they offer far more scope for the future development of democracy.

We may conclude, therefore, that in so far as the trend of international coöperation in Europe is influenced by internal political developments, it tends toward greater and more active intimacy between an increased number of sovereign states, and toward more openness, publicity, and universality in an atmosphere of wider republican freedom.

CHAPTER II

THE POST-WAR ECONOMIC EVOLUTION
OF EUROPE

In this chapter we shall attempt a rapid survey of
the recent economic evolution of Europe. Before
doing so, it may be well to recall that our general
concern is with the trend of international coöperation. By international coöperation we mean coöperation between nations represented by their respective
governments. So defined, our subject is essentially
political. Why then have we been led to insert a
special chapter on economic matters in a general
exposition of political interest?

It might be said that as man is not merely a
political animal, and as nations therefore are not
merely political herds, a study of international co-
operation is necessarily more than an inquiry into
political zoölogy. We shall not invoke any such considerations to justify what at first glance may seem
to be a digression from our main road. If we did, we
should for consistency's sake, have to trespass on all
the other fields of international coöperation. If we
claim as we do, that it would be irrelevant to our
main purpose to stray along the paths of literature,
art, philosophy, and science on each of which we
should meet instances of coöperation between individuals of different nationalities, while not irrelevant to touch on economic matters, it is on other
grounds.

Here international coöperation is not only individual. It is collective. Moreover, the economic fac-

tor has often so visibly and so decisively determined
political evolution that in order to understand the
trend of the latter, it is essential not to disregard
the former. As M. Theunis, the former Prime Minister of Belgium, who presided over the World Economic Conference with such exceptional distinction,
has said:

Economic conflicts and divergence of economic interest
are perhaps the most serious and the most permanent of all
the dangers which are likely to threaten the peace of the
world. No machinery for the settlement of international
disputes can be relied upon to maintain peace if the economic policies of the world so develop as to create not only
deep divergencies of economic interest between different
masses of the world's population, but a sense of intolerable
injury and injustice. No task is more urgent or more vital
than that of securing agreement on certain principles of
policy which are necessary in the interests of future peace.
And there is perhaps no question which, in comparison with
its intrinsic importance, has had so little careful and collective deliberation.[1]

International coöperation, as we have defined it,
while political in its agents and its methods, is
largely economic in its motives and in its results.
That is why we feel impelled to cast a glance at the
economic evolution of Europe since the War. Our
survey, however, will necessarily be hasty. We cannot attempt even to outline this most eventful evolution, nor to summarize the very numerous documents
published by the World Economic Conference of
1927, as Professor Patterson has so ably done in the
Annals of the American Academy of Political and

[1] Quoted by Sir Arthur Salter, *The Problems of Peace* (3d
series; London, 1929), p. 93.

Social Science.[2] Nor especially can we claim to have analyzed and digested all the enormous mass of material, some of it of exceptional value, which has been published in ever increasing quantities in the course of the last ten years. This rising tide of documentary material and of monographic studies is in itself as significant as it is embarrassingly overwhelming.

It is significant, as a symptom both of the uneasiness, restlessness, and novelty, which have characterized the economic situation in Europe in the last decade, and of the more and more persistent and systematic effort on the part of official and semi-official agencies to master its intricacies by dint of economic inquiry.

But it is embarrassingly overwhelming also, because it has led to a very real overproduction. Statistical and economic articles, memoranda, and reports of all kinds are published in order that they may be read, or at least consulted, by the authors of further monographs, and by others who would find therein detailed information concerning the state and progress of a given industry in a given province of a given country. But they should be, and often are, intended also for the instruction of those whose task it is to formulate general policies based on a synthetic conception of the economic situation as a whole. Now, unfortunately, the size of the human brain, at least in Europe, and the duration of human life, even in Europe, are not nearly as expansive as the budgets of governments, chambers of commerce, and other bodies who finance economic investigation.

[2] E. M. Patterson, *Europe in 1927, An Economic Survey* (Philadelphia, 1927).

An immediate and inevitable consequence is that the consumers of such literature cannot keep up with its producers, who, being for the most part salaried officials, are never checked by what economists call the effective demand of the market. The ultimate outcome, besides the protests of the tax-paying community who in the last analysis have to bear the burden of these operations, the indifference of the publishers who are wise enough to assume no risks whatever in connection with them, and the joy of the stockholders of paper concerns, who are the real beneficiaries thereof, is unfortunately much waste effort, at least for the present generation. Perhaps our children, profiting by the sins of their parents, will reap, in rich harvests of economic syntheses, the benefits of the statistical wild oats we are sowing today. But if wise sons make glad fathers, prodigal fathers have no reason to be glad before their sons' wisdom becomes profitable.

These remarks are, however, only partly pertinent here. My present purpose, as I have implied above, is very modest. Although it would no doubt be well served if I could already profit by the useful generalizations of the next generation, the available predigested material is sufficient to suggest a clear answer to the three very plain questions I shall ask.

Formulated in their simplest terms, which we shall somewhat elaborate as we attempt to answer them, these questions are the following:

First, are there more or fewer human beings in Europe today than before the War? Secondly, are they producing more or less food and other economic goods? Thirdly and finally, is there more or less international trade between them?

It is accordingly under the three headings of population, production, and trade that I shall seek to state certain fundamental facts of the recent economic history of Europe, and to show their bearing on the trend of international coöperation.

I

Population.

There is in all languages, as far as I am aware, an extremely irreverent saying about statistics and their relation to truth. I shall refrain from quoting it here. I would observe, however, that in order to present with assurance and without scruples, any social and economic statistics to a public audience, the first condition a lecturer must fulfill is absolute, blind ignorance. What strikes me most about statistics is not that they are boldly and wilfully mendacious, as—may I say?—a politician, but rather that they are delightfully and unwittingly deceptive as— if the ladies will permit—a woman. I am referring, of course, only to degenerate and cynical Old World politicians, and to charmingly frivolous Old World women. Most statistics are deceptive mainly because they are not comparable either to themselves or to other statistics.

This remark may seem strangely uncalled for and out of place at the beginning of a demographic study. Of all social statistics, those dealing with population, birth and death rates, and so on, are surely the simplest and therefore the most comparable and the least deceptive. That is undoubtedly true, but even here we cannot be too cautious. Thus, while compiling figures relating to the population of Europe from the most approved sources, such as the publications of the Office Permanent de l'Institut de Statistique and the *International Statistical Year Book* of the Economic and Financial Section of the League of Nations, I was struck by their irreconcilable discrepancies. These discrepancies were due to the fact that I had overlooked—or to be quite frank, that I had never known—that the boundaries and therefore the area and the population of the Europe of today were not the same as those of pre-war Europe. Europe is separated from Asia—or perhaps, would it not in every way be more correct to say, is connected with Asia?—by Russia, which was and is in part European and in part Asiatic. As the Soviet authorities have changed the internal frontiers between what was formerly the Asiatic and the European part of Russia, they have in fact changed the size of Europe. This, perhaps their most constructive achievement, is not less troublesome for the outer world than some others.

As the Europe of 1914 is not the Europe of 1919, but a continent about 5 per cent smaller, so the population of pre-war Europe cannot be compared with that of post-war Europe. In order to ascertain the rate of growth of population of the so densely peopled continent, we may compare 1900 with 1913, and 1919 with 1928, but not 1913 with 1919. It is therefore impossible to indicate with accuracy the effect of the World War on the population of Europe. To estimate that intermediate figure, we must consider the statistics of those countries whose boundaries the War did not alter, such as Great Britain, and those of others, such as France and

Germany, which have been so compiled as to permit of comparison.

Now, if we compare the population of Europe in 1900 and in 1913, we shall see that it increased at the average rate of about ten per thousand per annum. From 1920 to 1927 the per annum increase ratio was about six per thousand. Very roughly we can therefore say that the population was increasing nearly twice as fast before the War as it has been since.

That it did not decrease during the war is certain, although the ratio of increase was naturally less than either before or after. In France certainly, and in several of the present border states of Russia probably, there was a net decrease, but this was more than compensated by increases in all the other parts of Europe. If, therefore, we were to represent graphically the increase of the European population since the beginning of the century, we should be led to draw a curve rising rapidly from 1900 to 1913, continuing on an almost horizontal level from 1913 to 1919, and again rising appreciably since 1919, although less steeply than before the War.

At the beginning of May last, the third *Memorandum on Production and Trade,* of the Economic and Financial Section of the League of Nations, was published. Mr. A. Loveday, the eminent author of this important document from which I have drawn much of the statistical information contained in this chapter, while fully conscious of the impossibility of accurately comparing the pre- and post-war population of Europe, for the reasons above stated, presents the following table:

Changes in the Population of the World in the 14-Year Period 1913–1927.[3]

Continental Groups	Population in millions		Percentage movement		Percentage distribution	
	1913	1927	1913	1927	1913	1927
(a) Central and Eastern Europe						
Excluding Russia (U.S.S.R.)	165.6	173.3	100	104.5	9.3	8.9
Including Russia (U.S.S.R.)	303.7	323.8	100	106.6	17.0	16.6
(b) Rest of Europe	184.5	196.1	100	106.3	10.3	10.1
Europe, excluding Russia (U.S.S.R.)	350.1	369.4	100	105.6	19.6	19.0
Europe, including Russia (U.S.S.R.)	488.2	519.9	100	106.5	27.3	26.7
America						
North	105.0	129.2	100	123.1	5.9	6.6
Caribbean	30.1	31.7	100	105.3	1.7	1.6
South	55.9	78.7	100	140.9	3.1	4.0
Africa	130.7	145.1	100	111.0	7.3	7.5
Asia, excluding Asiatic Russia	968.6	1,033.9	100	106.7	54.3	53.1
Oceania	7.6	9.4	100	123.0	0.4	0.5
World	1,786.1	1,947.9	100	109.0	100.0	100.0

By Central and Eastern Europe, Mr. Loveday means all the countries situated to the east of the Rhine and the Alps, and to the south of the Scandinavian Peninsula. He excludes Holland and Finland, and includes not only European Turkey, but also the whole of the territory of the Union of the Socialist Soviet Republics, with Asiatic Russia, the population of which he estimates at about 30,000,000 persons. By North America, Mr. Loveday, who juggles with continents almost as dexterously as the

[3] League of Nations, Economic and Financial Section, *Memorandum on Production and Trade* (Geneva, 1929), p. 12.

Bolsheviks who have given him so much trouble, statistically speaking, means the territory to the north of Mexico. By Caribbean America, the region including Mexico to and including Panama, as well as all the islands in the Gulf.

In the light of this interpretation it will appear from the table that from 1913 to 1927 the population of Europe has increased by 6½ per cent; that of North America by 23 per cent; and that of the world by 9 per cent. As a consequence, the proportion of the world population living in Europe has, during this period of fourteen years, fallen from 27.3 per cent to 26.7 per cent.

The causes both for the general trend and for the temporary fluctuations of the recent demographic evolution of Europe are obvious. The general increase is due to the general excess of births over deaths, without exception, in all European countries, which since 1900 has more than made up for the overseas emigration. As for the slowing up of the rate of increase during the War which we have noted above, it was naturally due both to the increased death rate and the decreased birth rate, which, curiously enough, characterized the demographic evolution almost as clearly in the neutral as in the belligerent countries. Had the War not checked emigration from Europe, the depopulation which we have noted in a few countries from 1913 to 1919 might have become general. As to the decline in growth of the population since 1919, as compared with pre-war days, it is due to the fact that the birth rate has fallen so much faster than the death rate, that in spite of the decreased emigration, the annual demographic gain has been not much more than half of what it was from 1900 to 1913.

This fall in the European birth rate is assuredly a most significant phenomenon. Whether it be deplored as a symptom of moral and physical degeneracy, as it is for instance in the two Romes—that of the Palazzo Chigi and that of the Vatican—or welcomed as the expression of economic and social wisdom, as it is by those who hold that Europe is suffering from overpopulation, it can certainly leave indifferent no serious student of the situation.

If we seek to interpret the relative birth rates prevailing in different parts of Europe, we shall soon realize that they are susceptible of no simple explanation. In the following table we have grouped the various statistical areas for which comparable figures are available in increasing order of their birth rate. The figures, taken from a recent publication of the Permanent Office of the International Institute of Statistics, show the birth rate, the death rate, and the excess of births over deaths in almost all countries for 1926, and in a few countries for the previous year.[4] Figures relating to the birth registration area of the United States are given for purposes of comparison.

[4] *Aperçu de la Démographie des divers pays du monde* (The Hague, 1927).

Birth Rate, Death Rate, and Excess
of Births over Deaths for 1926.

Statistical Area	Birth Rate	Death Rate	Excess of Births over Deaths
	Per thousand inhabitants		
Sweden	16.9	11.8	5.1
Esthonia	17.7	16.	1.7
England and Wales	17.8	11.6	6.2
Switzerland	18.2	11.7	6.5
Greece	18.3	13.6	4.7
France	18.8	17.5	1.3
Belgium	18.9	12.8	6.1
Austria	19.2	14.9	4.3
Germany	19.5	11.7	7.8
Norway	19.7	10.6	9.1
Denmark	20.5	11.	9.5
Ireland	20.6	14.1	6.5
Scotland	20.9	13.	7.9
Luxemburg	20.9	15.2	5.7
Latvia	22.	14.7	7.3
Finland	22.3	13.5	8.8
North Ireland	22.5	15.	7.5
United States	22.6	11.3	11.3
Netherlands	23.8	9.8	14.
Czechoslovakia	24.6	15.6	9.
Italy	27.2	16.8	10.4
Hungary	27.3	16.6	10.7
Lithuania	28.4	15.3	13.1
Spain	29.7	19.1	10.6
Portugal	31.9	21.4	10.5
Rumania	35.2	21.	14.2
Bulgaria	37.	19.2	17.8
European Russia	44.2	29.9	14.3

A brief perusal of these figures suffices to show that they do not point to the action of any one single and simple factor. A closer examination may perhaps lead to the following generalization, which we venture to submit with due caution: other things being equal, the birth rate in Europe is lower in highly industrialized than in agricultural regions; in the north and west of the continent than in the east and south; in Protestant than in non-Protestant countries; and in densely than in sparsely populated areas.

We must emphasize, however, the qualification "other things being equal," because without that saving clause our generalization would clearly not be valid. Sweden, Norway, and Finland, it might be objected, are states with very low birth rates and an exceptionally low density of population, while Italy has a relatively high birth rate and a high density. Neither Belgium nor France nor Ireland is Protestant, and still they have low birth rates. Nor is Greece in northwestern Europe. It would be possible, I believe, but too fastidious, here to explain each of these exceptions by showing that in no one of them were other things equal. Of the four correlations above suggested, the least questionable is the first. If we compare the birth-rate figures with those indicating the proportion of the population gainfully engaged in agriculture, which we presented in our last chapter,[5] we cannot fail to be struck by the correlation between them. Agriculture and rural life, as they seem to favor or at least to allow political dictatorships, likewise favor and allow large families. Now Europe is rapidly becoming industrialized as we

[5] Cf. p. 40 *supra*.

shall have occasion to show presently. It is therefore
not rash to attribute in a large measure to this factor the rapidly falling European birth rate.

It may be noted, while seeking to explain the
falling birth rate of Europe, that we have produced
statistics which only show its effective status in 1926
or thereabouts. If we wish to avoid an error similar
to that into which many newspaper writers on economic subjects and even some economists have
fallen, by confusing the effects of a depreciating
with those of a depreciated currency, we must also
recall the changes the birth rate has undergone, at
least since the beginning of the century. We will
merely mention here the phenomenon which Doctor
Kuczynski has very well described in one of those remarkable little books in which the Institute of Economics of the Brookings Institution so usefully en-
lightens Europe about her own plight. It is what he
refers to as "a conspicuous trend toward a similar-
ity of birth rates," in the countries of western and
northern Europe.[6] While the average birth rate for
the five-year period from 1905 to 1909 was 32.3 per
thousand in Germany, 26.7 in England and Wales
and in Norway, 26.4 in Switzerland, 25.6 in Sweden,
25.1 in Belgium, and 20.1 in France, a quarter of a
century later it was in all these countries between
16.9 and 20. In what President Roosevelt might have
described as the race suicide race, the fastest western
European horses seem to be those which at the
beginning of the century were most heavily handi-
capped, and the slowest those which started nearest
the goal. Although as we have seen, a birth rate of

[6] R. R. Kuczynski, *The Balance of Births and Deaths,*
"Western and Northern Europe" (New York, 1928), I, 11.

less than 20 per thousand has not yet been reached by any state of southeastern Europe except Greece, which on account of her refugees is in a very peculiar position, the whole continent is tending in the same direction. With the single apparent exception of Portugal, which may be due to purely statistical causes, the birth rate has fallen appreciably everywhere in the last quarter of a century. The drop of over 12 per thousand in Germany is unique; 5 and 6 per thousand is the rule. Considering that this evolution, beginning before the War, hastened by the War, and continuing since the War, has taken place all over the continent, it may well be compared with a ground swell in mid-ocean, rather than with a passing and localized ripple.

Were it not for the concomitant but somewhat slighter drop of the death rate, Europe would actually be engaged in a process of depopulation. Even so, Doctor Kuczynski, considering, as one must, not only the birth and death rates, but the fertility rate as well, is led to the conclusion that the present trend is toward the extinction of the race. He writes at the conclusion of his introductory chapter:

If each woman has two children who become parents in their turn, the population will hold its own. If she has three such children, the population will increase by one-half within one generation. If she has less than two such children, the population will sooner or later decrease. With a fertility and a mortality as they prevailed forty or fifty years ago, the population then would have increased by one-half per generation in all countries of Western and Northern Europe with the exception of France and Ireland, where the population about held its own. With a fertility and a mortality as they prevail at present, the population of some smaller countries still shows a genuine growth, but the population of the larger countries, France, and especially England and Germany, is doomed to die out.[7]

This of course refers only to northern and western Europe. But as that is in all social respects the most advanced part of the continent, whose example the race is tending to follow everywhere, one cannot escape the conclusion that the Old World, in more ways than one, is truly growing old. The average age of its living population is steadily increasing. And if the present downward trend of its fertility continues, even the most drastic immigration laws the New World may enact will not prevent its ultimate depopulation.

This may sound alarming. In truth, however, it should alarm only those friends of Europe who think in terms, not of years nor even of generations, but of centuries, and who indulge in what one might call a quantitative conception of human values. As a matter of fact, Europe, by far the most densely peopled of continents, is still gaining in population. Whether the point of optimum demographic saturation has already been reached or exceeded is a question as difficult as it is important.

In the autumn of 1927 there met at Geneva a World Population Conference. It had been summoned by some American men of science and some American ladies of conviction who, prejudging the conclusions of the former, had hoped to find therein new arguments in favor of the birth control movement in which they were passionately interested. The conference discussed the problem of optimum population with special reference to Europe, but it cannot

[7] *Op. cit.* p. 4.

be said to have solved it.[8] It did, however, serve to
emphasize the complexity of the question, and to reveal an amazingly confused and contradictory state
of opinion. On the whole, I believe, the Americans
were to a man and especially to a woman, more or
less convinced that for the good of all concerned, and
primarily of America and of Europe itself, there
were too many Europeans in the world. The latter,
not unnaturally, hardly seemed inclined to share that
view.

It is not in the least surprising that the inhabitants
of a continent, peaceful, prosperous, and sparsely
settled as is America, should consider those of another, far less peaceful and prosperous, and far
more densely settled, as being too numerous to be
safe and happy. Nor is it, of course, surprising that
the latter should be somewhat reluctant to agree.
But this is distinctly not a matter to be settled according to personal, national, or continental prejudices. In the present state of our knowledge, no
one can say with assurance whether there be too few,
enough, or too many Europeans for their own economic welfare.[9] The example of America may seem
to point one way, but the fact that Europe has never
before been as densely populated, nor on the whole
as prosperous as today, may be taken as pointing in
the opposite direction. What is certain is that if a
few Europeans believe that their continent is over-
populated, and many others, for political and mili-

[8] See *Proceedings of the World Population Conference* (London, 1927).

[9] See my article entitled "De l'optimum de population" in the
Journal de Statistique et Revue Economique suisse, 63e année,
5e fascicule (Berne, 1927).

tary more than for economic reasons, complain that
their own country is underpopulated, no one is seriously alarmed at the ultimate consequences for the
whole of the continent, of the decreasing rate of
population growth in Europe.

What must be looked upon as more disquieting in
my opinion, is the fact that this rate varies appreciably from one country to another, and that the less
advanced nations are growing faster than the more
advanced. Whatever the ultimate consequences, this
fact, which is characteristic not only of Europe but
of the whole world, very directly affects the trend of
international coöperation today. Politically it accounts for the ambitions of the rapidly growing
states and the fears of their less rapidly growing
neighbors. Thus it has led to regional security pacts
on the one hand, and to the refusal of such general
agreements for the stabilization of the territorial
status quo as the Geneva Protocol of 1924 on the
other. The unequal national rates of population
growth are at bottom one of the most serious obstacles in the path of the League of Nations as at
present constituted. Equipped with every device for
the peaceful settlement of international disputes on
the basis of existing treaties, but deprived of the
legislative power peacefully to modify them, it appears in this respect as an essentially static institution in a dynamic world. This may help to explain
the respective attitudes adopted toward it by the
various states of Europe, as well as the efforts of its
boldest and most far-sighted friends to implement
Article 19 of the Covenant relating to the peaceful
revision of treaties.

Economically also, this different rate of demographic growth is important for the present and future of international relations. Such matters as international migration, labor legislation, and relative standards of living cannot fail to be affected thereby. Here, as in the political field, it tends to make organized international coöperation not only more difficult, but also more necessary. It is a constant cause of friction, and always a possible source of conflict.

The last subject which I wish to mention before leaving the topic of population and before proceeding to that of production, is the natural link between the two. It is important for our purpose here, to note the recent changes undergone by the population of Europe in what one might call its economic structure. The easiest and best, although by no means a fully satisfactory method of studying these changes is to compare the results of the various national censuses of population by occupational groups. The following table, extracted from the *International Statistical Year Book* of the League of Nations for 1927, is intended to show, by percentages of the total, the relative importance of the six main occupational groups before and after the War:

Population by Principal Occupational Groups.
(Percentage of Each Group in the Total.)

Countries	Date of Census	Agriculture, Fishing, etc.	Mining and Quarrying	Industry	Trade	Liberal Professions	Domestic and Similar Services
England	1911	7.7	6.9	38.7	13.4	4.2	15.1
and Wales	1921	6.8	7.5	39.7	13.9	4.4	11.8
Scotland	1911	11.	7.9	47.8	6.	4.	9.4
	1921	10.1	7.1	40.2	10.7	4.4	9.2
Germany	1907[10]	35.2	4.3	35.8	8.7	2.5	5.6
	1925	30.5	3.2	38.1	11.7	4.1	4.4
France	1906[10]	42.7	1.4	28.8	9.7	3.1	4.8
	1921[10]	41.9	1.3	28.4	10.4	3.5	4.
Belgium	1910[10]	16.4	6.1	42.1	14.5	3.6	6.3
	1920	19.1	6.6	39.9	10.7	3.6	5.
Holland	1909	28.4	1.	34.2	10.8	5.3	9.5
	1920	23.6	1.7	36.1	11.7	6.5	8.1
Switzerland	1910	26.8	0.3	45.4	10.9	4.4	5.9
	1920	25.9	0.3	44.1	11.7	5.3	6.2
Denmark	1911	41.7	– –	24.2	10.4	4.	10.3
	1921	34.8	– –	27.	10.8	5.5	13.3
Norway	1910	39.5	0.7	25.1	8.8	2.9	12.
	1920	36.8	1.5	27.4	11.1	3.5	9.1
Sweden	1910	46.3	0.6	25.1	5.4	2.7	8.3
	1920	38.7	0.8	28.8	7.9	3.6	7.1
Finland	1910	69.2	– –	10.6	2.1	1.2	2.2
	1920	68.9	– –	12.8	3.3	1.7	2.
Italy	1911[10]	55.4	0.7	25.9	5.6	2.7	3.
	1921	56.1	0.6	24.	6.4	3.	2.4

The other occupational groups listed in the *Year
Book* have been omitted because they are both less
important and less comparable.

That such a presentation is open to countless objections is only too obvious. In no two countries are

[10] Pre-war territory.

the terms adopted for defining the different groups
exactly alike. Furthermore, even in the same country, no two censuses are conducted on exactly paral-
lel lines. Besides, in some cases frontiers have
changed. Notwithstanding all these and several other
causes of error and of lack of adequate comparability, the above table does allow some general conclusions as to the changing economic structure of the
population of Europe.

It will be noted that with few exceptions, some of
which are obviously due to differences of tabulation,
the percentage of the population gainfully employed
in agriculture and in domestic and similar services
has fallen since the War, while that engaged in
mining, industry, trade, and in the liberal professions, has correspondingly risen. The broad significance of this fact is obvious. The industrialization
and commercialization of the population implies its
urbanization. The relative diminution of farmers
points in the same direction. The increased importance of the liberal professions is both a symptom
and a result of increased enlightenment and enhanced civilization. And finally the very general decrease in the figures relating to domestic and other
personal services, reflects both the impoverishment
of the employing middle classes, and the improvement in the conditions of the lower classes, from
which servants are recruited.

Although, to repeat, the above figures are incomplete, insufficiently comparable, and in other respects
statistically inadequate, still they do afford an interesting insight into the general trend of the social
and economic evolution of the principal European
countries since the War.

In conclusion, the answer to our first question referring to population may therefore be summed up as follows: there are today in the whole of Europe about 5 per cent more human beings than before the War, and their numbers are still increasing, although at an ever slower rate. The birth and death rates, whose general tendency is downward, vary in the different parts of the continent. They are, roughly speaking, lowest in the most advanced countries, that is in those which lead in the general march toward industrialization, commercialization, and urbanization which seems to characterize the present evolution of European civilization; and they are highest in those which are still predominantly agricultural and rural.

II

Production.

Does the slightly increased population of Europe produce more or less food and other economic goods, than were produced by their slightly less numerous predecessors before the War? If we were able completely and accurately to answer this, our second question, we should be in a very fair position to judge of the relative material welfare of pre-war and post-war Europe.

This would undoubtedly be so, because the annual production of a continent or of a country, much more even than that of an individual, is the approximate measure of their wealth. To be sure a continent or a country may, as an individual, have accumulated investments or accumulated debts, the interest on which will raise or lower the actual net income above or below their earned gross income. Whereas, however, this factor may be of quite decisive influence on the material fortunes of an individual, it is much less so in the case of a country and still less in that of a continent. There may be no relation whatever between the total net income and the gross earned income, say, of an English nobleman who has invested his title in the good graces of an American heiress, or of the scrupulously honest son of a bankrupt father. But there is always bound to be a direct relation between the annual production of a country or a continent and the amount of consumable goods at the disposal of their peoples.

If the number of Europeans has slightly increased since 1913, they will on the average be poorer than they were unless their annual production has also slightly increased. They will still be somewhat poorer if their production has increased only in the same ratio as their numbers, because from creditors of the world which they were in 1913, they have become its debtors. The tribute Europe received in interest payments from its debtors before the War, and that which it today owes its overseas creditors, is, however, so insignificant a part of its annual production, that it may almost be declared negligible, especially as it was and is compensated by new capital advances.

To make our meaning quite clear we will, anticipating our later detailed results, immediately indicate the general answer to our question as estimated in Mr. Loveday's memorandum. According to his figures we have seen that the populations of Europe, North America, and the world respectively, in 1927 were to those of 1913 as 106.5, 123.1, and 109 are to 100. Their respective total production indices for the two same years are given as 110, 128, and 121. We may therefore conclude that, in volume of production per head of population, the world has gained 11 per cent, North America 5 per cent, and Europe 3 per cent from 1913 to 1927.

The total production indices on which these conclusions are based represent, of course, little more than intelligent and rational guesses. No country possesses full returns of its total annual production, mineral, agricultural, and especially industrial. In the United States, whose vital statistics are still inferior to those of the most advanced European countries, economic statistics are much more developed—a perhaps rather significant contrast, by the bye. Even here, however, no complete record is kept of the yearly creation of wealth. For Europe and especially for the rest of the world, our information is still more fragmentary. How then, has it been possible to construct a production index which an economist may without impudence, although I admit not without some boldness, venture to quote even in these scientifically hallowed precincts of Williamstown?

I cannot here explain in detail the method devised and applied by Mr. Loveday, on whose data and on whose authority I rely no more, but also no less, confidently than he does himself. To sum it up in a few words, it is as follows: taking 66 commodities, whose annual production in weight or volume as well as value is known with a sufficient degree of approximation, he has transformed them into a homogeneous mass of value by multiplying the quantities of each produced by the average price of a unit in a given year. Adopting the year 1913 as a base, that is, taking the value of the total quantities of these 66 commodities in 1913 as 100, he expresses in percentages the corresponding total values of the other years considered. As these 66 commodities include all the main mineral, vegetable, and animal raw materials, such as coal, lignite, pig iron, steel, copper, lead, zinc, tin, aluminum, petroleum, tobacco, copra, cotton, flax, hemp, wool, rubber, and all the main foodstuffs, such as cereals, potatoes, meat, the result is a very comprehensive composite index. To regard such an index as the absolutely faithful expression of reality would be silly. But to disregard it as purely fanciful would, in my opinion, in the absence of a better method of estimating the progress of world production, be still sillier. I have therefore no scruples whatever in using it here, and I hope the reader will not only forgive me, but will also share the gratitude I feel to Mr. Loveday and his able staff for the intelligence, the care, and the tremendous labor involved in producing and applying it.

Let us now, before reverting to the total production index as the main source of our general conclusions, consider the trend of production in Europe, in North America, and in the world, first, of two of the most important commodities, then of all foodstuffs, of all raw materials, and finally of all foodstuffs and raw materials taken as a group.

The first commodity we shall choose for examination is cereals. Of course cereals are not, strictly speaking, one commodity, but rather at least five, because even if we disregard such minor varieties as spelt, we shall still have to consider wheat, rye,

barley, oats, and maize or Indian corn. Of these
wheat is the most important, in point of cultivated
area and of yield, both in the world and in Europe.
About half of the wheat of the world is grown in Europe, which has always produced appreciably more
than North America. Indian corn, which comes next
on the list, is, as its name and origin indicate, the
American cereal *par excellence*. More than half of
the world crop is grown on this continent. As for rye
and barley, very important for certain parts of Europe, they are almost negligible in America, while
oats, although grown in appreciable quantities in
the New World, are also a European commodity.

Considering these five cereals as a group, we may
note in the following table the varying relative importance of their crops in time and in space.

Distribution Percentage and Production Indices of Cereal Crops, Compiled by 1927 Values.

Year	Eastern and Central Europe excl. U.S.S.R.		Western and Northern Europe		Total Europe including U.S.S.R.		North America		World	
	%	P.I.	%	P.I.	%	P.I.	%	P.I.	%	P.I.
1927	16.3	85	12.9	97	42.	95	35.9	118	100	104
1926	16.8	88	13.	98	48.5	98	34.3	112	100	104
1925	17.3	91	14.2	108	48.7	99	34.8	115	100	105
1924	15.6	70	14.1	92	44.1	77	37.2	106	100	90
1923	16.3	82	13.7	100	42.8	83	39.1	124	100	100
1913	20.	100	13.8	100	51.7	100	31.7	100	100	100

This important table would call for many more
comments than we can devote to it here. We will
limit ourselves to the following few remarks.

Europe, which (including Soviet Russia) housed
over a quarter of the population of the globe in 1913,
produced over half of its cereal foodstuffs. It does

not follow, of course, that Europe's exports of grain exceeded its imports. On the contrary, as is well known, even before the War the Old World was dependent on the New for an appreciable part of its breadstuffs. The explanation is to be found in the fact that cereals are the food of the white race, and that the larger half of the human family which inhabits Asia, the great rice producing and consuming continent, are by taste, or rather by necessity, deprived of their daily bread. North America, which in 1913 was inhabited by less than 6 per cent of the total population of the world, already produced then more than 30 per cent of its cereals. While its proportion of the population of the globe had increased by less than 1 per cent, its relative share of the total grain production had increased from 31.7 per cent in 1913 to 35.9 per cent in 1927. This is a difference of more than 4 per cent. The position of Europe is precisely the reverse. While its proportion of the world population has decreased by about ½ per cent, its proportion of cereal production has fallen from 51.7 per cent to 47 per cent. Nothing could more clearly show the increasing dependence of the Old on the New World for its bread supply.

A further interesting change in the distribution of production has taken place in the interior of Europe. The East, that is mainly Russia, Rumania, Poland, Hungary, which had for several generations fed the West, has lost more than its share of the total production. The War, which reduced production in the East, on the whole stimulated it in the West. And what the War began, agrarian ownership reforms in the East and agrarian protection in the West have continued. For whether the breaking up of large estates in Russia and in the Balkans has reduced production as is commonly claimed by its victims, or only increased internal consumption as stressed by its advocates, one thing is certain: the exportable surplus of these countries has appreciably diminished. As trade figures are far less approximative and conjectural than production statistics, this fact can be asserted, even if not explained, with absolute assurance.

If we turn now from the distribution to the world production statistics, we are immediately struck by the slow total increase. It has been calculated that the average annual production of cereals in the world for the period from 1923 to 1927 is only 1 per cent higher than it was for the quinquennium before the War. The aggregate cereal index for 1928, which has not yet been fully estimated, probably exceeds 108, it is true. But even if we include that record harvest year in our calculations, the slowness of the progress is surprising, a progress much slower than that of the production of almost all other foodstuffs, and especially of sugar, potatoes, meat, and rice. In North America the progress has been appreciably greater, but even there it is less than that of the population, and only just suffices to make up for the general deficiency of Europe.

How and why, under these circumstances, there should be agricultural distress all over the western world, and a feeling of general overproduction of cereals, it is not easy to explain. According to all available statistics, the production of cereals has not increased as fast as the population of the world, nor of that part of the world inhabited by the bread-eating white race, even if we include therein, or to be more polite, add thereto, their grain-consuming cattle. Either our figures are fallacious, or the human and cattle diet has changed, or, what is more probable, the combined working of the law of diminishing returns, of the prevailing tariff policies of industrial protectionism, and of the change in the relative demand for cereal foodstuffs and for other commercial goods, has occasioned a narrowing of the margin between average cost and average prices. But that problem of the so-called agricultural surplus is both too intricate and too foreign to our purpose to be further discussed here.

The other commodity which we have singled out for especial, although also very hasty, consideration is coal. Here we stand on much firmer statistical ground. This is so both because the extraction of coal is almost exclusively localized in a few advanced countries and because the figures relating to production are far easier to compile and are therefore much less conjectural than those relating to agricultural crops. Besides, the unemployment and unrest prevailing in the coal fields of the world, and particularly of Great Britain, have given rise to so many inquiries of recent years that everything pertaining to the magnitude and the causes of the depression are clear, everything, except unfortunately, the possible remedies.

As is well stated in the recently published interim report by the Economic Committee of the League of Nations on *The Problem of the Coal Industry,* the coal production of the world has slightly fluctuated around the volume of 1,200,000,000 tons ever since pre-war days.

Between 1886 and 1913 the world consumption

and the world output had been advancing at the average rate of rather more than 4 per cent per annum. Since 1913, on the contrary, progress has been almost imperceptible, amounting to only about 4 per cent for the whole of the fifteen-year period down to 1928. Such, in spite of the great increase in population and industrial enterprise, has been the result of economy in the use of coal, by improved methods of combustion and of power generation, and by the resort to alternative sources of energy, such as oil and water-power.

The following table drawn up on the same lines as that shown above relating to cereal foodstuffs will bring out the essential facts of the recent coal situation:

Distribution Percentage and Production Indices of Coal Including Lignite Converted into Terms of Coal.

Year	Eastern and Central Europe excl. U.S.S.R.		Western and Northern Europe		Total Europe including U.S.S.R.		North America		World	
	%	P.I.	%	P.I.	%	P.I.	%	P.I.	%	P.I.
1928	20.2	112	27.	93	49.9	101	40.7	100	100	104
1927	19.4	110	27.3	96	49.1	102	41.7	105	100	107
1926	19.7	104	19.	62	40.8	79	49.4	116	100	99
1925	18.	95	27.7	91	47.1	91	43.2	101	100	99
1913	18.8	100	30.2	100	51.3	100	42.3	100	100	100

The most striking phenomenon shown by these figures is the already mentioned stability of world production. This is all the more striking, as it is hardly affected by many appreciable changes in its distribution among the various producing areas. To-day as before the War, about half the coal production of the world is extracted from European mines and about two-fifths from American mines. But in

1926 when the great British coal strike reduced the production of Europe by nearly 20 per cent, the American production rose by an almost equal fraction, only to fall again when the resumption of work in England and Wales restored Europe to her former position.

This fact alone would suffice to reveal the present characteristics of the coal situation: an almost stable demand appreciably inferior to the existing productive capacity.

There were before the War in Europe only seven European countries which produced more than one million tons of coal a year: the United Kingdom and Germany, whose aggregate production in 1913 amounted to 456 million tons out of a total of 587 million tons, France, Austria-Hungary, Belgium, Russia, and Holland. Today, as a result of the political changes, there are eleven, Poland, Czechoslovakia, Hungary, and Rumania having been added to the list. But before the War only the United Kingdom and Germany regularly exported more coal than they imported, whereas today Poland and Czechoslovakia have joined in competing for foreign markets. Besides, several countries such as France, Holland, and Spain have appreciably developed their own resources so that the former suppliers, and principally the United Kingdom, have suffered from the effects of a shrinking market.

On no one single point of economic interest has the demand for international action been more insistent than on this: Europe and the world are faced with a very real and chronic overproduction, that is, a situation in which the existing productive capacity of mines, ever ready to be exploited without

additional outlay of capital, is permanently superior
to the demand, and in which this demand has shown
itself to be singularly inelastic, neither expanding
with the fall, nor contracting with the rise, of prices.
International agreements, if the interests of the
competing states could be harmonized, could regulate conditions of labor and of transportation rates.
They could even serve to apportion markets and fix
prices. I am unable to understand, however, how
they can be expected to overcome the ever latent
overproduction and persistent unemployment without reducing output. The real cure, it would seem
obvious, can be effected only by the reëstablishment
of a sound equilibrium between supply and demand,
that is, by decrease of production or increase of consumption or by both. Now as long as the tendency
prevails in certain, if not in all, competing states,
to foster productivity by a protective tariff and by
a special transportation rate policy, there would
seem to be little hope for a concerted reduction of
output by means of international agreements. And
as long as it is not deemed possible to lower the
existing already depressed price level, it hardly
seems possible to expect an increased consumption,
except by an economic miracle. Such a miracle is,
of course, not out of the question if, by the industrial application of already effected scientific
discoveries, coal can be transformed and adapted to
new productive uses.

Although the coal problem is being constantly
studied in Geneva from the international point of
view, it is one of those problems which, in my humble
opinion, cannot be solved except by the elimination
of existing sources of supply or by the progress of

industrial technique, that is, by means applicable
nationally, as well as, if not better than, internationally.

After thus briefly considering the two essential
commodities of grain and coal, let us now, before
concluding this chapter, revert for a moment to the
combined production indices to which allusion has
already been made. We shall present in three successive tables, the results of Mr. Loveday's computa-
tion, first of the production of foodstuffs, secondly
of the production of raw materials, and thirdly, as
the summit of this boldly majestic economic pyramid,
of the combined production of foodstuffs and raw
materials.

Cereals and coal are among the most essential of
all commodities, as we in Switzerland, who lack both,
were made to feel cruelly during the War. Curiously
enough, however, their general production trend is
not that of either foodstuffs or raw materials considered synthetically. While, as we have just seen,
the total world production of both grain and coal
seems to lag behind the growth of world population,
the total production of foodstuffs seems to outstrip
it slightly, and that of raw materials more appreciably, and thus to point to a more optimistic conclusion.

In the following table this is shown for the
production of foodstuffs as a whole in the world,
which, from 1913 to 1927, has increased by 13 per
cent, whereas population is estimated to have gained
only 9 per cent:

Distribution Percentage and Production Indices of Foodstuffs Weighted by 1927 Values.

Year	Eastern and Central Europe excl. U.S.S.R.		Western and Northern Europe		Total Europe including U.S.S.R.		North America		World	
	%	P.I.	%	P.I.	%	P.I.	%	P.I.	%	P.I.
1927	16.5	97	12.1	106	41.7	106	23.2	120	100	113
1926	15.8	90	12.	101	41.	101	23.	115	100	109
1925	16.9	98	12.8	110	41.8	105	22.9	117	100	111
1924	15.4	82	12.5	99	37.9	88	24.1	113	100	102
1923	15.3	82	12.3	98	37.1	86	26.6	126	100	103
1913	19.1	100	13.	100	44.3	100	21.7	100	100	100

However, Mr. Loveday has further calculated that if we exclude China, whose unknown food production is not taken into account in the above table, and the Soviet Union, both from the population and the foodstuff figures, the growth of foodstuffs proves to be identical with the population growth. Not only in Europe, but even in America, population seems to be gaining on food while the opposite seems to be the case in Africa and Oceania.

This is not in the least surprising when we compare the production indices of the various varieties of foodstuffs. The figures for 1927, taking 1913 as a base at 100, are: cocoa, 216; cane sugar, 168; tobacco, 153; coffee, 141; potatoes, 135; tea, 118; meat, 116; beet sugar, 112; rice, 110; cereals, 104; and hops, 79. As a result the composite index figure based on these constituent elements naturally shows a greater increase in production in the tropical and semitropical parts of the world.

It will be noted that of all important foodstuffs, cereals have in general gained the least, whereas the production of meat in the world has become so much larger, that we may with assurance conclude that the per capita consumption of meat has also increased. This is true even in Europe, where the production per head is about the same as in 1913, but where imports of beef and lamb, notably from the Argentine and New Zealand, have greatly increased. This is a not insignificant symptom of the general rise in the standard of living which has undoubtedly characterized the European evolution of the last fifteen years.

The distribution and increase in the output of industrial raw materials is strikingly shown in the following table:

Distribution Percentage and Production Indices for Raw Materials Weighted by 1927 Values.

Year	Eastern and Central Europe excl. U.S.S.R.		Western and Northern Europe		Total Europe including U.S.S.R.		North America		World	
	%	P.I.	%	P.I.	%	P.I.	%	P.I.	%	P.I.
1927	11.4	118	18.	125	33.6	119	33.6	137	100	135
1926	10.6	104	14.3	95	28.7	97	37.6	146	100	129
1925	10.4	100	16.5	107	30.6	101	35.9	135	100	125
1924	10.	89	17.9	107	30.8	94	35.2	123	100	116
1923	8.3	70	17.2	97	28.1	81	38.4	127	100	110
1913	13.1	100	19.4	100	39.1	100	33.2	100	100	100

Nothing more clearly demonstrates the progress of economic civilization than the comparison of this table with the preceding one. Like all individuals except the very poorest and most underfed, nations—as they grow in wealth—tend to spend an increasing proportion of their income on industrial products. The fact, therefore, that the annual output of raw materials, out of which these products are made, has increased much faster than the annual output of foodstuffs since 1913, indicates that the world has effectively grown wealthier. Indeed it is probable that these figures understate the facts, as the undoubted progress in manufacturing technique tends constantly to increase the ratio between consumable commodities, which constitute real income, and the raw materials out of which they are made.

This gain is not confined to North America. Europe as a whole, and the west apparently more than the east, have had their share of it. But it has been greatest in Africa, Asia, and in Central America, mainly on account of the tremendous growth in the output of such materials as rubber, whose index in 1927 when compared with 1913, was 550, and petroleum, whose index was 322. *Per capita,* the increase in output of raw materials from 1913 to 1927 was 24 per cent for the world as a whole, 52 per cent in Africa, 51 per cent in Asia, 42 per cent in Central America, 18 per cent in western and maritime Europe, 12 per cent in the whole of Europe including Soviet Russia, and 11 per cent in North America.

The statement that the output of raw materials per head of population has grown faster in Europe than in the most advanced part of the New World in the course of the last fifteen years, must seem challenging to the point of impudence in the mouth of a native of that backward continent speaking at Williamstown. He will, however, I hope, be readily forgiven when he explains that it is due primarily to the very much lower output per head prevailing before the War. The admittedly overwhelming superiority of America in this respect is well shown by the following table presented by Mr. Loveday:

*Output of Industrial Raw Materials per Head in
Each Continental Group. (In Proportion to
the Average Output per Head in the
World in 1927.)*

Central and Eastern Europe excluding U.S.S.R.	128
U.S.S.R.	54
Rest of Europe	178
Europe	
Excluding U.S.S.R.	155
Including U.S.S.R.	126
North America	507
Caribbean	96
South America	147
Africa	48
Asia	36
Oceania	502
World	100

I know of no single short set of statistics that so
strikingly contrasts the relative wealth of the different parts of the world as this. When it is realized
that, North America being the creditor of the rest
of the globe, these figures understate the facts rather
than overstate them, Americans must surely be
proud of the place they occupy, and perhaps even be
tempted to regard with some leniency the occasional
defaults of their poverty-stricken debtors. The fact
that these debtors have of late been able slightly to
improve their relative position should arouse no
more alarm and jealousy among their opulent creditors, than an American financial magnate would feel
on learning that the immigrant schoolboy who sold
him his daily paper had doubled his income in a year,
whereas he himself had increased his by only 50 per
cent.

We now come to the last and most synthetic table,

that in which is shown the aggregate production of raw materials and foodstuffs:

Distribution Percentage and Production Indices of Aggregate Production of Raw Materials and Foodstuffs Weighted by 1927 Values.

Year	Eastern and Central Europe excl. U.S.S.R.		Western and Northern Europe		Total Europe including U.S.S.R.		North America		World	
	%	P.I.	%	P.I.	%	P.I.	%	P.I.	%	P.I.
1927	14.3	103	14.6	115	38.3	110	27.6	128	100	121
1926	13.6	94	13.	98	35.9	100	29.1	130	100	117
1925	14.3	99	14.3	108	37.3	103	28.1	126	100	116
1924	13.2	84	14.7	103	35.1	90	28.6	118	100	108
1923	12.6	79	14.2	98	33.5	85	31.2	127	100	106
1913	16.9	100	15.4	100	41.9	100	26.1	100	100	100

A rapid analysis of this table suggests the following remarks which may serve both as a summary and as a conclusion to this survey of production:

The production of the world, having steadily increased since 1923, has now reached a level about 20 per cent higher than that of 1913. That is less than the progress of North America which is estimated at nearly 30 per cent, but double that of Europe, estimated at 10 per cent. Although all the branches of the economic firm are moving forward, those managed by the younger and more enterprising partners in the New World, are forging ahead of the older establishments and are taking over an ever larger share of the business. This was especially true during the stress of the War and of the first post-war years. Since 1927, however, it would seem as if the parent house in Europe, partly financed from abroad, was again showing more activity and striving to regain its former relative position on

the market. In this endeavor western and maritime
Europe have so far been rather more successful than
their central and eastern hinterland.

III

Trade.

As the population of the world has increased since
1913, and as production has increased in a greater
ratio than population, one would not unnaturally expect international trade to have increased in a still
greater ratio. Such a conclusion would seem to be
justified by reason of the fact that, other things
being equal, the greater the wealth of a nation, the
greater will be the fraction of the domestic production consumed abroad, and the greater the fraction
of the imports in commodities consumed at home.
And such a conclusion would seem especially likely
for Europe since, as we have seen, the number of
sovereign states on the same territory has there increased by eight as a result of the War.

As a matter of fact, however, these abstract previsions do not seem to have fully materialized, if we
are to trust comparative trade statistics. The han-
dling and interpretation of such statistics are, it is
true, matters of extreme delicacy on account of price
and monetary fluctuations, lack of international comparability, changing methods of valuation of exports
and imports, and altering territorial units.

Adopting the conclusions of the latest *Memorandum on International Trade* of the League of Nations, as we may, because of the very able and careful calculations on which they are based, and as we

must, for lack of any other equivalent source, we note that "world trade in 1927 was 20 per cent greater than in 1913,"[11] although the increase in world production is estimated at 21 per cent.

The difference is quite negligible, given the many inevitable sources of error. If we compare the trade figures for Europe alone, however, the discrepancy is much greater. Whereas production in the period under consideration is estimated to have increased by 10 per cent, international trade increased not by more, as might have been expected, but by only 3 per cent. The corresponding figures for 1926—no increase in production and 9 per cent decrease in trade—are, at first glance, still more interesting.

Whatever the accuracy of these statistics the fact itself is not open to any doubt and may be verified by scrutinizing the position of almost all European states. Since the War production has outstripped international trade in Europe. And the explanation of this fact is no mystery. The development of international trade has been retarded by the deliberate will to retard it, at least as concerns imports. The greater national economic self-sufficiency which the War and the blockade imposed on Europe as a dire necessity, has since been more or less consciously pursued as an ideal by post-war European statesmanship. Considerations of national security, which Adam Smith himself had considered legitimate for the purpose—the old mercantilist ambition to defend and, if possible, to increase the national gold supply, the hope of combating unemployment by protecting the domestic labor market against ex-

[11] *Memorandum on International Trade and Balance of Payments* (Geneva, 1928), I, 13.

change and other dumping—are the main foundations on which this trade restriction policy has been
built up. True to mercantilist precedent it has on
the one hand been lenient in favor of imports of
foreign foodstuffs and raw materials, but more and
more merciless in its exclusion of manufactured
goods.

The relative diminution in the post-war trade of
Europe, compared with its pre-war trade or with its
production, is more noticeable in the east than in the
west, especially if we include Soviet Russia in the
former. The following table shows this clearly:

*Percentage Changes in Volume of Production
and Trade.*

	Production and Trade 1913	1925 Production	Trade	1926 Production	Trade	1927 Production	Trade
Eastern and Central Europe excl. U.S.S.R.	100	99	84	94	85	103	106
Western and Maritime Europe	100	108	100	98	100	115	110
Europe including U.S.S.R.	100	103	91	100	91	110	103
North America	100	126	139	130	150	128	155
World	100	116	107	117	110	121	120

It is estimated that "that part of the trade of countries with modified frontiers, or of newly founded
states, which might before the war have been domestic,"[12] was in 1927 about 4½ per cent of world
trade. As, with the exception of Ireland, all the

[12] *Memorandum on Production and Trade* (Geneva, 1929),
p. 51.

newly founded states are in central and eastern Europe, the trade figures for that continent group would therefore show a still much greater decline, were it not for the territorial changes which have rendered international an important fraction of the commerce which was formerly domestic. The shrinking of the foreign trade in eastern Europe is one of the most significant post-war phenomena. Beside the general impoverishment, reduced production, shattered currencies, and very restrictive commercial policies—factors which until two or three years ago were active all over Europe, but particularly so in the east—it was due also to two other specific causes. The first of these is agrarian reform. This movement swept over the whole broad belt of countries which separates the Soviet Union from the rest of Europe, from the Balkans in the north to the Black Sea in the south. The change in land tenure it brought about was more or less drastically effected in all the states arising out of, or territorially benefited by, the dismemberment of Austria-Hungary and Russia. This reform, although its motives were more social and national than economic, has had the most far-reaching consequences for the internal structure of the states concerned, as well as for their foreign trade. By the breaking up of large estates and the multiplication of peasant proprietors, the gross production of grain may or may not have been reduced, but there is, as we have already seen, no doubt whatever that the exportable surplus of those countries which prior to the War served to feed the rest of Europe has been cut down very appreciably. That is the first reason for the decline of the foreign trade of eastern Europe.

The second reason is a desire on the part of most of these young or rejuvenated states to become industrialized and more independent of the west. During and since the War textile mills and mechanical works have been set up behind often insurmountable tariff walls. They have been developed at the expense of the local consumer and indirectly at that of the exporting farmer. Thereby the production of national wealth has undoubtedly been retarded, but foreign trade has still more effectively been checked.

It is interesting to note, however, that all foreign trade figures for 1927 seem to show a reaction against the general tendencies prevailing since the War. From 1913 to 1926 the foreign trade of North America increased relatively faster than that of the world, that of the world faster than that of Europe, and that of western Europe faster than that of eastern Europe. From 1926 to 1927 all these relations have been reversed. Relative progress has been greater in eastern than in western Europe, in Europe than in the world, and in the world than in North America. Whether this be merely a passing accident, or the beginning of a return to a former state of equilibrium, remains to be seen. It would seem likely that a new state of equilibrium will be established, more favorable to America than that of 1913, but more favorable to Europe than that of 1926. This view of the future is based on the fact that America's remarkable progress since 1913 is neither fictitious nor accidental and that Europe is obviously recovering from what was an abnormal post-war depression.

The following table, extracted from the *Memoran-*

dum on International Trade,[13] shows the results of
these two successive changes in the percentage distribution of world trade in 1913, 1926, and 1927. The
figures relate to movements of merchandise only and
are based on recorded values reduced to dollars.

Percentage Distribution of the World's Foreign Trade.

	Imports			*Exports*			*Total*		
	1913	*1926*	*1927*	*1913*	*1926*	*1927*	*1913*	*1926*	*1927*
Central and Eastern Europe excl. U.S.S.R.	17.9	13.3	17.	17.4	13.8	14.2	17.7	13.6	15.6
Western and Maritime Europe	40.	37.3	36.5	33.5	29.1	30.6	36.8	33.3	33.6
Europe including U.S.S.R.	61.5	51.8	54.6	55.2	44.1	46.1	58.4	48.1	50.4
North America	12.4	17.6	16.4	15.8	20.7	19.9	14.1	19.1	18.1
World	100	100	100	100	100	100	100	100	100

Besides well illustrating the point just made, this
table might suggest many other comments of interest. We can here call attention to one only. It will
be noted that Europe's percentage of the trade of the
world, which has since 1913 been reduced from 58.4
per cent to just about 50 per cent, has always been
appreciably greater in imports than in exports. Correspondingly, the converse has been the case for the
rest of the world in general and for North America
in particular. Of the twenty-seven European states
considered, there is only one, Czechoslovakia, whose
exports have always exceeded her imports; six,
France, Russia, Poland, Finland, Yugoslavia, and
Lithuania, whose balance of trade is in a state of
approximate equilibrium, and twenty, that is, all the

[13] *Op. cit.,* p. 39.

others, whose imports always exceed their exports. North America and the United States have, of course, had consistently active trade balances ever since the War as well as for a generation before. The phenomenon has therefore remained the same, but its causes have radically changed.

Before the War the active trade balance of the United States represented in the main, besides immigrant remittances and tourist expenditure, interest and repayment on foreign loans. Today, however, as the former American debtor has become Europe's creditor, her excess of exports cannot be accounted for in the same way. Doubtless the increase in tourist expenditure will have much more than made up for the probable decrease of immigrant remittances. But numerous and lavish as are American ladies abroad, and admittedly generous as their husbands are wise enough to be, they cannot, in spite of their combined meritorious and happily not altogether unsuccessful efforts, spend enough to pay for the excess of American exports to Europe, plus the interest due by Europe on her debts.

The new investments of American capital in the Old World, while postponing the evil day of settlement, naturally render the problem ever less susceptible of a simple solution. Whether that solution be found in increased imports to the United States, or in decreased exports from the United States, it cannot but create a still closer solidarity and interdependence of interest between the two continents, which, peopled by the same peoples, are separated only by a sea which is yearly becoming more like a lake.

It is, of course, possible to suppose also, that American investments abroad will continue until Europe will have become an American-owned and American-visited museum, from which no other returns will be expected than those which a private golf course yields its opulent proprietor. But even so, the connection will be ever closer between creditor and debtor, because what could be dearer to the heart of an American businessman, overburdened with cares and millions, than the only place in the world where he can forget his professional worries and really enjoy himself?

Before closing this chapter let us turn back once more from this imaginary rural playground of the future to the overcrowded workshop that Europe is today, still endeavoring, and as we have seen, still succeeding, in improving the lot of her teeming millions by hard productive labor.

Our last point will again illustrate the growing interdependence of Europe and the United States, which we have just noted.

There are today three states which may be said to dominate the foreign commercial relations of Europe. These three states are Germany, the United Kingdom, and the United States. Together they supply between 32 and 33 per cent of the total imports into European countries, and absorb between 32 and 33 per cent of their exports. For fourteen out of the twenty-six European states, Germany is the most important source of supply. These fourteen include six of Germany's nine neighbors, the four Balkan and the Scandinavian states, Russia, Bulgaria, and Rumania. Germany is, moreover, the second most important source of supply for four other

European states, that is, Italy, Austria, Hungary, and Portugal. The United Kingdom is the most important source of supply for two European states, the Irish Free State and Portugal and the second most important for seven, including France and Germany. The United States is the most important for six states, that is, the United Kingdom, Germany, France, Italy, Spain, and Greece, and the second most important for nine other states.

As concerns markets, the United Kingdom is the most important for thirteen European states including Germany, France, Bulgaria, and Russia. Germany is the most important for seven, including Italy, Poland, and Czechoslovakia, and the United States is the most important for Greece.

If instead of counting customers and furnishers we weigh European demand and supply, our conclusions will be the same. The following table shows the relative importance of these three commercial masters of Europe, both before the War and in the last two years for which figures are available:

Percentage of Total Imports.

	1913	1926	1927
To European states from:			
United States	13.2	15.2	13.9
United Kingdom	8.4	7.4	8.
Germany	17.5	11.3	10.3

Percentage of Total Exports.

	1913	1926	1927
From European states to:			
United States	5.3	7.	6.6
United Kingdom	13.7	15.	14.5
Germany	16.9	8.7	11.2

We find that today the United States comes first
as a source of supply, her exports to the states of
Europe representing 13.9 per cent of their total imports, Germany being second, and the United Kingdom third. The order is reversed as concerns markets, the United Kingdom coming first as buying
14.5 per cent of the total European exports, Germany being second, and the United States third.

We see further that the War has improved the
position of the United States, both as a source of
supply and as a customer of Europe, whereas it has
on the whole appreciably weakened that of her two
commercial rivals. We note finally that a reaction
seems to have set in in 1927, tending slightly toward
the restoration of pre-war conditions.

This statistically well-established, enhanced importance of the United States on the markets of Europe may at first surprise an American reader. Of
recent years so much has been said of the relative
decline of Europe, both as a consumer of American
exports and as a producer of American imports,
that it may seem strange to hear a movement stressed
which apparently tends in the opposite direction. The
explanation is, of course, to be found in the gigantic
growth of the foreign trade of the United States.
While increasing in comparison to that of European
countries, this trade has increased so much faster
with other parts of the world, that commercial relations with Europe seem to have diminished. As a
matter of fact, however, if we disregard the abnormal war period, they have, absolutely and not relatively speaking, never been as important as today,
and although steadily declining in proportion to that
of other continents, are still much more important

than that of any other, and almost as important as that of the rest of the world together. This is clearly shown by the following table, extracted from an American source.[14]

Foreign Trade of the United States.

Year	Total Value in Millions of Dollars	With Europe Value in Millions of Dollars	Europe's Percentage
Exports			
1876–1880	677	562	83.1
1901–1905	1454	1051	72.3
1910–1914	2166	1350	
1926	4809	2310	48.
1927	4865	2314	47.6
Imports			
1876–1880	493	248	50.3
1901–1905	972	498	51.3
1910–1914	1689	836	49.5
1926	4431	1286	29.
1927	4185	1276	30.5

IV

Conclusion.

In reviewing this all too long, and still all too hasty, survey of the post-war economic evolution of Europe, I cannot but be impressed by all the topics I have not even mentioned. Nothing has been said about interallied debts and reparations, about monetary fluctuations and commercial policies, about industrial unemployment and agricultural unrest, about international cartels and international banking, and nothing whatever about the great change

[14] *Commercial Year Book,* 1928 (Washington, 1928), I, 114.

in the distribution of wealth which in most countries, impoverishing the middle classes and improving the lot of the manual laborers, has on the whole, I believe, tended toward greater social equality. What I have said, however, may be summed up in a very few sentences:

Since 1913 the population of Europe has increased, not as fast as before the war, nor as much as elsewhere. Production has also increased, not as much as in other continents but still faster than the population, thereby creating an increase in *per capita* wealth. As for international trade, it has declined until very recently. Since 1927, however, although still appreciably below the level of production, it has again risen above its own level of 1913. In this general, although irregular, forward movement which can thus be noted all along the line of social and economic activity, the relations of the United States to Europe have become both more intimate and less exclusive, as have so many other relations in this post-war world.

PART II

THE METHODS AND RESULTS OF
COÖPERATION

CHAPTER III

COÖPERATION OUTSIDE THE FRAMEWORK
OF THE LEAGUE OF NATIONS

HAVING in the preceding chapters outlined the political and economic evolution of the states of Europe, we turn now to the methods and results of coöperation between them.

When two or more states agree to engage in some form of international coöperation, they normally do so with some definite end in view. It is natural, therefore, to classify the different modes of international coöperation according to the dominant aims pursued by those who engage in it. These aims are almost as numerous and as varied as are the aims of the foreign policy of each state taken separately, since few are powerful enough to undertake anything in the foreign field alone. When we glance over the long list of topics which have been dealt with at diplomatic conferences in the course of recent times, we shall realize, however, that they can all be grouped under one of two general headings. Whether the subjects discussed were political, military, legal, commercial, social, humanitarian, or technical, the fundamental aim pursued was always, in the last analysis, in some way to enhance the security or to promote the prosperity of the contracting parties. Security and prosperity, which are to the state what life and health are to the individual, are, therefore, the two great national goals which may be said to characterize the two general types of international coöperation.

Besides, there always has been since 1919 the still
not completely solved problem of the execution of
the peace treaties. While coöperating to solve it the
victors of the War, as well as the vanquished, were,
of course, unmindful neither of their security nor
of their prosperity. However, given the very peculiar, formally prescribed, and transient nature of
this especial task, it is convenient and legitimate to
treat it by itself.

We would thus have three types of international
coöperation characterized by their aims: the international execution of the peace treaties, the international promotion of national prosperity, and the international quest for national security.

The modes of international coöperation may also
be classified according to other criteria: According to the number of participating states, we may
distinguish bilateral, plurilateral, and general, if
not universal, coöperation; according to the circumstances in view of time, intermittent, periodical, and
continuous coöperation; according to the quality of
its personal agents, diplomatic, technical, or govern-
mental. And finally we may classify the forms of
international coöperation according to its methods
of organization, on a national or on an international
basis.

We may sum up these various possible classifica-
tions in the following table:

International Coöperation

Criterion   *Modes*
I. Aims   (a) execution of treaties
                 (b) promotion of prosperity
                 (c) enhancement of security

Criterion	*Modes*
II. Numbers	(a) bilateral
	(b) plurilateral
	(c) general
III. Times	(a) irregularly intermittent
	(b) periodic
	(c) continuous
IV. Agents	(a) by professional diplomats
	(b) by special delegates
	(c) by responsible heads of government
V. Organization	(a) on a national basis
	(b) on an international basis

Past history has recorded examples of all these various types of international coöperation. The Napoleonic Wars gave rise to the Holy Alliance to assure the permanency of the peace settlement. Countless commercial treaties and defensive alliances have been concluded for the promotion of prosperity or for the enhancement of security. Of arbitration conventions between two signatories, of plurilateral agreements between states bordering on the same international river, and of general gatherings such as The Hague Peace Conferences, there have been many. Occasional meetings, such as visits of prime or foreign ministers, recurrent gatherings, for instance the Pan American Conferences at which governments are usually represented by especial delegates, are examples of intermittent and periodic coöperation, as the professional activities of ordinary diplomats are examples of continuous coöperation. Usually all such coöperation was organized and financed separately by the various coöperating states, but international bureaus, such as those for the protection of literary property, or of the Postal Union, are instances of internationally organized and financed coöperation.

All these forms were practiced before the War, and none have been abandoned since. What is, however, quite novel, and therefore more instructive and significant for the post-war period, is the creation of an entirely original mode of coöperation, characterized by the combination of several, if not all, of the former methods. An institution has been set up, international in its organization and finances, open to all states, and frequented by almost all, where all international aims can be and are simultaneously and continuously pursued, and where professional diplomats, especial technical delegates, and foreign and prime ministers assemble at frequent intervals throughout the year. That institution is the League of Nations.

As it is not destined to replace but merely to supplement the other modes of international coöperation, and as these are not only surviving, but are more generally and more frequently resorted to than ever before, we shall consider them first. This chapter will accordingly be devoted to an outline of recent international coöperation in Europe outside the framework of the League of Nations. But since, as I have said, this League, although primarily of American authorship, is both the most significant product and the most characteristic method of post-war European coöperation, we shall consider its origins and evolution in our last chapter.

It may seem strange but it is an undoubted fact that the coexistence in Europe for the last decade

of the two methods of international coöperation—
the old traditional and the new League methods—
has given rise neither to serious conflicts nor to any
clear division of labor between them.

The execution of the peace treaties has been
carried on both without and within the League of
Nations. International attempts to promote prosperity have been made at Genoa and elsewhere, as
well as at Geneva. And security has been sought
after both by bilateral arbitration treaties, plurilateral defensive alliances, and disarmament agreements on the one hand, and by general conventions
dealing with the same matters on the other.

In discussing international coöperation first without and then within the League, we shall therefore
have to traverse the same ground twice, or, to use a
maritime simile, we shall sail twice around the sea
of European coöperation. On each trip we shall visit
each of the three countries bordering on that sea, but
we shall stop over at different harbors. We shall
thus have occasion to note that the same cargoes
are handled both by one great general transport
corporation, and by many smaller and more special-
ized, but not less active, firms. As a rule each goes
about its business without considering its competi-
tors. In some instances particularly unwieldy or
dangerous cargoes have been left or turned over to
the larger concern by its minor rivals. Such was the
case notably in several frontier matters concerning
Austria, Hungary, Czechoslovakia, Poland, Lithuania, and in the liquidation of the estate of the Genoa
Conference after its demise. In at least one instance,
that of the Corfu affair, there was some mutually
troublesome competition. But more often, as in the

promotion of conciliation and arbitration treaties, and in the relations between the drafting of the Geneva Protocol of 1924 and of the Locarno Conference of 1925, there has been much wholesome and stimulating emulation and reciprocal helpfulness.

On the whole we shall see that the big corporation is taking over more and more of the business of its smaller rivals, but that from the very nature of things it can never absorb them entirely. As the amount of international freight to be carried is continually increasing there is shipping enough for all and no danger of predatory monopoly, but every incitement to friendly combination.

I

The Execution of the Peace Treaties outside the Framework of the League of Nations.

The treaties of peace concluded in 1919 were not in all their provisions, and could not be, immediately and finally applicable. Therefore several tasks of international delimitation, arbitration, control, execution, and temporary administration remained to be performed once the peace conferences had adjourned and the results of their labors been accepted. Certain of these tasks, such as those concerning the Saar Basin, minorities, and mandates, were expressly intrusted to the League. Others, such as those dealing with reparations, plebiscites, and the disarmament of the vanquished, were turned over to especial interallied commissions. But the treaties themselves provided for no one organ of international authority to supervise and control the whole settlement. At the beginning of the first volume of his *Survey of International Affairs,* Mr. Arnold J. Toynbee described the manner in which the difficulty thus arising was met in terms so clear and so concise that I prefer to quote, rather than by paraphrasing to weaken and to lengthen his statement.

After mentioning the various interallied bodies provided for under the treaties of peace with Germany, Austria, Hungary, and Bulgaria—including, for Germany alone, five Delimitation Commissions, four Plebiscite Commissions, commissions for the navigation of the Rhine, Danube, Elbe, and Oder, commissions for such matters as the repatriation of prisoners of war and the distribution of railroad material, the commissions for the government of Danzig and the provisional government of Memel, the interallied commission in control of the occupied territory in Germany, the Commission for the military control and disarmament of Germany, and the Reparation Commission, Mr. Toynbee continues:[1]

It was clearly necessary . . . to set up some permanent organization to which these Commissions could report and which could come to decisions on the innumerable questions that would (no doubt) arise. It had already been deter-

[1] A. J. Toynbee, *Survey of International Affairs, 1920–1923* (London, 1927), pp. 1 *et seq.* As all students of international affairs are aware, this and the following volumes of the same series, published under the auspices of the British Institute of International Affairs, are an inexhaustible mine of accurate information. One cannot too highly praise the spirit, care, and ability displayed in the preparation and publication of these works, which reflect the greatest credit both on the remarkable institution and on the eminent author responsible for them. Many of the facts recalled in this chapter are drawn from this source, hereunder referred to as *S.I.A.*

mined, during July, 1919, to establish for this purpose a Commission which should sit in Paris and should be the official representative of the Principal Allied and Associated Powers for the purposes of the interpretation and execution of the Treaties. It was eventually decided that the members of this Commission should be the Allied Ambassadors to France, and in consequence, it received the name of the Conference of Ambassadors. This Conference came into existence immediately after the exchange of ratifications, but there has not been published, and there does not in fact appear ever to have existed, any formal instrument setting up the Conference and determining its functions and limitations. It held its first meeting on the 26th January, 1920. From that time onwards it continued to hold meetings, as a rule once a week, and it established a secretariat and offices of its own. Unfortunately, information is not available for giving a consecutive account of its activities, since, except for brief *communiqués* to the French press, there has been no systematic and regular publication either of its agenda or of its decisions. None the less, it is possible to give some general indication of its functions and methods.

In addition to the French representative, the Conference consisted of the Ambassadors in Paris of Great Britain, Italy, and Japan. The American Ambassador was generally present, at any rate during the first months, but he was there for the information of his Government and took no formal part in the proceedings. The French representative was the Chairman; at the first meeting M. Millerand, the Prime Minister, was present; afterwards his place was taken by M. Cambon.

In order to understand the duties of the Conference, it is necessary to consult the texts of the Peace Treaties. In these texts it is laid down repeatedly that certain action shall be taken by the Principal Allied and Associated Powers. The plebiscite regulations, for instance, will be found in every case to lay down that, after a plebiscite has been taken, the frontier shall be fixed by the Principal Allied and Associated Powers. The articles regarding Danzig set forth that the Principal Allied and Associated Powers undertake to establish the town of Danzig as a Free City, and also to negotiate a treaty between the Polish Government and the Free City of Danzig. The military clauses ordain that the manufacture of arms and other war material in Germany shall only be carried out in factories or works the location of which shall be communicated to and approved by the Governments of the Principal Allied and Associated Powers. The chapter on penalties gives to the Allied and Associated Powers the right to bring persons accused of having violated the laws and customs of war before military tribunals. In fact, it may be said that almost every chapter of each Treaty contains provisions of this kind, the characteristic feature of which is that the Treaty cannot be carried out without a formal decision made by the Allies in coöperation with one another. Briefly, it may be said that the Ambassadors' Conference was the organ set up to carry out all these and any other clauses of the Treaties;[2] and, so far as can be ascertained, they confined themselves almost exclusively to these definite functions.

The Supreme Council, that is, the body representing the five Principal Allied and Associated Powers which had negotiated the four European peace treaties, held its last regular meeting on January 21, 1920, when it formally empowered the Conference of Ambassadors to act. But this latter body presently found itself in the position of a subordinate deputy, rather than in that of a full successor, to the former. Although the Conference of Ambassa-

[2] With the important exception that the Reparation Commission was an independent body reporting directly to the Allied Governments, while there also seems to be some doubt as to the extent to which the Conference of Ambassadors controlled the Rhineland High Commission.

dors has been sitting continuously for nearly a
decade, the Supreme Council was intermittently revived whenever circumstances of particular importance or urgency were held by the British or French
Prime Ministers to render its intervention necessary
or opportune.

To recall in detail the activities of these two bodies
and of all of their subsidiary interallied organs, including the practically independent Reparation Commission, would be to write the main chapters of the
recent political history of Europe. Our aim is much
more modest. We wish but to outline the main trend
of that history. For that purpose we will note first
the general procedure adopted by these various
interallied bodies, as indicating the nature of the co-
operation of the states they represented; secondly,
the final settlement of most of the questions be-
queathed to them by the treaties; and thirdly, the
general tendency from coercion to negotiation and
compromise which was followed for the solution of
these problems which force alone was found impotent to solve.

In the peace treaties which they drafted the five
great victors constantly referred to themselves as
the "Principal Allied and Associated Powers." The
term is neither modest nor strictly accurate. As their
co-belligerents do not seem, at least openly, to have
resented the subordinate position to which they were
thus condescendingly relegated, we, having no reason to be more royalist than the King of the Bel-
gians, for instance, shall not quarrel with the first
adjective. But the second is distinctly misleading.
"Allied" implies an alliance and an alliance implies
a treaty. Now as the enemies of the Central Powers

never concluded a treaty of alliance among themselves, and as the only legal tie which bound at least some of them to each other—the undertaking not to conclude a separate peace—was dissolved by the coming into force of the diplomatic instrument in which the expression "allied" is used, it is obviously more convenient than proper.

As the victors constituted no true alliance, each of them, of course, retained not only his absolute sovereignty, but even his untrammeled independence of the others. When, therefore, the peace treaties provide, as they frequently do, that certain matters shall be left to the discretion of the Allied and Associated Powers, they necessarily mean to the discretion of each and every one of them. Unless where the contrary is expressly stated, the ulterior collective decisions of the Allied and Associated Powers had, therefore, to be unanimous in order to be valid.

The authors of the treaties were so conscious of this that in several minor instances—rulings of Boundary and Plebiscite Commissions, and even certain findings and decisions of the Reparation Commission, were cases in point—they declared the vote of a majority to be sufficient.

In consequence, for the last ten years the Supreme Council and the Conference of Ambassadors, in carrying out the peace treaties, were either unanimous or impotent, that is, obliged to procrastinate. Unanimity was easily achieved when, as in most routine decisions and in most cases of deliberations on new boundaries, no opposed French and British interests were at stake. To be unanimous proved difficult in the Supreme Council or the Conference of Ambassadors, when, as in many instances in their dealings with Germany about disarmament and reparations and the administration of the occupied territory, the French policy of strict and relentless execution of the Treaty of Versailles clashed with the more conciliatory British tendency to subordinate everything to economic reconstruction and peace. Even here, however, some common ground could usually be found, because each party felt that, much as the other was unreasonable or inconsistent, formal agreement on an unsatisfactory basis was less dangerous than open disagreement. When unanimity could not be attained, the resulting deadlock was always fraught with most unfortunate consequences. Either, as in the territorial discussions about Eastern Galicia, Vilna, and Memel, it led to violence and *faits accomplis,* which the interallied authorities were then obliged unanimously but weakly to sanction. Or, as in the case of Upper Silesia, it could be overcome only by recourse to the League of Nations and to a settlement of which the most that can be said is that it is better than none. Or, as in the great Franco-British controversy over German reparations and sanctions, culminating in January 1923 in the occupation of the Ruhr, it produced what was almost a complete collapse of the Entente, and certainly a suspension of friendly relations. In this latter case the isolated action of France, followed with grim resignation by Belgium and with obvious reluctance by Italy, was of doubtful legality. But whether it was justified under the Treaty of Versailles, as the French claimed, or not, as was held by the British jurists, it was certainly not a collective interallied undertaking, but an individual venture of some of the former enemies of Germany.

If we now cast a glance over the whole field of problems which, unsolved by the peace conferences themselves, were by them entrusted for settlement to organs of interallied coöperation, we shall note that they fall into three groups. There are those which are today completely and finally solved, those which have received a temporary solution, and those which still await solution. To the first group, by far the largest, belong most of the territorial questions, as well as those relating to the allocation of mandates, the disarmament of the defeated powers, and the treatment of war criminals. By final settlement we do not, of course, mean settlements for all eternity— we are speaking historically and not metaphysically —nor even settlements regarded as final by all the interested parties. We refer only to such settlements as have been sanctioned by legally binding, formally accepted decisions which renewed negotiations or war alone could overthrow. Thus the delimitation of the Polish Corridor or of the frontiers of the new Hungary may not be and are not in fact considered final by the majority of the German and of the Hungarian peoples. But the decisions concerning them have been made once for all by the competent interallied bodies and have been formally, even if reluctantly, concurred in by the Governments of the defeated states.

Problems temporarily solved are those concerning which the solution has been found and accepted for a limited period, at the end of which changes are expressly anticipated. The territorial status of the Saar Basin, the *régime* of Upper Silesia, and the foreign military occupation of Germany have given rise to such problems and solutions, which are, for-

tunately for the stability of the new Europe, rather
rare.

Unfortunately less rare, but on the whole not numerous, are the still unsolved problems. Some of
them, such as the regulation of the status of the
Lower Scheldt by common agreement between Belgium and Holland contemplated in the peace treaties,
but not yet realized, are only intermittently considered, because they are not of first-rate European
importance. But others, such as the Polish-Lithuanian question or the settlement of reparations have
not yet been solved in this first post-war decade in
spite of the ablest, most persistent, and most patient
interallied efforts. While it may be confidently hoped
that all of them will be solved in the course of the
coming decade, it would be excessively optimistic to
expect that within the same period the greatest
shadow which still darkens the future of Europe will
be dispelled.

The shadow I refer to is that of the Bolshevik
Colossus standing in somber reticence on the very
threshold of the old continent, a terrifying and dis-
mally sad figure of helpless violence and inhuman
fanaticism. This great state, potentially vigorous
and powerful, but actually benumbed by addiction to
the drugs of false doctrines and paralyzed by ex-
cesses of intrigue, has as yet proved quite uname-
nable to all forms of wholesome and constructive international coöperation. To ask whether it will soon
sincerely join in such coöperation, is to ask whether
it is likely soon to reform its internal policies. One
thing is obvious. As long as the rulers of the Soviet
Union feel obliged to keep up the hopes of their followers by holding out to them the prospect of a

world revolution, prepared and favored by Moscow, they can be neither willing nor acceptable partners in the great enterprise of peace reconstruction which is being attempted in Europe and which can succeed only if based on at least a minimum of mutual confidence and good will.

The slow, irregular, but still persistent growth of these feelings of confidence and good will in Europe in the course of the last decade, is clearly shown by the changing reciprocal attitudes of the former enemies within it. In order fully to understand the progress made since 1919 it is necessary, even though it be unpleasant, briefly to recall the feelings which animated the victors and the vanquished on the morrow of the Armistice.

When the last shot had been fired in France on November 11, 1918, the War was over. But peace was not at hand.

While during the first half of 1919 the victorious but disgruntled and well-nigh ruined Allies were bitterly discussing among themselves what was to be the fate of their defeated enemies, the latter, faced with revolution and starvation, were awaiting the verdict in impotent silence. When the German delegation was finally summoned to Versailles they came and were treated as convicted but not yet sentenced criminals. Having protested against their proposed sentence, as being contrary both to the terms of the armistice and to justice, they were, on June 16, 1919, told in no uncertain terms by the victors, that "they utterly fail to understand the position in which Germany stands today." After this promising prelude the letter in which the final conditions of peace were explained to them continued: "In the view of the

Allied and Associated Powers, the War which began
on August 1, 1914, was the greatest crime against
humanity and the freedom of peoples, that any nation calling itself civilized, has ever consciously com-
mitted.'' Therefore, to quote but a few lines more
from this sixty-page arraignment, the victors declared:

Justice, . . . is the only possible basis for the settlement
of the accounts of this terrible war. Justice is what the German Delegation asks for and says that Germany had been
promised. Justice is what Germany shall have. But it must
be justice for all. There must be justice for the dead and
wounded and for those who have been orphaned and be-
reaved that Europe might be freed from Prussian despot-
ism. There must be justice for the peoples who now stagger
under war debts which exceed £30,000,000,000 that liberty
might be saved. There must be justice for those millions
whose homes and land, ships and property German sav-
agery has spoliated and destroyed.

That is why the Allied and Associated Powers have insisted as a cardinal feature of the Treaty that Germany
must undertake to make reparation to the very uttermost
of her power: for reparation for wrongs inflicted is of the
essence of justice.

As justice thus understood led to demands of economic sacrifice which no one generation, no matter
how industrious, could possibly hope to satisfy, and
to demands of territorial and moral sacrifice besides,
with which no people, no matter how prostrate,
could honestly agree fully to comply, the inevitable
result was, to reverse an American historical phrase,
an ''era of bad feeling.'' That the era of intolerably
bad feeling, which undoubtedly ensued in Europe,

was to last less than a brief decade, no optimist in the summer of 1919 would have dared to prophesy.

It is against this horizon as a background—a horizon black with mutual hate and suspicion and overtopped, as by fiery volcanoes, by the bloody recollection of the grimmest war of history—and it is with a treaty imposed by a vindictive victor on a resentful foe as a starting point, that one should consider the recent evolution of international coöperation in the Old World.

A few facts and a few dates will suffice as milestones on the road of reconciliation, to indicate the direction and the pace of progress.

The Treaty of Versailles was signed on June 28, 1919. Peace, however, was legally restored only six months later, when the Treaty, having been ratified by Germany and by three of the Principal Allied Powers, in accordance with the provisions of its final article 440, came into force on January 10, 1920. It was then that diplomatic relations were resumed between the former enemies by the mutual accrediting, first of *chargés d'affaires,* and then, six months later, of ambassadors in their capitals.

A large and important part of Germany, the whole left bank of the Rhine and three bridge heads on the right, was, however, still under military interallied occupation. On April 6, 1920, this occupation was even extended by the French to Frankfurt and Darmstadt, that is, beyond the temporary limits fixed by the treaty. This isolated action of the French was taken as an additional sanction against Germany, whose troops had entered Rhenish Westphalia to put down a revolutionary strike. As the British were inclined to condone Germany's move,

which—although strictly illegal—seemed justified
by the extraordinary circumstances, they strongly
protested against the attitude of their French Allies.[3]
This interallied crisis was but the first serious symptom of a state of affairs which, beginning on the morrow of the armistice, has lasted until the present
day.

As already observed in another connection, the
British, whose territorial security was no longer
threatened, have always sought to restrain the
French and to convince them that the common interest was better served by a policy of conciliation,
calculated to regain the good will of their former
enemies, or at least to avoid unnecessary bitterness,
than by the use of force. For this main reason
Franco-British relations have on the whole, during
the last decade, always been the function of Franco-
German relations, becoming more intimate when the
latter became less unfriendly, and cooling off again
with each new manifestation of Franco-German hostility.

At the beginning of July, 1920, after the French
had evacuated the Frankfurt zone, the eighth interallied conference took place at Spa. It is mentioned
here because, unlike all the preceding and many of
the following meetings of the Supreme Council, it
was attended by the Germans on a footing of formal
equality.[4] Although the atmosphere at Spa was anything but cordial, and although in the following year
there was a renewed temporary extension of the
occupied area in which Great Britain this time co-
operated, it did represent the first attempt to substitute discussion and compromise for strict coer-

[3] *S.I.A., 1923,* pp. 91 *et seq.*   [4] *Ibid., 1920–1923,* p. 13.

cion as a method of solving the reparation and disarmament problems.

In the meanwhile, in December, 1920, Austria and Bulgaria had joined the League of Nations. Their admission by the unanimous First Assembly, and that of Hungary in September, 1921, by the Second, were significant both in themselves and as an example which, however, was to be followed by Germany only five years later.

The year 1922 began as auspiciously as it was to end disastrously. At the Cannes Conference on January 6, 1922, the Supreme Council adopted a resolution introduced by Mr. Lloyd George to the effect that:[5]

The Allied Powers in conference are unanimously of opinion that an Economic and Financial Conference should be summoned in February or early March, to which all the powers of Europe, including Germany, Russia, Austria, Hungary and Bulgaria should be invited to send representatives. They regard such a Conference as an urgent and essential step towards the economic reconstruction of Central and Eastern Europe. . . . A united effort of the stronger Powers is necessary to remedy the paralysis of the European system.

This reconstruction conference met at Genoa on April 10, 1922, but the political horizon had darkened since the beginning of the year. The French Prime Minister, M. Briand, was already weakened even in January by the part he had played at the Washington Conference—an international gathering which, if not as catastrophic in its consequences as a brilliant American journalist has pronounced it to be, was certainly less triumphantly successful than

[5] *Ibid.*, p. 21.

most of his American readers seem to have believed.[6]
M. Briand's agreement with Mr. Lloyd George at
Cannes cost him his office and before the Genoa Conference met he had been succeeded by M. Poincaré.
Now M. Poincaré was, by his whole conception of international relations, their aims, and their methods,
as opposed to the Genoa Conference as he was
temperamentally unfit to coöperate with its author,
his British colleague, Mr. Lloyd George.

Antagonized by France, unsupported by the
United States, who had refused the invitation to
participate in the Conference, the British Prime
Minister, whose aim it had been to reintegrate Germany and Russia into the European system, was
obviously defeated when on April 16 these two
powers concluded their separate agreement at Rapallo.

There followed months of bitter interallied disappointment and difficulties and of growing French
irritation against Germany. The beginning of 1923
witnessed the French invasion of the Ruhr, and a
whole dismal year was spent in exhausting the possibilities of this most terribly destructive attempt
to gain peace by coercion.

During this time not only were France and Germany at war in so far as it is possible to wage real
war on a defenseless foe, but France and Great
Britain were so estranged that only by the great
tact and patience of Mr. Lloyd George's conservative successor in office, was an open breach avoided
between the former Allies. Their representatives
never met in conference on reparations from Jan-

[6] Frank Simonds, *How Europe Made Peace without America*
(New York, London, 1927), pp. 185 *et seq.*

uary 4, 1923, until September 19 of the same year. Even on the latter occasion—a personal visit paid by Mr. Baldwin, the British Prime Minister, on his way from Aix-les-Bains to London, to his French colleague M. Poincaré—the best the official *communiqué* issued after the brief interview, could announce, was:

It is not to be expected that in the course of one meeting, M. Poincaré and Mr. Baldwin were able to settle upon any definite solution, but they were able to establish a common agreement of views and to discover that on no question is there any difference of purpose or divergence of principle which could impair the coöperation of the two countries upon which depends so much the settlement of the peace of the world.[7]

Only when a few days later, on September 27, 1923, the German Government abrogated its ordinance of passive resistance, did a new, but still faint, dawn of hope break. It was eagerly welcomed not only in London and Paris, but also in Washington, where the sinister course of European affairs had been followed with obvious misgivings. From this day may be dated the beginning of a new era of reconciliation, first between France and Great Britain, and presently also between Germany and her former enemies. In the most recent edition of his remarkable book, Dr. Isaiah Bowman has observed:[8]

Despite British opposition to the occupation of the Ruhr, it now seems certain that this was the ultimate act necessary of performance to bring not merely Germany, but Great

[7] *S.I.A., 1924,* p. 339.
[8] Isaiah Bowman, *The New World* (4th ed.; London, 1928), p. 10.

Britain and even France as well, to a realization that only in joint action could a lasting remedy be found.

Whether the proof offered by the Ruhr enterprise of the sterility of mere force, was, as Doctor Bowman implies, necessary or not, it was certainly convincing.

On its morrow everyone, even in France, realized that another way out of the reparation tangle had to be found. The proposal of an impartial inquiry into Germany's capacity to pay, made by Mr. Hughes in his New Haven speech of December 29, 1922, and indorsed by Mr. Coolidge on October 11, 1923, was eagerly taken up in London, and although not without hesitation, finally accepted in Paris. This led to the appointment of the Dawes Commission at the end of December, 1923, to the exchange of extraordinarily cordial and frank letters between the new British Prime Minister, Mr. MacDonald, who has the undying merit of having initiated it, and M. Poincaré, in January and February, 1924.

The change which had come over Europe as a consequence of the resumption of methods of conciliation cannot be more clearly shown than by the words uttered by the heads of the British and German governments when the former welcomed the latter to the London Conference on August 5. Speaking of the results of the labors of the Dawes Commission, Mr. MacDonald said:

We are all anxious that the responsibilities which the report imposes upon us should be accepted not because they must be, but because there is a common desire to make a serious and honest attempt to fulfill obligations to which signatures are attached, and to attach signatures after discussion in which each party has been fairly heard. Such agreements carry moral obligations as well as legal ones.

To which the German Chancellor, Doctor Marx, replied:[9]

We see here the way which will and must lead our people to freedom and peace, and at the same time afford a possibility of their working together with other peoples in the joint reconstruction of Europe. The restoration of mutual confidence is the first essential for the fruitful coöperation of the nations. If the Conference succeeds, as we confidently hope it will, in preparing the ground for the attainment of this great end, then the whole German people, as soon as the vital conditions for its free economic activity have been restored, will devote its whole strength to carrying out the many obligations which the Experts' Plan requires from it.

The Conference, as is well known, did succeed, and on August 16, 1924, Mr. MacDonald could congratulate himself and the world on being able to offer, as he said in his concluding speech, "the first really negotiated agreement since the War."[10]

From this point on events moved, if not as briskly as those ignorant of the complexities of international multilateral coöperation may have hoped, at least with gratifying rapidity.

On August 30, 1924, the London Agreements were signed. On September 3, Mr. S. Parker Gilbert was appointed as Agent-General for Reparations Payments. In October the loan to the German Government was floated in New York, London, Paris, and in other financial centers, and everywhere oversubscribed. On October 29 the Reparation Commission

[9] *S.I.A., 1924*, p. 374.   [10] *Ibid.*, p. 384.

announced that the economic and fiscal unity of Germany had been reëstablished. On November 15 the railroads of the occupied and invaded areas were handed over to the new German Corporation created under the Dawes Plan, and two days later the military evacuation of the Ruhr was completed.

In February, 1925, the negotiations began which were to lead to the Locarno treaties in October of the same year, and to Germany's admission to the League of Nations as a permanent member of the council less than a year later. The dissolution on January 31, 1927, of the Commission of Military Control in Germany, may be taken as the final step in the process of political reconciliation.

Of course, this progress cannot be held to be entirely completed until some equality in armaments shall have been reëstablished, if possible, on or near the plane of the vanquished, until all German territory has been evacuated—which according to the Treaty of Versailles will not be before 1935—nor until all reparation payments will have ceased— which will be when the United States says the word. But already today, after the successful negotiations of the Experts' Committee of 1929, on which Germany, unlike in 1924, has been fully represented, western Europe may be said to have overcome the War.

If we recall the extracts from the Allied letter of June, 1919 to the German Peace Delegation, which I quoted a moment ago, it is impossible to deny the tremendous progress that has been made in the course of the last decade on the road toward truly peaceful coöperation between equal and free nations in the execution of the peace treaties.

II

The Promotion of Prosperity outside the Framework of the League of Nations.

Although the League of Nations has always had a hand in the execution of the peace treaties, and although, as we shall see in our last chapter, the Principal Allied Powers have tended to unload on Geneva an ever increasing share of their responsibilities in the liquidation of the War, the larger part of this field remains essentially theirs. The main task of the Supreme Council and of the other inter-allied bodies, was to complete in peace the work the victors had begun in the War. As it was they who had sown the seed, it has very naturally been for them to reap the harvest of their victory.

To promote national prosperity and national security through the organization of international co-operation, on the other hand, is the most important function of the League. However, as the execution of the peace settlement was the main task of the Supreme Council, but not their monopoly, so the promotion of prosperity and security has not been internationally pursued only within the framework and through the organs of the League. We have, therefore, in this chapter, still to consider these two topics as dealt with by the states of Europe outside of Geneva.

If we disregard for the moment the action of the League of Nations, we shall note that Europe has sought to promote the prosperity of its constituent states by two sets of international measures, multilateral and bilateral. The multilateral method was pursued in the various pre-war international organi-

zations and unions, and some few regional meetings
such as that of the successor states of the Hapsburg
monarchy held at Porto Rosa in 1921, which we are
content merely to mention, and at the more ambitious
but unsuccessful Genoa Conference. The bilateral
method was that employed in the negotiations of the
countless commercial treaties by which the individual states of Europe have sought to readjust their
economic relations with one another.

About the extra-League attempts at multilateral
coöperation for the promotion of prosperity, we
shall say but little, both because they were neither
novel nor very fruitful, and because these international rivulets generally tended to flow into the main
stream at Geneva. And about the bilateral economic
negotiations we may be very brief also, both because
it would be impossible to analyze them in detail
without adding another volume to the long list of
monographs already devoted to post-war commercial policy[11] and because their chief characteristic
was the subordination of the economic to the political and to the military, that is, of prosperity to
security.

The Genoa Conference which sat for five weeks
from April 10 to May 19, 1922, was attended by
thirty-four national delegations. Of these twenty-
nine represented European states including Germany and Russia. As the United States had, much
to everyone's regret, declined the invitation to par-

[11] An excellent concise review of the most recent developments
in this field is to be found in a memorandum prepared by the
Secretariat of the League of Nations for the second meeting of
the Economic Consultative Committee, League Document, Economic and Financial (1929), II, 12.

ticipate, and as the five non-European delegations all came from various parts of the British Empire, the Genoa gathering was both the most inclusively and the most exclusively European Conference that has ever been held since the War. Its essential object, the economic reconstruction of the Old World, was as European as its composition. And its spiritual father, the British Prime Minister, was the most picturesque and, in spite of his many obvious failings and shortcomings, perhaps the greatest war and post-war statesman of Europe. In a speech delivered in the House of Commons on the Conference, a week before its opening, on April 3, 1922, Mr. Lloyd George, whose last important international venture this huge gathering of European heads of governments was to be, thus pictured the state of the continent he had set out to save:[12]

The Conference has been called to consider the problem of the reconstruction of economic Europe, devastated and broken into fragments by the desolating agency of war. Europe, the richest of all continents, the continent which possesses the largest amount of accumulated wealth and certainly the greatest machinery for the production of wealth, the largest aggregate of human beings with highly civilized needs, and with highly civilized means of supplying those needs, and therefore Europe, the best customer in the world and of the world, has been impoverished by the greatest destruction of capital that the world has ever witnessed. If European countries had gathered together their mobile wealth accumulated by centuries of industry and thrift on to one pyramid and then set fire to it, the result could hardly have been more complete. International trade has been disorganized through and through.

[12] J. Saxon Mills, *The Genoa Conference* (London, undated), p. 10.

The recognized medium of commerce, exchange based upon currency, has become almost worthless and unworkable; vast areas, upon which Europe has hitherto depended for a large proportion of its food supplies and its raw material, completely destroyed for all purposes of commerce; nations, instead of co-operating to restore, broken up by suspicions and creating difficulties and new artificial restrictions; great armies ready to march, and nations already overburdened with taxation having to bear the additional taxation which the maintenance of these huge armaments to avoid suspected dangers renders necessary.

Nothing could be more ambitious nor more generous than the aims Mr. Lloyd George had set himself and the Conference when he had proposed its summoning at Cannes in January. Europe was to be reunited economically by commercial agreements, and appeased politically by a joint undertaking to refrain from aggression. Russia and Germany were to be readmitted as equal partners into the system of European nations. Thereby all would be benefited. Great Britain's two million unemployed would be restored to productive labor as the European market would be reopened to British exports. Germany would reëquip Russia industrially, and so be able to pay her reparations to France and to her Allies out of the profits of her enterprise. France, no longer worried about Germany's professed incapacity to pay, would be assured of Great Britain's full support in breaking down, if necessary, Germany's supposed deliberate reluctance to pay. And in order still further to allay France's suspicions about the intentions of her chief enemy and of her principal Ally, Mr. Lloyd George was prepared to offer her on behalf of Great Britain, a formal treaty of guar-

anty against the direct and unprovoked aggression
of Germany.

The scheme undoubtedly lacked neither boldness
of conception nor statesmanlike vision. But even before the Conference met two accidents had occurred
which must have shaken even its author's faith in
its ultimate success. In France, as we have seen,
M. Briand had been obliged to pay by his forced resignation the penalty for having, although timidly,
shared this faith. His place had been taken by
M. Poincaré whose every fiber revolted against the
conciliatory aims and the impatiently revolutionary
and intolerably illegal methods of his abhorred British colleague. The new official attitude of France was
so unfriendly to the projected Conference that her
attendance at one time seemed doubtful and her co-
operation was bound to be more critical than constructive. The other primary misfortune was the
abstention of the United States. In a speech delivered before the National Liberal Council in January, 1922, Mr. Lloyd George, while replying to
critics who had reproached him with not placing the
Conference under the auspices of the League of
Nations, had given as the main reason for his independent action, the inevitable refusal of the United
States to accept an invitation emanating from Geneva. "There are two great nations," he had declared, "whom, if you are going to establish peace,
and going to get the economic reconstruction of the
world, it is necessary to get there."[13]

Now the two great nations whose coöperation at
Genoa was, late in January, held to be "necessary"
by Mr. Lloyd George, were Russia and the United

[13] J. Saxon Mills, *op. cit.*, p. 21.

States. The Russians came, it is true, not only willingly, but with great alacrity. But they came as pugnacious claimants and not in the least as the prodigal sons whom their British host would have hopefully greeted, and whom the other guests might have politely tolerated.

The story of the Conference cannot be retold here. In his final speech on May 19, 1922, Mr. Lloyd George declared it to have been "one of the most remarkable conferences ever held in the history of the world . . . for ever an inspiring landmark on the pathway of peace."[14] But Mr. Lloyd George appears to be one of those fortunate individuals whom only a personal failure personally admitted can reduce to despondency, who is temperamentally unable to admit a personal failure, and who therefore lives in a state of almost continuous enthusiasm. And this enthusiasm is never more rapturous than when he is commenting on his own doings, which is nearly all the time. In spite of all the magnetism of his rare personality, however, the contagion of the former British Prime Minister's infectious enthusiasm remained rather narrowly circumscribed in space and especially in time.

Looking back dispassionately on the results of the Genoa Conference we may note that they were of two kinds, political and economic. The political results were transient in so far as they were beneficial and durable only in so far as they were unfortunate. The Conference indirectly fostered the German-Bolshevik intimacy and delayed rather than hastened the Franco-British *rapprochement*. The eco-

[14] J. Saxon Mills, *op. cit.*, p. 273.

nomic results, on the other hand, were immediately slight, but ultimately fruitful.

When the wind of time, blowing over the battlefield of Genoa, had dispersed the smoke clouds of oratory and the dust of intrigue and animosity, there became visible among the corpses of many defeated political hopes and exploded social fallacies, a few modest common-sense economic and financial truths. The resolutions embodying them were taken up later by the technical organizations of the League of Nations, to which they had been submitted by the Conference itself, and some of them, such as those relating to freer and more stable economic intercourse and to economic statistics, have given rise to important international conventions.[15]

While the Genoa Conference was by far the most spectacular incident in the recent history of multilateral international coöperation to promote prosperity without the framework of the League, it was by no means the only instance of such coöperation. On the contrary, all the important pre-war international public unions such as the International Telegraphic Union, the Universal Postal Union, the International Union of Railroad Administrations and many others, have resumed and often intensified their activities, which the War had either interrupted or hampered.

At the peace settlement it was anticipated that the League of Nations was sooner or later to absorb or at least to control them all. Therefore Article 24,

[15] *The Genoa Conference and the League of Nations,* memorandum by the Secretary-General, League Document C. 423. M. 257. 1922.

which reads as follows, was inserted into the Covenant:

1. There shall be placed under the direction of the League all international Bureaux already established by general treaties if the parties to such treaties consent. All such international bureaux and all commissions for the regulation of matters of international interest hereafter constituted shall be placed under the direction of the League.

2. In all matters of international interest which are regulated by general conventions but which are not placed under the control of international bureaux or commissions, the Secretariat of the League shall, subject to the consent of the Council and if desired by the parties, collect and distribute all relevant information and shall render any other assistance which may be necessary or desirable.

3. The Council may include as part of the expenses of the Secretariat the expenses of any bureau or commission which is placed under the direction of the League.

The program thus outlined has only been very partially carried out. Two main obstacles stood in the way of complete administrative centralization under the League. The most important of these obstacles was the lack of universality of the League. It was naturally not to be expected that states which, while parties to the pre-war treaties setting up the international unions in question, were not welcome at Geneva or not willing to join the League, should consent to the projected change. Besides, the states on whose territory and under the immediate influence of whose governments the old international bureaux had been placed, were as a rule very reluctant to see the privileges that they thus enjoyed curtailed. Up to the present only four of them, none of first-rate importance, have been placed under the control of the League. They are the International Bureau for Assistance (Paris), the International Hydrographic Bureau (Monaco), the Central International Office for the Control of Liquor Traffic (Brussels), and the International Commission on Air Navigation (Paris).

On the other hand, formal or informal coöperation has been agreed upon between the League and most of the others. This coöperation has been effected either by what might be called the interlocking of administrative organs, as in the case of the *Office International d'Hygiène Publique* in Paris, or by mutual representation in an advisory capacity of especially appointed delegates, as in many of the others.

Even when no effective coöperation has resulted, the League of Nations, by the mere emulation of its example and by the exchange of information, has tended to promote progress among these bureaux, and to accelerate the pace of their labors.

An especial section in the Secretariat is intrusted with the duty of keeping in touch with them. A general idea of the scope, if not necessarily of the real importance of international coöperation without the framework of the League, may be gained by a perusal of the *Handbook of International Associations* published by this section. According to the latest edition of this *Handbook*, there are in existence twenty-four separate public international organizations based on treaties and financed by the states which created them. Besides, the *Handbook*[16] men-

[16] *Handbook of International Organizations,* League Document XII. B. Bureaux.

tions about 475 non-governmental international institutions, of which only a few receive official subsidies, but of which the most are purely private organizations of very unequal importance.

Of far greater immediate signficance for the welfare of Europe than either the oratory of the Genoa Conference or the continuous activities of all these organizations, has been that form of international coöperation which is represented by the negotiation of bilateral commercial treaties.

When two states engage in conversations for the purpose of regulating their reciprocal trade relations, they may be said to be collaborating on the international plane for the promotion of their common benefit. It is in some such terms that the negotiators habitually define their purposes at the beginning and at the end of their labors. If, however, we consider realistically what takes place during the weeks and months of actual discussion between them, we are forced to dismiss such a definition as diplomatically but quite excessively euphemistic. This is particularly true of most of the post-war European commercial wrangles.

In the first place, every national delegation is usually so absorbed by the defense of its own interests and so oblivious of those of the other, that even if all goes well the result can never be more than a compromise acceptable to each party. It would be a mere accident if such a compromise were ever identical with the greatest common economic advantage of both. Secondly, and this is particularly characteristic of post-war commercial negotiations in Europe, this advantage is seldom realized, because it is not often exclusively or even chiefly sought after. When either or both parties to a commercial negotiation are animated by the desire to protect certain so-called "key" industries at all costs, it is not surprising that the price of security thus purchased should have to be paid in terms of lost prosperity. Thus the certain and permanent interests of peace are deliberately sacrificed to the doubtful interests of unlikely war.

The consequences of both of these two causes have been further intensified by the action of a third factor which does not seem to have received the attention it deserves, and which, in my own country at least, and also elsewhere, I believe, has certainly tended to favor a protective and restrictive trade policy. The organization, not only of the various industries and crafts, but also of agriculture, into associations for the defense of their professional interests, with highly trained staffs of officials on the one hand, and the parliamentary influence of these bodies on the other, has led governments to rely on them for the formulation of their commercial policy. Often, indeed, the especial delegations intrusted with the actual negotiations, are composed of the heads or permanent secretaries of these associations. Under these circumstances it is natural that the various producers' interests should be better safeguarded than those of the whole consuming community. Now it is a well-known fact that the greater the producers' and the lesser the consumers' influence on trade policy the better the chances of protectionism.

Protectionism has been favored also by such general circumstances as abnormal war investments and fluctuating currencies, before whose immediate consequences even convinced free traders have been obliged to bow their heads in sorrowful resignation. The war and the blockade, as we have seen above, led to the creation and development of costly industrial plants which no responsible government could abandon to the sudden destruction which would have befallen them on the morrow of peace, with the restoration of completely free competitive conditions. As for unequally fluctuating currencies, their effect was to favor temporary and abnormal exports from countries affected by inflation, to their financially sounder neighbors, to whom they transmitted their disease in the shape of unemployment. That the latter countries should have sought to protect themselves by restrictive or even by prohibitive measures, was as natural as that they should have refused to limit their freedom by concluding long-term commercial treaties with most-favored-nation clauses.

As a result of all these various converging circumstances, the post-war commercial negotiations of Europe have so far resembled international war more than international pacific coöperation.

The World Economic Conference was summoned by the League of Nations in 1927 mainly to put an end to that state of affairs and to restore economic peace. In its report it noted, deplored, and condemned the abnormal height, the undue complexities, and the hopeless instability of most existing customs tariffs, as well as the many instances of irritating international discrimination which still prevailed eight years after peace had been concluded.

On all these four points the Economic Conference of 1927 was unanimous and insistent. But on all these four points the League's Economic Consultative Committee, created to continue the action of the Conference, in its recent *Report* of May, 1929, could note but little progress and could but reiterate the recommendations of its parent body.[17]

The making of commercial treaties, it is true, had proceeded actively, the total for the year 1928 being forty-two as against thirty in 1927. As a result, "the network of commercial treaties thus noted is an indication of the persistent instability of the tariff situation. The Economic Conference has been informed in 1927 by one of its experts who had examined 180 recently negotiated treaties, that in all but twenty-seven, the treaty was changeable within a year."[18] In the 1929 report of the Consultative Committee we read that "another feature of the year . . . is that these treaties are still for very short periods only, indeed in most cases for not longer than a single year."[19] Besides these forty-two short-term commercial treaties, only six of which contain tariff provisions and many of which reëstablished the right of their authors to raise their duties, thirty-four still more provisional agreements or *modus vivendi* were concluded in 1928, whereas only three had been signed in 1927. While formerly fluctuating currencies—perhaps the chief reason for this instability of customs tariffs—have very generally been stabilized

[17] *Report of the Economic Consultative Committee on Its Second Session* held at Geneva from May 6 to 11, 1929, League Document, II Economic and Financial (1929), II, 23.

[18] Sir Arthur Salter in *Problems of Peace* (2d series; London, 1928), p. 119.

[19] *Application of the Recommendations of the International Economic Conference,* Report on the Period May, 1928, to May, 1929, League Document, II Economic and Financial (1929), II, 12, 9.

in Europe, their evil consequences have not yet sub-
sided. The Consultative Committee, having recalled
the recommendations of the Economic Conference
that "states should refrain from making frequent
and sudden changes in their customs duties," regret-
fully noted that "these resolutions have not as yet
passed beyond the stage of recommendations."

The situation as regards the simplification of the
customs formalities and the abolition of what has
been termed indirect or administrative protectionism does not justify more optimism than as regards
stability. Here also the Economic Conference had
uttered wise words of warning, the Economic Committee pursued useful investigations, and the League
sponsored an especial convention. But real progress,
which in the last analysis depends on the good will
of the governments in their reciprocal relations, was
and remains exasperatingly slow.

As far as the actual level of tariffs is concerned,
it was estimated at the Economic Conference that it
was on the average 30 per cent higher than before
the War.[20] After analyzing in its report the causes
and consequences of this change, the Conference had
emphatically declared: "the time has come to put
an end to the increase in tariffs and to move in the
opposite direction." A year later, in 1928, the Consultative Committee, whose liberal convictions seem
to be slightly less firm and less unanimous than were
those of the parent body, but which still deplores the
prevailing excessive protectionism, was able to report that the upward tendency of tariffs had been
checked and that a beginning had been made with
stabilizing the situation by means of commercial

[20] Sir Arthur Salter, *op. cit.*, p. 120.

treaties. At its recent session in May, 1929, the new facts before it did not allow it to repeat even this very modestly hopeful statement. Some reductions there had been in the course of the year, notably in Sweden and in Germany, but they were at least neutralized if not outbalanced by increases elsewhere. In its report we read:

It is noteworthy that the proposals for the most sweeping increases of tariffs should come from those nations whose tariff indices are already among the highest in the world. Among other countries the protectionist pressure is not at present taking the form of a demand for a general upward revision, but for changes here and there. The effect of this is not as yet sufficient to upset what appears to be . . . a temporary condition of equilibrium. But if the pressure continues, these converging movements may have a cumulative effect and make the position of low tariff countries difficult. Indeed, if the tendency is not checked, it must sooner or later lead to the position which prevailed before the Conference of 1927; the world would then be faced with another period of tariff competition instead of a steady reduction towards a state of equilibrium at a lower level.[21]

On one point only do the recommendations of the Economic Conference seem to have been followed by almost unanimous, effective action by the states to whom they were addressed. The adoption of the most-favored-nation clause which the Genoa Conference in 1922 had already urged and whose importance the Economic Committee of the League has repeatedly stressed, has come to be the rule in the negotiation of bilateral commercial treaties. ''With

[21] *Report of the Economic Consultative Committee* (1929), p. 6.

one exception," says the 1929 report of the Economic Consultative Committee, " these (42 new commercial) treaties, following the precedent of 1927, all embody the most-favored-nation clause—in most cases in an unlimited form."

It is obvious that this change, in doing away with unfair and therefore particularly irritating international discrimination, presents very notable advantages for the prosperity and even for the peace of the world. It is less clear, perhaps, but it is equally certain, however, that it may constitute an obstacle on the road leading toward a general reduction of tariffs. That this difficulty did not escape the attention of the Economic Consultative Committee is shown by the following statement, which it made a point of adding to its cordial endorsement of the clause in its last report, and which it is hoped may not pass unnoticed in Washington:

The high tariffs of countries which, while not prepared to effect any reduction in their own duties, claim the unconditional application of the most-favored-nation clause, tend to make other countries hesitate to include important reduction of duties in bi-lateral treaties concluded by them.[22]

Without further pursuing this rapid survey of European tariff policies, as implemented by bilateral commercial treaties, we may and we must conclude that they are both unsatisfactory and very significant.

That it is contrary to the economic interest of Europe as a whole, and contrary also to the economic

[22] *Report of the Economic Consultative Committee* (1929), p. 13.

interest of each of its twenty-seven constituent national units that most, if not all of them, should be carrying on an ill-disguised commercial war with each other, in the vain hope of attaining an every-day-more-impossible state of self-sufficiency, even the most dogmatic of American protectionists will readily recognize. The growing realization of this truth in Europe, especially in the light of America's prosperity, internal free trade, and external sky-scraping tariffs, explains the increasing demand for some sort of European customs union. That such a demand will receive some measure of satisfaction in the near future is uncertain, and in my opinion, unlikely. I deem it unlikely especially on account of the growth of intercontinental trade which we have noted in our last chapter, of the imperial connections of the United Kingdom, and of the uncoöperative policy of the Soviet Union. But uncertain and unlikely as it may appear, it is highly significant as a reaction both against what is often referred to in Europe as America's growing economic imperialism, and against Europe's internecine commercial warfare.

This warfare in itself is symptomatic of the still prevailing state of European unrest, and of the persistent suspicions which still animate a large number of the states of the Old World. We are thus naturally led to consider the various measures of international coöperation for the promotion of security outside of the League, which is to be the subject of the last part of this chapter.

III

The Promotion of International Security outside the Framework of the League of Nations.

The feeling of national security is based either on the confidence that nothing threatens the state from without or on the conviction that possible external menaces can and will be successfully dealt with if they should turn into open aggression.

As a matter of fact the national security of no state rests exclusively on the first of these two pillars. Even the United States, Canada, Argentina, and Denmark, to take the example of some of the most fortunate states, who have every reason not to feel threatened from without, base their national security in part on the ultimate protection against possible attack afforded by certain definite factors: the United States, on her navy and army and on her potential military resources; Canada, on the support of Great Britain and on the friendly assistance of her great neighbor to the south; Argentina, on her geographic position and perhaps even on the much maligned Monroe Doctrine; Denmark, on the solidarity of Europe and on the protection of the League of Nations.

However, we must recognize that the various states of the world enjoy an extremely varying measure of natural security, that is, security irrespective of any deliberate steps taken in order artificially to enhance it. The most threatened states are those who possess advantages, territorial or other, of which they might be deprived by the hostile action of a powerful and envious rival. The greater and the more coveted these advantages, the more numerous, the more powerful, and the more envious such rivals on the one hand, the lesser on the other, the natural security of the states that possess such advantages and such rivals.

If this be so, it is obvious that the nations of Europe as a whole should feel less secure than those of the New World. This statement might well bring forth a protest from nationals of certain Central American republics. I should the less quarrel with them on that score, as their dissent would but confirm the truth of my previous remark on the basis of natural security.

However, and barring this admitted exception, the greater number of individuals and of sovereign states on the surface of Europe, the greater consequent length of national frontiers, combined with the greater ethnical and linguistic variety and the lesser consequent degree of social homogeneity, all tend to increase the possibilities of international friction and thereby to weaken, not only the subjective feelings, but also the objective facts of national security in the Old World.

If, instead of contrasting the Old World as a whole with the New, we look into Europe itself, we shall find that both the feelings and the facts of natural national security are far from being everywhere the same. They are slight in those countries which, according to our above statement, enjoy the greatest and most envied advantages within the reach of jealous rivals. As a rule therefore, all those states that have benefited territorially by the War, would, in the absence of any artificial protection, feel and be most exposed to attack. This is the case notably

for France and her continental allies. Having today
nothing to gain by further expansion, since their
victory has brought them all that military victory
can bring under modern conditions, they have everything to fear from aggression, since successful re-
venge would free their former enemies from the
bonds of economic servitude and from the humilia-
tion of territorial dismemberment. France's natural
security is particularly precarious. Her rich and
thinly peopled territory, her immense colonial empire, and her reparation credits would, were she not
particularly protected, as we shall see, inevitably
make of her the prey, not of her former enemy to the
East, but also of her poorer and hungrier Latin sis-
ter to the South.

So much for what, for want of a better term, we
have called natural security. It is, we repeat, not
that which prevails today, but that which would prevail had nothing been undertaken to strengthen it.
Let us now inquire how natural insecurity can, by
deliberate policy and by conscious effort, be turned
into effective and real security.

It can be done either by reducing the danger of
external aggression or by increasing the chances of
successful defense. The victorious powers and all
the European states that deemed themselves especially menaced, have done both. To reduce the danger of external aggression, the victors have dis-
armed their former enemies, concluded various kinds
of non-aggression treaties, and developed the machinery for the peaceful settlement of international
disputes. To increase the chances of successful defense, they have maintained or even increased their

military establishments and they have concluded among themselves treaties of mutual assistance.

It will be observed that all these various measures to enhance national security, except national armaments, are international measures. They constitute a large part of the activity and of the program of the League of Nations. But they include also many other bilateral and multilateral agreements negotiated and concluded outside of Geneva. It is to the consideration of these latter measures that we shall devote the rest of this chapter, reserving the efforts of the League to promote security for the end of this book.

Of disarmament as a means of reducing the dangers of external aggression we shall say but a word here. In so far as disarmament has been imposed on the vanquished, we have already referred to it while dealing with the execution of the treaties of peace. And in so far as it has been proposed as a general international measure we shall revert to it while discussing the League of Nations. The only disarmament, besides that forced on the defeated by the peace settlement, that has so far been effected by international agreement since the War, is that which the world owes the Washington Conference of 1922. As the Five Power Naval Treaty of February 6, 1922, was in reality an Anglo-American-Japanese affair, in which France and Italy took a minor and rather reluctant part, its consideration hardly falls within the scope of a study on recent European coöperation.

There remain therefore to be examined here three distinct topics which, although far from being unrelated to each other, can nevertheless be discussed separately. These topics are, in the inverse order of what I believe to be their political importance of to-day, although not, I hope, of the future: treaties of non-aggression; treaties of conciliation, arbitration, and judicial settlement; and treaties of mutual guar-anty.

If a state could be assured that no other state would ever, under any conditions, take up arms against it, its national security would of course be tremendously enhanced thereby. This consideration is at the bottom of all non-aggression pacts, what-ever their diverse forms. In pre-war days it led to neutrality treaties, such as those in which Switzer-land and Belgium, for instance, were assured by some of their great neighbors and some other great powers, not only that they would be protected if attacked, but also and primarily that they would not be attacked.

Since the War the same idea is to be found, as we shall see later, in the Covenant of the League of Nations and in various resolutions voted by succes-sive Assemblies. But it is to be found also in a large number of bilateral and multilateral treaties con-cluded without the framework of the League.

In the numerous cases in which, in the course of the last years, two European states have bound them-selves to submit each and every dispute which may arise between them to conciliation, arbitration, judi-cial or some other form of pacific settlement, they have sometimes explicitly, and always implicitly, thereby concluded a non-aggression pact.[23]

When in 1922 the thirty-four nations assembled

[23] For the text of such treaties registered with the League of Nations, cf. League Document C. 653, M. 216 (1927), V.

at Genoa adopted the then famous Peace Pact, they
too agreed to a non-aggression convention. For what
else is an undertaking formulated in the following
terms:

In order to enable the work of the Commission to be
carried on in tranquillity and in order to restore mutual
confidence, engagements will be entered into binding the
Russian Soviet Government on the one hand, and the other
participating Governments on the other hand, to refrain
from all acts of aggression against their respective territories.[24]

The aim is always the same, "to restore mutual
confidence," that is, to enhance the feeling of security, and the means are not different, "to refrain
from all acts of aggression." And that the hopes
aroused by this provisional peace pact were not less
sanguine than they always have been, before and
since, whenever responsible Governments, by solemnly condemning aggression, thereby allow political oratory to proclaim the advent of a new era of
assured tranquillity, is shown by the following words
uttered by Mr. Lloyd George after the formal acceptance of the resolution:

We have signed a pact of peace. It is a provisional one.
It is for months—no, it is for longer than that. We have
decided to have peace amongst warring nations. Once you
establish it, nations are not going back upon it. We have
decided to give peace a trial on our hearthstones, and when
she has been there for several months, we will not turn her
out again. The psychological effects upon the principles of
the peoples of the world will be electrical. The thrill of
peace has gone through the veins of Europe and you are

[24] J. Saxon Mills, *op. cit.*, p. 260.

not going to get nations lifting up hand against nations again.[25]

At the end of the same year 1922, the German Chancellor Cuno proposed another non-aggression pact to be concluded between the four great powers of western Europe. This suggestion, which, shortly before the occupation of the Ruhr, had been communicated by Berlin to Washington for transmission to Paris, was formulated in a single sentence. As read by Mr. Hughes to the French Ambassador, M. Jusserand, on December 21, 1922, it was as follows:

The German, British, French and Italian Governments solemnly engage themselves towards one another and promise the United States not to make war among themselves for a generation (say for thirty years) unless the matter is decided by popular vote, which should make war virtually impossible.[26]

The idea, which M. Poincaré promptly brushed aside as a "clumsy manoeuver" intended to free Germany from the pressure which it might be necessary to bring to bear on her to secure the execution of the reparation and disarmament clauses of the Treaty of Versailles, was repeated and revived later in various forms by the Wilhelmstrasse. It finally led, through the correspondence initiated on February 9, 1925, by the Luther Cabinet, to the Locarno agreements.[27]

[25] Speech of May 19, 1922, J. Saxon Mills, *op. cit.*, p. 278.

[26] Cf. British Command paper, Cmd. 1812, Miscellaneous, No. 3, (1923). *Interallied Conferences on Reparations and Interallied Debts*, p. 70.

[27] Raymond Leslie Buell, *Europe: A History of Ten Years* (New York, 1928), p. 105.

In these agreements the essential element of the
original idea was adopted in a very much modified
and less simple form, it is true. Not only did all the
participating powers set up an elaborate system of
conciliation and arbitration for the peaceful settlement of their disputes, but on October 16, 1925, Germany and France, and Germany and Belgium concluded the following non-aggression pact in Article 2
of the famous Treaty of Mutual Guaranty between
Germany, Belgium, France, Great Britain, and Italy:

Germany and Belgium, and also Germany and France,
mutually undertake that they will in no case attack or invade each other or resort to war against each other.

This stipulation shall not, however, apply in the case of:

1. The exercise of the right of legitimate defence, that
is to say, resistance to a violation of the undertaking contained in the previous paragraph or to a flagrant breach of
Articles 42 or 43 of the said Treaty of Versailles, if such
breach constitutes a non-provoked act of aggression and by
reason of the assembly of armed forces in the demilitarized
zone immediate action is necessary.

2. Action in pursuance of Article 16 of the Covenant of
the League of Nations.

3. Action as the result of a decision by the Assembly or
by the Council of the League of Nations, or in pursuance
of Article 15, par. 7 of the Covenant of the League of Nations, provided that in this last event the action is directed
against the state which was first to attack.[28]

In spite of these qualifications we are here in
presence of a *bona fide* non-aggression pact. Personally I should even be inclined to say that these

[28] Quoted from the Locarno Conference, *World Peace Foundation Pamphlet* (Boston, 1926), IX, No. 1, 56.

very qualifications make the undertaking more definite and more binding, because they show the intention and the courage of the signatory powers to
face the real facts of the situation and not to evade
difficulties which cannot be suppressed by verbal
preterition.

We come now to the latest and most important of
non-aggression pacts concluded outside the framework of the League of Nations, the so-called Kellogg
Pact of August 27, 1928. Although the treaty is
usually known under the name of the American Secretary of State who negotiated and signed it and
although it bears with his the signatures of the representatives of Japan and of all the overseas de-
pendencies of the Empire, it cannot be overlooked in
a study on recent international coöperation in Europe. Not because it was initiated by M. Briand and
not because it was signed in Paris, but because it
binds almost all the states of Europe, it has become
an essential part of the public law of the Old World.

Although heralded by much rhetoric about the
outlawry of war and although containing in its terms
a solemn renunciation of war, the Kellogg Pact is
nothing if not a multilateral non-aggression treaty.
M. Briand was therefore fully justified in declaring,
in his speech of August 27, 1928, the day of signature, that "all the signatories of the Locarno
Treaties were entirely familiar with the concept of
the renunciation of war as an instrument of national
policy."[29]

The Kellogg Pact is a vitally important treaty on
account of the part which the United States took in

[29] Quoted from James T. Shotwell, *War as an Instrument of
National Policy* (New York, 1929), p. 183.

its drafting and on account of the signatures it
bears. In spite of my very best efforts, however, I
cannot bring myself to see in it a new revelation of
world policy. Its signatories undertake two obligations. In Article 1:

The High Contracting Parties solemnly declare in the
name of their respective peoples that they condemn recourse to war for the solution of international controversies, and renounce it as an instrument of national policy in
their relations with one another.

And in Article 2:

The High Contracting Parties agree that the settlement
or solution of all disputes or conflicts of whatever nature
or of whatever origin they may be, which may arise among
them, shall never be sought except by pacific means.

The first obligation is negative and vague. The
second is positive and vague. And as for the consequences of the possible violation of either, they are,
as expressed in the preamble of the document, that
the culprit ''should be denied the benefits furnished
by this Treaty,'' which is certainly no less vague.

Now this vagueness has its obvious advantages.
It has allowed the least coöperative and most nationalistic of governments and parliaments to accept
the treaty without much ado. It is significant in this
respect that the briefest and one of the first affirma-
tive replies to be received by the State Department
bore the signature of the European statesman who
has since, in his recent polemic with the Pope, declared that it was his considered policy to bring up
his youthful fellow citizens as ''conquerors'' and as
''warriors.''

The concision of the wording of the Kellogg Pact has the additional advantage of allowing the "man in the street" to become familiar with its terms and thus of favoring the generation of the "thrill of peace," which Mr. Lloyd George spoke of at Genoa. This is a very real advantage if the peace thrill urges those who experience it on to constructive action. It may also be a very real danger, however, if it leads men to entertain the illusion that peace is a cheap blessing that may be had for the asking, and not an almost inaccessible ideal, that requires of the generation that would achieve it the most strenuous, persistent, and self-sacrificing moral and intellectual efforts.

I fully appreciate that this is heresy and little short of blasphemy in the eyes of the uncompromising members of the "outlawry of war" school. At the risk of delighting the pugnacious cynics who enjoy nothing so much as the spectacle of a spirited controversy between equally sincere and ardent friends of peace, I cannot here avoid briefly taking issue with the advocates of the doctrine that war can be effectively abolished by vague declarations. In order to understand the trend of European coöperation, it is essential to realize why the simple method of invoking peace in order to establish it has been deemed insufficient, although by no means useless, abroad.

The objections to the Kellogg Pact—I repeat, not as a means of focusing public opinion on the problem of war and peace, for as such it was very generally welcomed, but as a sufficient basis of national security—may be brought under three heads.

The first objection relates to the uncertainty as to

what the Kellogg Pact prohibits and as to what it permits. The second objection relates to the absence of any indication as to the nature of the "pacific means" which are to be substituted for war as a method of settlement of international disputes. The third objection relates to the lack of any definite provision for the unlikely but unfortunately not impossible event of violation. Let us examine at least the first of these three objections a little more closely.

Almost everyone on both sides of the Atlantic condemns aggression and almost everyone recognizes the justification of self-defense. Wars are therefore of two kinds, aggressive and defensive. This is so absolutely and so rigorously true, that we can express it by the arithmetical formulae: all wars = wars of aggression + wars of defense; or, wars of aggression = all wars − wars of defense; or wars of defense = all wars − wars of aggression. Now a war of defense is undoubtedly a "war for the solution of international controversies" and an "instrument of national policy." As such it is expressly prohibited by the wording of the Kellogg Pact, but implicitly justified in the minds of its authors and signatories. Is such an ambiguity not most deplorable in the drafting of a solemn international agreement on which, if it is to be taken seriously, as it should be, the fate of the world may depend?

The natural reply most often made to this objection is the very great difficulty of discovering a simple and clear definition of aggression or self-defense. No serious student of international affairs will, of course, deny this tremendous difficulty, even, or perhaps especially, if he has witnessed the drafting of the famous Protocol of Geneva in 1924. But

the difficulty is not in the least avoided or overcome
by the general terms of the Pact. The solution of the
problem is not thereby discovered. It is merely
postponed. It is postponed to the next grave international crisis when, as usual in international crises,
haste, passion, and contradictory information will
certainly render absolutely impossible what is today, under infinitely less unfavorable conditions,
already sufficiently difficult.

Let us suppose that, being ill in bed, you have a
bottle of morphia within your reach, of which you
know nothing except that taken under certain circumstances and in certain doses it may mean death,
but that taken under other circumstances and in
other doses it may mean salvation. Would it be wise
in such a predicament not to consult a physician and
a chemist immediately, but to adjourn the examination of these circumstances and doses until, alone, in
the midst of night, you awoke in a fit of frightful
pain and paralyzing fever, to make a decision on
which your life may depend?

In view of the gravity of the problem, of its terrible reality, and of its very difficulty, the following
statement, made by one of the leaders of the outlawry school is absolutely incomprehensible to me,
as it would, I believe, be to every European who read
it. In a chapter entitled "Self-defence and Outlawry," written before the drafting of the Kellogg
Pact, but dealing with exactly this point, Dr. Charles
Clayton Morrison says:

Outlawry absolutely has no point of contact with the
question of the right of self-defence. If self-defence is
right, it is right under outlawry. If it is wrong, it is wrong

under outlawry. The outlawry of war both transcends and cuts under the whole question of "defensive" versus "aggressive" war. All distinctions between "kinds" of war are "blotted out."[30]

It so happened that, in the course of the preparation of these pages, I had stopped on this point on May 30 last. I was, I must confess, somewhat uneasy about my own intelligence and about my ability to understand American thought since on so vital a matter I had been obliged to admit my complete failure to grasp the meaning of an obviously enlightened and sincere American author. I was consequently much relieved when, on the following morning, picking up at my club the continental edition of the *Daily Mail* of May 31, I found therein an account of President Hoover's admirable Memorial Day address delivered at Arlington. President Hoover was reported as having said:

that if the Kellogg-Briand peace pact was to fulfil its high purpose they "must clothe faith and idealism with action." If this covenant [he continued] be a genuine proof that the world has renounced war as an instrument of national policy, it means the abandonment of the aggressive use of arms at once by every signatory nation and it becomes a sincere declaration that all armaments shall be used hereafter only for defence. Consequently, if we are honest, we must consider our naval armaments and the armaments of the world, in the light of their defensive, not their aggressive use.

I was all the more relieved and delighted by this clear and frank statement of the eminent head of

[30] Charles Clayton Morrison, *The Outlawry of War, a Constructive Policy for World Peace* (Chicago, 1927), p. 209.

the American Government, thus emphasizing the contrast between aggressive and defensive use of force, as, with many other Europeans, I had been somewhat puzzled by a passage in the last Armistice Day speech of his predecessor. On November 11, 1928, that is, in the midst of the discussion of the pact which bears the name of his Secretary of State, President Coolidge had declared:

> To be ready for defence is not to be guilty of aggression. . . . We do not need a large land force. . . . When we turn to the sea the situation is different. We have not only a long coast line, distant outlying possessions, *a foreign commerce unsurpassed in importance and foreign investments unsurpassed in amount, the number of people and value of our treasure to be protected,* but we are also bound by international treaty to defend the Panama Canal.[31]

Now if the protection, by the American navy of American lives and even of American capital abroad, is consistent with the renunciation of war as an instrument of national policy, the distinction between defense and aggression is still more difficult than it was thought to be in Europe. But I fully agree that that difficulty is very considerable in any case. Indeed I believe it to be insurmountable in the absence of a preëstablished and preaccepted system for the peaceful settlement of all international disputes and conflicts, as contemplated, but unfortunately as not yet set up, under the Kellogg Pact.

This second deficiency as well as the absence of sanctions which, in the eyes of Europe, is the third

[31] Quoted from the *New York Times* (November 12, 1928), p. 2. The italics are mine.

objection to the Pact as a sufficient basis of national security, have been so often discussed that I shall refrain from dwelling on them here.

The cause of peace and of American-European coöperation in pursuance of peace has since the War had no more devoted, more able, and more useful advocate than my friend Professor James T. Shotwell. It is therefore both a particular delight for every European to find himself in full agreement with most of what he has written about the Kellogg Pact and a real and very agreeable duty to seize every occasion to pay a public tribute of gratitude to all his generous and successful endeavors on behalf of its conclusion. One passage, however, in his above-mentioned book in which he deals with the European view of the Kellogg Pact, seems open to some question. He writes:

The apparent divergence between European and American interpretations, was, after all, not so serious as opponents of the treaty seemed to think. It was chiefly due to the fact that the Pact of Paris had been vague upon the point which Europe emphasized and definite where Europe had been vague. There are two things in the suppression of war, the suppression itself and the substitution of something else for it. Europe had been developing the substitution; America insisted upon the renunciation. This was the basis of the whole misunderstanding.[32]

We shall presently have something to say of the attempts of Europe at developing "the substitution." But what we have said already about her efforts not to outlaw or to renounce war in the abstract, but to combat, and in order to combat suc-

[32] James T. Shotwell, *op. cit.*, p. 191.

cessfully, to define aggression, may be held to defend her against the reproach of vagueness also on this point. But as it would be most ungracious in a European to accept Mr. Shotwell's compliment and to question his criticism of Europe, while disagreeing only with his eulogy of America's policy, I would suggest the following formula which he would not, I believe, repudiate: America has been insistent on her desire to renounce, but reticent about defining the object of her renunciation, while Europe has been hesitant about renouncing, before knowing what she was being asked to renounce.

As I see it, the Kellogg Pact, as a weapon to combat war, is comparable to the individual total abstinence pledge, as a weapon to combat drunkenness. If, as in our marshy, wet Europe, one has not the courage to prohibit the production and consumption of liquor as a crime and to punish all delinquents by calling on the police to arrest them, it is sound policy to encourage the individual drunkard to renounce liquor as an instrument of personal exhilaration but of social disturbance. It is well, however, in that case to place all intoxicating drinks without his reach and to supply him liberally with soft beverages, lest, becoming very thirsty, he should renounce his renunciation, on the plea that he had no alternative means of protecting his life against the threat of drought.

Replace drunkards by states in my irreverent simile, liquor by cruisers, and soft drinks by methods of pacific settlement, and you have, I truly believe, Europe's general opinion on the Kellogg Pact. To declare the pact useless, would be as stupid and as wicked as to condemn the total abstinence pledge method, which has undoubtedly helped to reform countless individuals and to alleviate much human misery. But to declare it sufficient to do away with war, would be as rash as to deny the superiority of effectively enforced prohibition as a means of combating intemperance. As long as the latter method remains impracticable, everyone should be deeply grateful to the authors of the Kellogg Pact, who have most certainly helped mankind to make one step forward on the long and steep road to permanent international peace, which must remain the ultimate goal of our common endeavor.

Aside from non-aggression pacts and often in connection with them, the states of Europe have sought and found in conciliation and arbitration treaties another means of enhancing their national security by reducing the chances of armed conflicts. Although all such treaties have not been negotiated with the express purpose of avoiding war, they do provide for the machinery required for the pacific solution of international problems which diplomacy proves unable to solve amicably.

In the course of the last ten years 106 such bilateral treaties have, up to the 1st of June, 1929, been registered with the Secretariat of the League of Nations.[33] They vary in content and detail, of

[33] Cf. *Arbitrage et sécurité, étude méthodique des conventions d'arbitrage,* etc., 2e éd., revue et augmentée (Geneva, 1927). League Document C. 653 M. 216 (1927), V. The information contained in this volume, which relates to arbitration treaties registered before December 15, 1927, has been supplemented and brought up to date by communications for which I am indebted to MM. Nisot and Giraud, of the Legal Section of the Secretariat.

course, but they all have as their object the establishment between the signatories of a system of conciliation, arbitration, or both. Some of them absolutely exclude, while others merely suspend, the resort to arms, but both types of treaties provide for the submission of disputes to the examination and report of an impartial body.

As is well known, international conflicts may be of two kinds. The first are of a juridical or justiciable nature. They are those enumerated in Article 13 of the Covenant, which, roughly speaking, correspond to those referred to in the Locarno treaties as disputes ''with regard to which the parties are in conflict as to their respective rights '' The others are so-called non-justiciable or political disputes. The first are susceptible of a judicial or an arbitral solution. The second are, strictly speaking, susceptible only of an arbitral settlement, although they may even then be submitted to the Permanent Court of International Justice, judging *ex aequo et bono,* as they are, for instance, under the provisions of the Italian-Swiss Treaty of December 20, 1924. In all cases the difficulty may or may not first be referred to a conciliation commission, whose decisions will be final only if accepted by both parties.

As the treaties in question relate either to conciliation or to arbitration (including or not judicial settlement), or to both conciliation and arbitration, as they may deal either with juridical disputes alone, with non-juridical disputes alone, or with both at the same time, and as they may or may not contain clauses excluding certain matters from the purview of the conciliators or arbiters, they offer a great variety of types, which may be classified in a number of different ways. In the following table we shall distinguish only those which deal with arbitration alone, with conciliation alone, or with both arbitration and conciliation. We shall further distinguish those concluded between two European states (E), between an European and a non-European state (EA), and between two non-European states (A). The years noted are those of signature.

Bilateral Treaties.

Year of signature	Arbitration	Conciliation	Arbitration and Conciliation	Total
1919	....	1 EA	....	1
1920	....	....	1 EA	1
1921	....	....	1 E	1
1922	1 EA	....	....	1
1923	3 E, 4 EA, 2 A	1 EA	....	10
1924	3 E, 4 EA	9 E	3 E	19
1925	4 E, 1 EA	4 E	10 E	19
1926	7 E, 1 A	1 E	14 EA	23
1927	....	....	6 E, 1 EA	7
1928	1 E	1 E, 1 EA	12 E	15
1929	3 EA	1 E, 3 EA	2 E	9
Total	34	22	50	106

This table shows the extraordinary increase in bilateral arbitration and conciliation treaties concluded since the War and especially since 1923. If we summarize its results according to continental groups, disregarding the year of signature, we shall have the following picture. In the course of the last ten years there have been registered with the League of Nations these treaties:

Concluded between:	Arbitration	Conciliation	Arbitration and Conciliation	Total
European states	18	16	48	82
European and non-European states	13	6	2	21
Non-European states	3	..	..	3
	34	22	50	106

It is very apparent from these figures that the trend toward the establishment of permanent machinery for the peaceful settlement of international disputes, which is noticeable all over the world, has been much stronger in Europe than elsewhere. These figures do not, of course, give an entirely true description of this trend, since they refer only to treaties registered with the League, as registration is compulsory only for members of the League, and as the proportion of the states members of the League is greater in Europe than in other continents. But even allowing for a few bilateral treaties which may have escaped registration, having been concluded between two states neither of which belonged to the League, the result would not be essentially different.

Especially if we take into account, as we must, the well-known fact that far-reaching reservations, which have almost entirely disappeared from European treaties, are still maintained in most American conventions, we are fully justified in the assertion that, even disregarding the League of Nations, Europe is leading the world in the legal organization of international peace. The following list, showing the total number of bilateral treaties of the three above-mentioned types, which have been signed by

the various states and registered with the League
in the course of the last ten years, is very enlightening:

Sweden	34	Esthonia	19	France	7	Japan	2
Finland	32	Portugal	19	Italy	7	Rumania	2
Denmark	31	Haiti	18	Guatemala	4	Yugo-	
Switzerland	30	Uruguay	18	Paraguay	4	slavia	2
Germany	26	Ethiopia	14	Chili	3	Greece	1
Belgium	23	Bulgaria	13	Czecho-		Siam	1
Norway	23	Spain	13	slovakia	3	Liberia	1
Austria	22	Great		Hungary	3	Peru	1
Holland	21	Britain	12	Latvia	3	Ireland	1
United		Poland	9	Lithuania	3	Argentine	1
States	20	Brazil	7				

At the head of the list come most of the small
states of Europe. Being both law-abiding and weak,
the pacific settlement of international disputes is
both their ideal and their interest. Then come Germany and the United States of America as the first
of the world's Great Powers. As no country need
less count on law for its national security than the
United States, its arbitration policy is a convincing
tribute paid to its respect for right. When it will
have consented to drop or to limit the reservations
in its arbitration treaties, as would seem consistent under the Kellogg Pact, it will clearly assume
the position of moral leadership in international relations, which is the ardent hope both of many of its
greatest citizens at home and of all its friends
abroad. The European Great Powers and their victorious allies, with the exception of Belgium, all
come farther down on the list. This may lead one
to believe that they still rely less on right than on
might for their security.

A rapid examination of the recent treaties of

guaranty or of mutual assistance, with which we
shall close this chapter, tends to strengthen rather
than to weaken this suspicion. Such treaties are intended to enhance national security less by directly
diminishing the danger of war, as non-aggression
pacts and arbitration conventions, than by reducing
the chances of defeat in case of war. Their negotiators and their advocates will, of course, claim that
they thereby indirectly also tend to avoid war by
frightening off all would-be aggressors. This claim,
which has ever been raised in favor of defensive
alliances, as well as in favor of strong national
armaments in the past, may or may not be founded
in future. That will depend on the reaction of such
measures on the state of mind and on the policy of
such supposed would-be aggressors who, not always
conscious of aggressive designs themselves, may
well feel threatened more than reassured by coali-
tions among their neighbors.

The story of the relations between alliances and
regional agreements on the one hand, and the League
of Nations on the other, is a long and complicated
one. It cannot be fully told here. It is necessary, however, in order to understand how certain European
states, although members of the League and as such
protected by the provisions of the Covenant and
especially by Article 10, came to conclude mutually
defensive conventions among themselves, to refer
briefly to the origin and evolution of these relations.
We may also thereby gain an idea of the comparative political reality and effective potency of the
Covenant and of special treaties.

That, before the Armistice, President Wilson,
in whom history will ever recognize the principal

founder of the League of Nations, held special alliances to be incompatible with the exigencies of the new peace era which he hoped to inaugurate, is certain.

In his famous speech of May 27, 1916, delivered before the League to Enforce Peace, he had already noted with obvious approval that "repeated utterances of the living statesmen of most of the great nations now engaged in war have made it plain that henceforth alliance must not be set up against alliance, understanding against understanding, but that there must be a common agreement for a common object." In his address delivered before the Senate of January 22, of the following year, he had declared on his own behalf: "There must be, not a balance of power, but a community of power; not organized rivalries, but an organized common peace." This point is particularly stressed in the closing words of this memorable address. "I am proposing," said President Wilson in his peroration, "that all nations henceforth avoid entangling alliances which would draw them into competitions of power, catch them in a net of intrigue and selfish rivalry, and disturb their own affairs with influences intruded from without. There is no entangling alliance in a concert of power."

In his speech of September 27, 1918, his last important utterance before the Armistice, which is clearly leveled at the Associated Powers as much as at Germany, he stated as the third point of his "practical program" for peace: "There can be no leagues or special alliances or special covenants and understandings within the great and common family of the League of Nations."

Even after President Wilson arrived in Europe, he still adhered firmly to this doctrine. Speaking in London on December 28, 1918, he said:

. . . The center and characteristic of the old order was that unstable thing which we used to call "balance of power" . . . a balance which was determined by the unstable equilibrium of competitive interests. . . . The men who have fought in the war . . . are determined that that sort of thing should end now and for ever. It is very interesting to me to observe how from every quarter, from every sort òf mind, from every concert of counsel, there comes a suggestion that there must now be not a balance of power, not one powerful group of nations set up against another, but a single overwhelming powerful group of nations who shall be the trustees of the peace of the world.

And two days later, at Manchester, he further declared:

If the future had nothing for us but a new attempt to set the world at a right poise by a balance of power, the United States would take no interest, because she will join no combination of power which is not a combination of all of us.

In view of these very clear and oft-repeated assurances, it is not surprising that President Wilson should have willingly agreed to the suggestion contained in the British so-called Phillimore Plan for a League of Nations, to insert an article in the Covenant expressly abrogating all international treaties inconsistent with its provisions. This article, formulated in the Phillimore Plan, slightly redrafted by President Wilson, and adopted with some further verbal amendments, reads as follows in the actual Covenant:[34]

Article 20.

1. The Members of the League severally agree that this Covenant is accepted as abrogating all obligations or understandings *inter se* which are inconsistent with the terms thereof, and solemnly undertake that they will not hereafter enter into any engagements inconsistent with the terms thereof.

2. In case any Member of the League shall, before becoming a Member of the League, have undertaken any obligations inconsistent with the terms of this Covenant, it shall be the duty of such Member to take immediate steps to procure its release from such obligations.

When this article came before the League of Nations Commission meeting at the Hotel Crillon on February 10, 1919, it gave rise to a most interesting discussion.[35] Did it permit alliances? And if so, which? Some members considered its terms to allow the making and concluding of defensive alliances. M. Hymans of Belgium seem inclined to go even farther and not to condemn all offensive agreements. Others held opposite views. President Wilson was, as often, rather enigmatic, declaring that "an alliance shall not be held valid unless it is recorded" and approved "by the court of public opinion."

Mr. Miller commenting on this discussion writes: "No one was objecting to a clause against treaties inconsistent with the Covenant. It was agreed to without dissent or even proposal of amendment.

[34] David Hunter Miller, *The Drafting of the Covenant*, 2 vols. (New York, 1928), II, 6, 15.

[35] Cf. *ibid.*, pp. 279 *et seq.*, 447 *et seq.*

But every one wondered just how far the new limitation would extend in practice.''[36]

Before this article had been fully adopted, however, a very important event took place which, without affecting its wording, was profoundly to influence its political significance. When the draft Covenant, which already contained it, was published on February 14, 1919, no mention of the Monroe Doctrine was to be found therein. American opinion was aroused lest this article, in combination with Article 10, might be interpreted as encroaching on that cardinal principle of American policy. On President Wilson's return to Paris, after his brief trip home, he therefore proposed to add the following clause, which has become Article 21 of the actual Covenant.

Article 21.

Nothing in this Covenant shall be deemed to affect the validity of international engagements such as treaties of arbitration or regional understandings like the Monroe Doctrine, for securing the maintenance of peace.

This addition, of course, provoked much critical comment in the Commission.[37] The French, in particular, feared that it would weaken America's obligation under Article 10 to come to the support of European states which might be the object of external aggression.

President Wilson, realizing the political importance of reassuring his countrymen by explicitly declaring the Monroe Doctrine to be compatible with the Covenant, insisted and prevailed. But at the

[36] D. H. Miller, *op. cit.*, I, 199.
[37] *Ibid.*, pp. 442 *et seq*.

same time he inevitably thereby weakened his own position as an opponent of especial agreements. Having demanded and obtained this concession to American feeling, he could not consistently refuse to others what he had claimed for himself.

It was while the discussions on this point were proceeding at the Crillon Commission that it became known that he was favorably considering the possibility of granting France the additional guaranty which she desired through a triple alliance with the United States and the British Empire.[38]

It was primarily in order to deter France from her ambitious plans with respect to the left bank of the Rhine, that President Wilson and Mr. Lloyd George, on March 14, 1919, offered her this additional guaranty. The French, in a lengthy memorandum dated February 25, had sought to convince their American and British partners that Germany's western frontier should not extend beyond the Rhine. Basing their contention on purely strategical considerations, they had attempted to prove that all other measures of protection, including the League of Nations, were insufficient.[39]

M. Tardieu, who had seconded his chief, M. Clemenceau, in the prolonged interallied debates on this point, asserts in his book on the peace settlement that the French "arguments relating to the insufficient security afforded to France by the Covenant of the League of Nations had convinced Mr. Wilson." In any case, the outcome of the discussion was the offer to France of two especial treaties by the Brit-

[38] *Ibid.,* pp. 377 *et seq.*
[39] André Tardieu, *La paix* (Paris, 1921), pp. 165 *et seq.*

ish Empire and the United States according to which
these powers "shall be bound to come immediately
to her assistance in the event of an unprovoked
movement of aggression against her made by Germany." These two twin treaties were to come into
force only when both had been ratified. As the
American Senate failed to take action on the American treaty, they both remained dead letters.

Nevertheless, the drafting of these conventions
was profoundly significant. For President Wilson
it indisputably implied the recession from the attitude he had taken in all his above-quoted utterances.
Here was clearly "an entangling alliance," one of
those "special covenants . . . within the great and
common family of the League of Nations" which he
had expressly condemned. Here was unmistakably
an attempt to set up "one powerful group of nations . . . against another," "a combination of
power which" was distinctly not "a combination
of all of us." To be sure, as stated in the preamble of
the draft treaties, it was inspired "by the desire to
maintain the Peace of the World." To be sure, it
was intended to be of but a provisional nature and
to come into force only after it had been "submitted
to the Council of the League of Nations and . . .
recognized by the Council, acting if need be by a majority, as an engagement which is consistent with
the Covenant of the League." These provisions all
show that President Wilson's League conscience
was uneasy about the step he was taking in signing
this especial treaty, which could be justified only on
the admission that the protection afforded by the
Covenant was insufficient. It was undoubtedly a

significant step down from the high position he had previously taken.

It was, after the especial mention of the Monroe Doctrine, the second breach in the wall which, in his original conception, was to have afforded all nations an equal and reciprocal guaranty.

Through this breach, many other defensive alliances concluded between members of the League have since passed, both a symptom and a cause of the weakness of the Geneva institution.

France was the first nation to avail herself of this possibility. She did so with particular alacrity, since the faith of her first post-war ministers in the League was not very ardent. Moreover, she felt sorely abused and ensnared by the refusal of the American Senate to ratify the Versailles Treaty, in which she had made such concessions to President Wilson's views, the Covenant which was to protect her, and the assistance agreement in favor of which she had given up her territorial designs on the Rhine frontier.

France therefore turned first to Belgium with whom, on September 7, 1920, she concluded a military understanding. The terms of this understanding have never been published, but an exchange of letters between the French and Belgium governments approving it has been registered with the League of Nations. From these letters and from the covering note by which they were communicated to the Secretary-General, we learn that "the understanding in question is purely defensive and has reference exclusively to the case of a non-provoked aggression." Its object is stated as being "to reinforce the guarantees of peace and security resulting from the Covenant of the League of Nations."[40]

Of the treaty of guaranty which Mr. Lloyd George offered France on behalf of Great Britain at Cannes in 1922 we have already spoken. It was haughtily refused by M. Poincaré under the doubtful pretext that, not being reciprocal, it was contrary to the dignity of France to accept it. The real reason was obviously that the price demanded by Mr. Lloyd George in terms of British influence on French policy was deemed excessive.

France concluded a more general political treaty with Poland. In this document, signed on February 19, 1921, and registered with the League of Nations more than two years later, on July 19, 1923, we find, besides political and economic clauses providing "for joint action and mutual support," the following Article 3, which constitutes the basis of another defensive alliance:

If, contrary to the expectations and to the sincerely pacific intentions of the two contracting States, they or one of them saw itself attacked without provocation on their part, the two Governments would act in concert with a view to the defence of their territory and to the safeguarding of their legitimate interests.

With Czechoslovakia, France concluded a "treaty of alliance and friendship" on January 25, 1924. This is both an agreement of mutual assistance in

[40] This and several of the following quotations are taken from a pamphlet entitled *Post-War Political Alignments* published in 1923 by the World Peace Foundation. In this excellent short monograph the relevant texts are very conveniently presented and well explained.

case of any violation of the peace treaties or of any attempt at monarchical restoration in favor of the Hapsburgs and the Hohenzollerns, and an arbitration convention.

France, furthermore, concluded two identical treaties of mutual guaranty with Czechoslovakia and Poland at Locarno on October 16, 1925, a treaty of friendship with Rumania on June 10, 1926, and a similar agreement with the Kingdom of the Serbs, Croats, and Slovenes on November 11, 1927. In these last two agreements we find, besides provisions concerning mutual assistance, a reciprocal non-aggression pact similar to that concluded at Locarno between Germany, France, and Belgium.

It is interesting to note that, while the first Belgian, Polish, and Czechoslovakian agreements are only incidentally and in very vague and general terms declared by their authors to be "in conformity with the Covenant of the League of Nations," the four latter conventions all contain several specific provisions precisely defining their relations to the Covenant. This change in spirit and in wording is striking. It evinces the greatly enhanced political importance which is attached to the Geneva institution since the reëntry of Germany into the European family, at the Locarno Conference.

While the former treaties may be said to have been concluded as substitutes for the Covenant, the latter tend to supplement and to implement rather than to replace it. However, there is no doubt whatever as to the historical and political importance of all these treaties. France, dissatisfied with the insufficient protection afforded by the League of Nations and disappointed in her hopes of an Anglo-

American guaranty, sought to create a system of defensive alliances against the "hereditary enemy." For that purpose she first enlisted the support of Germany's three other principal neighbors, Belgium, Poland, and Czechoslovakia. Then, at Locarno, she secured the guaranty of Great Britain and Italy, and finally she established relations of mutual assistance with the allies of her allies, Rumania and Yugoslavia. It is behind this quadruple line of defenses that she has gradually consented slightly to reduce her armaments. France today may be compared with a medieval fortified town, whose citadel, manned by a powerful, although partially demobilized garrison, is surrounded by four concentric circles of walls, around which lie the still waters of the moat dug by the authors of the Kellogg Pact.

In the shadow of this formidable fortress, Mr. Benes of Czechoslovakia has built the smaller but also quite impressive castle of the "Little Entente." For his country, also, the League of Nations, deprived of the support of America, did not seem to afford sufficient protection against the possible hostile reactions of vindictive foes.

For Czechoslovakia the most dangerous prospective enemy was not Germany, of whose pre-war territory she had received only a little over one hundred square miles and who was already vigilantly watched over by France, Belgium, and Poland; nor was it Austria, completely prostrate and placed under the strict supervision of Italy and Yugoslavia. The real danger Czechoslovakia saw in Hungary, of whose pre-war Magyar population from over half to three-quarters of a million were subjected to her rule[41] and whose people are almost unanimous and extremely relentless in their hostility to the Treaty of the Trianon.

Turning therefore first to Yugoslavia and then to Rumania, similarly although perhaps less especially threatened by the very existence of a mutilated Hungary, Mr. Benes concluded with them, on August 14, 1920, and on April 14, 1921, respectively, two almost identical "defensive conventions." Nothing could be clearer than the meaning of these treaties by which the signatories "in case of an unprovoked attack on the part of Hungary" undertake "to assist in defence of the Party attacked" and to refrain from concluding "an alliance with a third power without preliminary notice to the other."

The Little Entente founded by these two treaties was completed by the conclusion of a similar defensive convention between Czechoslovakia's two allies on July 2, 1921. The main difference between this and the two preceding documents was that it provided for bilateral mutual protection also in case of an unprovoked attack by Bulgaria, which was both Rumania's and Yugoslavia's neighbor but not Czechoslovakia's.

Resting firmly on the basis of these three treaties, the Little Entente since 1920 has remained an active and important factor in the political situation of central and eastern Europe. Since then three circum-

[41] Estimates vary. Disregarding both Hungarian and Czechoslovakian figures, we note that Mr. I. Bowman, *op. cit.*, p. 329, places the number of Magyars in Slovakia at 750,000 and M. Mousset, *La petite entente* (Paris, 1923), p. 12, states that there are about 600,000 Magyars in Czechoslovakia, 350,000 in Yugoslavia and 500,000 in Rumania.

stances have affected and, on the whole, strengthened it.

The first of these circumstances is the actual test
to which the treaties were put when, on October 22,
1921, ex-King Charles returned for the second time
in six months to Hungary. Whereas his first expedition in March, 1921, had been frustrated by the action of the Conference of Ambassadors, this second
crisis was boldly met by the Little Entente. Desirous
not only of preventing the military consequences
which were bound to follow if the challenge of the
pretender to the crown of Hungary was left unanswered, but also of asserting itself in the face of the
great western powers, who were inclined to regard
it as a mere instrument of their own policy, the
Little Entente, under the leadership of Mr. Benes,
informed the world that it considered the "presence
of the ex-King on Hungarian soil to be a *casus
belli.*"

This prompt and bold move was in every respect
successful. It led to the retirement of King Charles,
to the acquiescence of the Great Powers, and above
all to the strengthening of the bonds of solidarity
between the three allied states.[42]

In the second place the defensive conventions
which had been concluded for two years, were renewed in 1922 and have now, since the Belgrade
Conference of May, 1929, become practically permanent. At the same time they have been reinforced
first by the promise of general mutual political and
diplomatic support, then by commercial agreements,
and finally by far-reaching conciliation and arbitration conventions.

[42] A. Mousset, *op. cit.*, pp. 60 *et seq.*

The third circumstance which must be noted in connection with the evolution of the Little Entente is that constituted by the various international understandings into which, with their mutual consent, their members had entered with other powers. Besides recalling their bonds with France, we may mention that Czechoslovakia has concluded political treaties with Poland, Austria, and Italy; Yugoslavia with Italy and Greece; and Rumania with Italy and Poland.

Of all these treaties the Polish-Rumanian is perhaps the most important. What Germany is to France and her allies, what Hungary is to the Little Entente, Soviet Russia is to Poland and Rumania, that is the possible enemy, the common fear of whom has created and cemented their political intimacy. The "Convention for a defensive alliance" concluded between Russia's two largest European neighbors on March 3, 1921 goes still farther than the Little Entente treaties. Not only have the two signatories undertaken "to assist each other in the event of being the object of an unprovoked attack on their present Eastern frontiers," but they have so completely identified their respective destinies that, in case of a defensive war against the Soviets, they have agreed "not to negotiate nor to conclude an armistice or a peace without the participation of the other State."

As the Little Entente is related to the principal allied powers, the Polish-Rumanian alliance to the Little Entente, so the so-called Baltic Entente is related to the Polish-Rumanian alliance. The Baltic Entente, composed of Poland, Esthonia, Finland, and Latvia (but not Lithuania) is based on one plurilat-

eral treaty signed in Warsaw, on March 17, 1922.
Its aims are also defensive, but much less definite
and defiant than those of the three other groups.
"In case of an unprovoked attack upon any of"
the signatories "by another State, they will adopt a
benevolent attitude towards the State attacked and
will immediately agree upon the course of action"
to be pursued.

Our purpose in referring to these various defensive alignments outside the League of Nations, is
not to give a complete picture of the present state
of Europe. Were it so, we should have to touch on
many other topics, such as the German-Russian,
Polish-Lithuanian, and other international relations.
We should, moreover, have to devote considerable
space to the enterprising policies of Italy. Italy, the
most youthful of the Great Powers and the hun-
griest of the victors, gaining a foothold in the
Balkans by her peaceful penetration in Albania,
attempting first to dominate, then to undermine the
Little Entente, and pressing her active negotiations
with Yugoslavia, Rumania, Poland, Bulgaria, Hungary, Greece, and Turkey, has as ever sought to
enhance her international position by winning the
indispensable friendship of Great Britain and by
endeavoring to convince the world in general, and
her great rival France in particular, of the necessity
of granting her, in the interests of peace, certain
territorial and other concessions.

The consideration of these subjects would lead us
into the vast field of the dynamics of European
politics. We are however merely concerned with its
statics, that is, with the efforts made to promote

national security, or, as the defeated nations would put it, to protect the conquests of the victors.

These efforts, as we have seen, have been pursued outside the League of Nations and not only within it, as we shall see in our last chapter. During the first years after the signature of the peace treaties and until Locarno they have moreover been pursued in a spirit and by methods which it is not always easy to reconcile with the methods and the spirit of the Covenant. Secret military agreements, exclusive alliances which, in view of the Little Entente's spontaneous action against Hungary in 1921, cannot even be held to be purely defensive, unreserved promises to lend mutual diplomatic and political support, undertakings to remain neutral in cases where a candid interpretation of the Covenant would seem to call for positive action, and many other similar symptoms show quite clearly that the first post-war years were far from fulfilling the hopes of a "new era" in international affairs, which President Wilson had so insistently demanded and so confidently predicted during the War.

From 1925 on however a great change is noticeable. While the first assemblies of the League of Nations had been occupied in seeking to adapt the Covenant to the exigencies and realities of the political situation, the negotiators of the various defensive treaties were from then on obviously striving to adapt their regional agreements to the legal exigencies of the Covenant. Thus they repaid the concessions made by the League between 1920 and 1924 in terms of concessions made to the League from then onward.

The trend of international coöperation in Europe

during the last decade is therefore irregular in this as in other respects. After the exhaustion of the War and the disappointments of the Peace Conference, a period of bitter reaction set in. Relentless coercion in the execution of the peace treaties, narrowly discriminatory protectionism in the field of international economics, and military alliances as the main bulwark of national security prevailed. It was as if the War had been fought in vain, that, resembling the French royalists after the fall of Napoleon I, Europe had forgotten nothing and learned nothing. During this dismal period the prostration and isolation of the defeated alone prevented the formation of threatening counter alliances.

Then, after the failure of the Ruhr adventure, a more conciliatory state of mind gradually began to assert itself. It came to be realized that force alone could not solve the problems of the Old World, and with the spirit of friendliness and the ideals of justice, Europe seemed to rediscover the League of Nations, which had been founded to foster the former and to serve the latter.

In spite of this decided change in which no one who prefers justice to violence and peace to war will hesitate to see a change for the better, the great question of the future of Europe as of the world still remains unanswered. That question relates to the ultimate reality in international affairs.

If, in the future, as in the past, since the earliest beginnings of human history, brute force is in the last analysis to dominate international relations, then that ultimate reality will ever be found in the policy of balance of power based on national armaments. In that case, arbitration may still be resorted

to as a means of settling minor quarrels, the League
of Nations as a convenient clearing house for international operations, and the outlawry of war as a
method of reducing the economic weight of armaments. But the last decision will always rest with
Mars.

If, on the contrary, violence is to be banned from
international society, as it has in the course of the
last half millennium by gradual steps been banned
from civil society, then unconditional arbitration
will be recognized as the final means of settling all
disputes. National armaments will be suppressed
and replaced by a police force at the command of
a supreme international authority. Then at last
Themis will rule the world.

The present League of Nations is as yet far from
being the supreme international authority. It is little
more than the clearing house above referred to. It
has, however, never abandoned that higher ambition
which was that of its noblest and most far-sighted
founders and which remains the hope of all those
who, in the cosmic duel between Mars and Themis,
have never despaired of the ultimate triumph of the
goddess of justice.

It is to the origin and early evolution of that
remarkable institution that the closing chapters of
this book will be devoted.

CHAPTER IV

COÖPERATION INSIDE THE FRAMEWORK OF THE LEAGUE OF NATIONS

I

The Changing Structure of the League.

FOUR years ago I was privileged to present to the Williamstown Institute of Politics a sketch of the League of Nations as I saw it.[1] As my analysis dealt only with fundamentals and as nothing has led me to change my point of view since, the picture then outlined still faithfully reflects my present opinions. It is not my purpose to redraft that picture nor to limit my discussion to the important events Geneva has witnessed in the course of the last four years. I would rather, adopting another plan, show how the League has developed during the first decade of its existence.

To do this is not in any sense to digress from my main subject. As we have seen already, international coöperation in Europe has increasingly been carried on at Geneva, and as we shall see presently, the League of Nations has increasingly, although not exclusively, become a league of European nations. To inquire into the evolution of the League is therefore to consider one of the most characteristic aspects of the trend of post-war international coöperation in Europe.

Although the League is neither a state, nor a

[1] Cf. *International Relations as Viewed from Geneva* (New Haven, 1925).

superstate, nor even a confederacy of states in the ordinary sense of the latter term, it is a political institution. Like every political institution, it may be judged according to what it is and according to what it does. It must therefore be studied both in its constitutional structure and in its functions, that is, its activities and policies. Accordingly we shall in this chapter consider the evolution of the structure of the League and in the next and last, the growth, extension, and dominant tendencies of its activities and policies.[2]

Constitutional law is an essential, but it is certainly the dullest branch of political science, as, I imagine, human anatomy is an essential, but probably the least inspiring branch of medicine. Life alone is interesting. But life cannot be fruitfully studied except in the bodies it animates. And the study of these bodies, political and physical, can and should be rendered interesting if we see in them not merely legislative texts to be analyzed and flesh and bones to be dissected, but organs to be considered with a view to the functions for which they have been created and by which they are constantly being modified. It is in this spirit that we shall seek to describe the changing structure of the League of Nations.

1. *The Members of the League.*

By far the more vital organs of the League of Nations are, as its very name indicates, the nations

[2] I owe it to the reader to say that I have already dealt with these topics in my lectures delivered in 1926, 1927, and 1928 before the Geneva Institute of International Relations. Cf. *Problems of Peace* (London, 1927, 1928, 1929).

which constitute its membership. They are both the stuff of which the League is made and the masters which dictate its policies. Their numbers, importance, geographical position, and political tendencies are therefore of prime significance.

The ideal that the League should be all-inclusive in membership was doubtless at the bottom of the minds of its principal founders when they first set out to speak about it. In his address before the League to Enforce Peace, delivered on May 27, 1916, President Wilson, for instance, had spoken of ''a universal association of the nations.''

As the time of the drafting of the Covenant approached, however, this ideal conception was, if not generally abandoned, at least held in reserve for an indefinite future. In his Fourteen Points speech of January 18, 1919, President Wilson had already used the much vaguer term of a ''general association of nations.'' The first ''suggestion for a Covenant of a League of Nations'' drafted by Colonel House on July 16, 1918, provides for ''states not parties to this convention,'' as had the British plan prepared by Lord Phillimore's commission before March 20, 1918, which Colonel House had consulted. In fact, this British plan was based on the idea that membership in the League was first to be confined to the States allied in the War, with the possible addition of a few neutrals.[3]

The reasons which led to this restriction were threefold. In the first place, the state of mind prevailing among the Allies generally, and in France and Belgium in particular, made it very difficult for them to conceive of an immediate peaceful associa-

[3] D. H. Miller, *op. cit.,* I, 6; II, 5 *et seq.,* 9 *et seq.*

tion with their enemies. Secondly, the American proposal to incorporate the Covenant in the peace treaties seemed destined to exclude also the neutrals which, as I know, was very far from the intentions of its author. And thirdly, the fact that certain Latin-American governments, the most important of which was that of Mexico, were not recognized by several powers, including the United States, and were therefore unwelcome even in Washington, seriously hampered President Wilson in his advocacy of a universal League.

That he remained to the end, however, the chief champion of this conception is shown by the part he took in the drafting of the actual Covenant. When at one of the last meetings of the Crillon Commission, on March 22, 1919, M. Léon Bourgeois of France and M. Hymans of Belgium urged the adoption of a provision by which the "honor of having been the founders of the League of Nations should be reserved for those states which had participated in the war," President Wilson, supported by Lord Robert Cecil, opposed this restrictive view. On the contrary he "believed that it was best to avoid giving the League the appearance of an alliance between victorious belligerents, in the first place because it was a world league; in the second place because such a policy would lead to an exclusive spirit in considering the claims to admission of new members."[4]

When the Covenant was finally adopted by the Peace Conference of Paris on April 28, 1919, its

[4] Extracted from the Minutes of the Commission quoted by D. H. Miller, *op. cit.*, II, 341.

Annex provided that forty-five states might belong to the League as original members.

Of these, thirty-two, the victorious belligerents, were to join as signatories of the Treaty of Versailles and thirteen, former neutrals, were "invited to accede to the Covenant." Of the thirty-two victors, twenty-eight effectually joined by ratifying the Treaty of Versailles; one, China, who refused to take this step, by ratifying the Treaty of Saint-Germain; while three, the United States of America, Ecuador, and Hedjaz remained aloof. All of the thirteen neutrals invited to accede to the Covenant promptly did so.[5] Six further states were admitted in 1920, three in 1921, one in 1922, two in 1923, one in 1924, and one in 1926. The total membership of the League today would therefore be fifty-six, if Costa Rica and Brazil, by seceding in 1926 and 1928 respectively, had not reduced it to fifty-four.

It might be interesting to analyze these figures from many points of view, as the evolution of the League is naturally bound to be influenced in its course by the composition of its membership. In the limited space at my disposal, I shall make only three observations.

They refer to the three main tendencies discernable in the development of the League, which may be defined as its Europeanization, what for want of a less barbaric term I shall call its "debellicisation," that is, its gradual emancipation from the memories and consequences of the War, and finally its universalization.

[5] Cf. Manley O. Hudson, "Membership in the League of Nations," *American Journal of International Law,* Vol. XVIII (July, 1924), No. 3.

In 1920, when the League was founded, sixteen out of a total of forty-two original members were European states, that is, 38.1 per cent. Today, twenty-seven out of a total of fifty-four members are European, that is, exactly one-half. Of the fourteen states admitted by the successive assemblies, eleven were European; they were the four ex-enemy states, the four new Baltic states, Luxemburg, Albania, and the Irish Free State. Today, if we disregard the Soviet Union and such tiny political units as Liechtenstein, San Marino, Monaco, and Andorra, we may say that the whole of Europe has joined the League.

In America, in spite of two admissions, Costa Rica in 1922 and San Domingo in 1924, the evolution has tended in the opposite direction. Mexico has never acceded to the Covenant. The United States and Ecuador have, as aforesaid, remained aloof. Costa Rica decided to resign in 1924 and Brazil in 1926. Besides, the Argentine Republic was represented only at the beginning of the first assembly and has not put in an official appearance at any of the succeeding assemblies. Although she has never formally resigned, has up to the present year fully met her financial obligations, and has been represented on several technical committees, she can hardly be held to be a full-fledged member of the League. Besides, the coöperation of Peru and Bolivia has until the Assembly of 1929 been so intermittent and so casual as to be little more than nominal.

As for Asia and Africa, except for the admission of Abyssinia in 1923, the participation of these two continents in the affairs of the League—although constant—has not been active.

It is therefore a fair generalization to say that, since its creation, the League has undergone a process of Europeanization.

The second point to which I wish to call attention is the change resulting from the gradual entrance into the League of the states defeated in the Great War. The Covenant was drafted by the victors in 1919, and it would have been surprising if it had not been drafted primarily in their interest. All the permanent and all but one of the non-permanent seats on the Council were to be occupied by themselves. But already in 1920 two of the defeated powers, Austria and Bulgaria, were admitted to the League. In 1922 Hungary followed, and Sweden, a second former neutral, was elected to the enlarged Council.

Furthermore, in 1926 four former neutrals, the Netherlands, Chili, Colombia, and Salvador, were elected as non-permanent members in the place of the two, Spain and Sweden, who until then, had alone represented that part of mankind which was not associated with the military triumphs of 1918. In 1927, it is true, three of these four were again replaced by ex-belligerents, but in the elections of 1928 the three vacant seats were all attributed to ex-neutral states, Spain, Persia, and Venezuela. Thus, in the short space of nine years, a league of victors became a league of nations.

The third tendency which deserves notice is the universalization of the League. The importance of this tendency is not measured merely by its increased formal membership, but also and still more by the increasingly frequent and active participation in its labors of non-member states. Thus, for instance, at the Conference on economic statistics,

over which I had the honor to preside in December
1928, I had the privilege of welcoming official delegations from seven non-member states, including the
United States, the Soviet Union, Brazil, Mexico,
and Turkey. Moreover, these delegations and particularly that from the United States, very ably
headed by Dr. Dana Durand, took an extremely useful and on many points a truly leading part in the
deliberations of the Conference. This example of co-
operation, which I mention solely because I was in
a position to witness it personally, is typical of what
has become a general habit in the course of the last
years at Geneva. And that such coöperation is not
confined to minor technical matters is shown by the
again extremely useful and again truly leading part
taken by the American delegations at the successive
meetings and particularly at the last meeting of the
Preparatory Committee of the coming disarmament
conference.

The facts therefore fully warrant the statement
that the League of Nations, in spite of several ab-
stentions and of two resignations, is steadily tending toward the ideal of universality of which its
founders had dreamed.

That they should have pursued the ideal of universality as the ultimate goal, is very natural. Whether
the League of Nations be merely the useful clearing
house of international affairs of which we have
spoken at the end of our last chapter, or whether it
be destined to become the supreme arbiter and
pacificator of the world, it cannot completely serve
either purpose unless it be or become universal.
Neither a telephone company nor a fire engine service can do for an urban community all they are

intended to do for its convenience or its safety, if they have no access to certain parts of the town.

If Europe were without commercial and other relations with the rest of the world and if the last war had not shown that under contemporaneous conditions international conflicts were limited to certain continents neither in their causes nor especially in their effects, nor consequently in their possible remedies, Europe might well be content with the League of European Nations it has already almost completely established. But, as we have seen in our first chapters, the trend of political and economic coöperation tends toward the suppression or at least the lowering of barriers, national and even continental. Therefore, the League of the future seems bound, sooner or later, in some shape or other, to become, as President Wilson had said and as it is already in many respects, if not in legal form, "a world league."

2. *The Council.*

After the Members of the League, its most conspicuous, if not necessarily its most important organ is the Council.

Very early in the process of the drafting of the Covenant it was recognized that the constitution of the League of Nations would have to provide for two bodies, one on which all members would or could be represented and another small enough to allow for the prompt transaction of business. The first of these bodies has become the Assembly and the second the Council.

As to the composition of the Council, the authors of the Covenant were at first divided. All were of course agreed that the Great Powers should always be represented thereon. But some of them, and notably Lord Robert Cecil, apparently influenced by the example of the Supreme War Council or Versailles Council of Prime Ministers, and by that of the Peace Conference itself, suggested that they alone should enjoy permanent representation, other states being by them invited to send representatives to the Council when matters affecting their interests were under discussion.[6]

On the other hand, General Smuts had proposed to add to the permanent delegates of the Great Powers on the Council, four other members to be elected in rotation from two panels representing the intermediate and the minor powers. This view was, of course, supported by the representatives of all the latter in Paris, many of whom, and particularly Mr. Pessoa of Brazil, would have preferred a still stronger representation and none of whom would have been content with less.[7]

In the Covenant as finally recommended by President Wilson and adopted by the Peace Conference these two conflicting conceptions have been combined. The Council was to be composed of the representatives of the five victorious Great Powers and of four others, representing smaller states, to be elected by the Assembly. Besides, any state whose interests are especially affected by matters discussed by the Council "shall be invited to send a repre-

[6] Cf. Lord Robert Cecil's plan of January 14, 1919, the British Draft Convention of January 20, 1919, and Lord Eustace Percy's draft. D. H. Miller, II, 61, 108, 119–120.

[7] D. H. Miller, *op. cit.,* II, 41, 257 *et seq.,* 301 *et seq.*

sentative to seat as a member" during their consideration.

When the first Council met in January, 1920, it
was composed of the representatives of four Great
Powers and of four other states. The principle
set up a year before, according to which the Great
Powers were always to be in a majority of at least
one, was already violated as a result of the absence
of the United States. Since then it has been further
violated in 1922 by the admission of two additional
elected members, and in 1926 by the increase from
ten to fourteen of the total membership of the Council. Today the Great Powers have again five permanent seats, Germany having occupied that left
vacant by the United States. But they are surrounded by nine other states, who are therefore in
a majority of four.

This evolution is curious and interesting; but it is
not, as might at first be thought, significant of any
real change in the relative importance of the various
categories of states represented on the Council. In
1920, on a Council of eight, four minor powers and
two non-European states were represented. Today,
on a Council of fourteen, there are represented nine
minor powers and six non-European states. No one
who has closely followed the development of the
League, however, would say that the importance of
the Great Powers and of Europe has diminished at
Geneva. In fact, the very opposite is obviously the
case. And, paradoxical as it may appear, it is just
because the Great Powers and the states of Europe
have come to realize that, in the absence of the
United States, whatever the majority on the Council, they were the true masters of the League, that

they welcomed or at least accepted without any apprehension an evolution which threatened their numerical preponderance. In 1922 and again in 1926 the Council was enlarged and modified in its structure, not in order that it might more truly represent the majority of the League, but merely in order to forestall resignations on the part of states who intimated that they would remain in the League only if assured of permanent or at least of intermittent representation on what is to some extent its governing body.

Whether the future will justify this enlargement of the Council is extremely doubtful. While it has temporarily appeased certain appetites, it has whetted certain others, assuredly not belying the French saying: *"L'appétit vient en mangeant."* While it has contributed to retain Poland in the League and to induce Spain to withdraw her resignation, it has sufficed neither to hold Brazil nor to attract Argentina. As all weak measures of this kind, it has, I believe, on the whole increased rather than reduced the number of disappointed electoral ambitions by creating more wants than it could satisfy.

Its most serious consequence, however, in my opinion has been to divorce responsibility from power. Now as power and responsibility, although they may be formally divorced, are inherently inseparable, the enlargement of the Council, which has led Cuba and Salvador to sit as equals beside the British Empire and France, has tended to create and fortify within it an inner circle of Great Powers whose decisions, when unanimous, are in fact, if not in legal theory, final. That is why, although apparently favoring the small at the expense of the large, it has been less opposed or less reluctantly accepted by the great than by the minor states.

On the other hand, it has made possible the introduction of a scheme of rotating regional representation which General Smuts had already advocated in 1918 and which all the Assemblies prior to 1926 had vainly sought to adopt. Thus, the Little Entente, the Nordic group, including the Scandinavian, the Baltic States, and Holland, Latin America, and Asia tend to agree on representatives who succeed one another in regular order and who, in a certain measure, speak and act as mandatories not only of their own state but also of their group as a whole.

On another very important point the hopes and the predictions of General Smuts have come true, after having been disappointed for several years. In his most remarkable pamphlet published in December, 1918,[8] General Smuts had written:

> The Powers represented on the Council should send to it representatives of the highest authority and standing. These representatives should be a Prime Minister or Foreign Secretary. . . . If the most important leaders in the Governments of the Powers attend the sittings of the Council as often as possible, and proper consultation of others interested takes place the Council cannot fail to command the highest prestige and authority. . . . The more confidence it commands, the less will be the inclination among the Powers to enter into private intrigues or understandings apart from the regular machinery of the Council.

Such "private intrigues or understandings" have unfortunately not been avoided, partly, as I see

[8] Entitled *The League of Nations, A Practical Suggestion* and reprinted in D. H. Miller, *op. cit.*, II, 23 *et seq.*

it, on account of the excessive enlargement of the
Council. Nevertheless there is no doubt that its
prestige and authority have been considerably enhanced by the regular attendance, since 1924, of a
large number of Foreign Secretaries, including as a
rule those of France, of Great Britain, and, since
1926, of Germany. The change in this respect is
significant, both as a symptom of the increased importance which governments and parliaments attach
to the League and as a means of improving its
efficiency and of accelerating the rhythm of its deliberations.

The following figures, which show the proportion
of prime ministers and foreign secretaries attending Council meetings from 1920 until 1929 are, I
believe, one of the best statistical demonstrations of
the growing political importance of the League of
Nations, which can be produced.

	Number of Council Sessions	Number of States Rep-resented	Number of Prime and Foreign Min-isters among Council Members	Proportion of Prime and Foreign Minis-ters to Number of Council Members
1920	11	8	11	12.5 per cent
1921	4	8	0	0 per cent
1922	7	8	0	0 per cent
1923	5	10	0	0 per cent
1924	5	10	9	18. per cent
1925	5	10	18	36. per cent
1926	6	10 & 14	28	43.7 per cent
1927	5	14	34	48.6 per cent
1928	5	14	30	42.8 per cent
1929	4	14	20	36.1 per cent

If, disregarding the non-European members of
the Council, we limit our inquiry to the representatives of European states, we shall have the following, still more striking figures.

	Number of Council Sessions	Number of European States Represented	Number of Prime and Foreign Ministers among European Council Members	Proportion of European Prime and Foreign Ministers to Number of European Council Members
1920	11	6	11	16.6 per cent
1921	4	5	0	0 per cent
1922	7	5	0	0 per cent
1923	5	6	0	0 per cent
1924	5	7	9	25.7 per cent
1925	5	7	18	51.4 per cent
1926	6	7 & 9	28	62.2 per cent
1927	5	8 & 9	34	79.1 per cent
1928	5	8	29	72.2 per cent
1929	4	8	20	62.5 per cent

Let us now consider the same figures relating to the first nine ordinary Assemblies.

	Number of States Represented	European	Number of Prime and Foreign Ministers among Delegates	European	Proportion of Prime and Foreign Ministers among Delegates to Number of Delegations	
					Total	European per cent
1920	47	21	6	5	12.8	23.8
1921	45	24	8	8	17.7	33.3
1922	48	25	9	9	18.7	36.
1923	50	26	7	7	14.	26.9
1924	51	26	22	21	43.1	80.8
1925	50	26	18	18	36.	69.2
1926	49	26	18	18	36.7	69.2
1927	49	26	22	22	44.9	84.6
1928	50	27	21	19	42.	70.4
1929	53	27	27	27	50.9	100.

If we now represent the percentage of the three above tables in a combined graph, we shall have the following picture.

Proportion of Prime and Foreign Ministers in Council and Assembly.

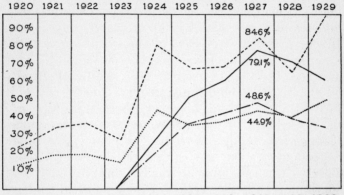

—·—·— Proportion of prime and foreign ministers to number of Council members.

————— Proportion of European prime and foreign ministers to number of European Council members.

·········· Proportion of prime and foreign ministers to number of Assembly delegations.

------- Proportion of European prime and foreign ministers to number of European Assembly delegations.

Besides showing clearly a marked trend in the development of the League of Nations since 1924, these figures call attention to a phenomenon of the greatest political significance. As they indicate, it has become the habit of several of the leading statesmen of most of the greatest states of Europe to spend together, in a small Swiss town, about two out of every twelve months. During one of these two months they enjoy the company of several of the leading statesmen of the minor European countries.

These periodic meetings of those most directly responsible for the foreign policy of the Old World under conditions of daily contact and of real informality are, of course, the occasion for countless diplomatic and personal conversations between them. In strict legal theory each of these statesmen, to be sure, is but the spokesman of one absolutely sovereign state, which is entirely free, within the limits of its treaty obligations, to do exactly what it pleases. As a group, however, these statesmen are the spokesmen of Europe whose constituent parts, independent though they may be in law, are interdependent in fact and cannot fail to be still more closely drawn together by the constant intimacy and continuous collective action of their political leaders.

Every adult citizen is legally his own master. But every member of a family is socially conscious of a certain measure of responsibility for and to his near relations, who live under the same roof or in the same neighborhood. Likewise the statesmen of Europe, conferring together for weeks every year at Geneva on behalf of their respective countries, are both legally free to pursue their own national policies and politically bound in so doing to consider the interests of their colleagues.

If I were to be asked by which means the League of Nations has so far most effectively served the cause of peace in the world and especially in Europe, my answer would not be doubtful. I should reply: Not by its efforts in favor of disarmament, of arbitration, and of mutually guaranteed security, but by the habits of international conversation and coöperation it has engendered among the governments of Europe and the statesmen of the world.

3. *The Assembly.*

What we have just said applies particularly to the Council. This is so both because its meetings are more intimate and because its members are the representatives of the most important European states, those with whom the responsibility for the peace of the continent ultimately rests. But it is true also of the Assembly, whose annual ordinary sessions lasting from three to four weeks, have become the main political event of the year.

Before the League was founded, everyone interested in its constitution realized that some all-inclusive body would have to be set up to elect its officers and to vote its budget. But what that body would be, nobody knew. Was it to be a purely formal and rather impotent and inarticulate meeting of diplomatic plenipotentiaries, as the Peace Conference in plenary session had been? Or would it turn into an irresponsible and an oratorical world debating club? Or could it really be made to voice the public opinion of the world and to bring the pressure of this opinion to bear on those immediately responsible for international policy?

Of all of the principal authors of the Covenant, General Smuts, on this as on many other points, proved to be the most far-sighted and the most boldly constructive. While the plans of the Phillimore Commission, of Colonel House, and of President Wilson contemplated a general diplomatic conference, at which the states would be represented by their ambassadors and ministers accredited with the government of the states at whose capital the League was to have its seat, and while Lord Robert

Cecil merely proposed besides the at least annual meeting of the Great Powers a quadrennial meeting of all the constituent states,[9] General Smuts had far higher ambitions for the Assembly. In his famous pamphlet he wrote:

There will have to be a general conference or congress of all the constituent States, which will partake of the character of a parliament, in which public debates of general international interest will take place. In this body all the States may be considered equal and should vote as States. . . . In all cases the resolutions of the conference will only have the force of recommendations. Even so, however, the conference may be a most useful body and may become a most powerful and influential factor in moulding international public opinion. The League will never be a great success unless there is found as its main support a powerful public opinion. . . . The debates periodically taking place in the general conference might well become of immense importance in this great task of forming and educating a strong body of international opinion behind and in support of the League in its work. For the first time in history people will hear great subjects discussed on an international platform, and the narrow national influence of the local Parliament and still more of the local press will gradually be neutralized and a broader opinion and spirit will be fostered. The representatives of the States on such a conference should be viewed largely from this point of view of favourably influencing and educating public opinion in all constituent countries. The Powers should not grudge strong representations to the smaller States, as in any case the resolution will only be in the nature of recommendations to the national Parliaments.[10]

[9] D. H. Miller, *op. cit.*, II, 4, 7, 12, 61.
[10] *Ibid.*, pp. 39 *et seq.*

These lines, written two full years before the first Assembly met, give an astonishingly true picture of what that remarkable body is and seems likely ever more to become. Its periodic meetings, its consultative character, its main function as a focus of what has come to be called the spirit of Geneva and as an educator of national opinion, the publicity and parliamentary tone of its debates, and the relatively important part played in it by the representatives of the minor states, all these traits, which subsequent history has gradually revealed, General Smuts foresaw with a truly prophetic eye. For once—the fact is so rare in the evolution of the League that it should be noted—it was the statesman with the boldest imagination and the highest ambitions who was right in his previsions. Coming from a minor state, General Smuts naturally did not share his British, American, and French colleagues' rather contemptuous views of the international rôle of small countries, views which the sight of the Peace Conference seemed somewhat to justify. And coming from a free and from a new state, with no diplomatic service and no diplomatic traditions, he naturally and very rightly placed the political importance of parliamentary and of public opinion above that of ambassadors and ministers.

Article 3 of the Covenant, which is the legal basis on which the Assembly rests, merely provided that it was to meet ''at stated intervals and from time to time, as occasion may require.''

The great importance assumed by the Assembly as an organ of the League is due primarily not to the provisions of this Article, but to three decisions which it took itself in the course of its first sittings

in December, 1920. It then decided, first, to meet
annually in ordinary session, secondly, to sit in
public, and thirdly, to vote the annual budget of the
League. The more one studies the evolution of the
Assembly, the more one is struck by the far-reaching
consequences of these three decisions. Thanks to
its annual meetings, at which the elections to the
Council are held and the work of the Council discussed, it exercises a very strong influence over the
smaller body. Thanks to the publicity of its debates,
it has established and maintained contacts with the
public opinion of the world which, as General Smuts
had foreseen, is obviously the true backbone of the
League. And thanks to the position it has assumed
as the supreme budgetary authority, it will, unless
all parliamentary precedents prove deceptive, effectively control the future development of the League.

The true nature of the Assembly is extremely
hard to define. This is so, not only because, as a
youth who has not yet chosen his future profession,
the Assembly has not yet fully found itself nor decided on its own destiny, but also because it resembles no historical antecedent. It is certainly
neither a court of justice, nor an international executive, nor a legislature. It is not a court of justice
because, among other reasons, its members are
not independent individuals, but representatives of
governments, to whom they are responsible for
their actions. It is not an international executive,
because, among other reasons, it is too numerous
and too unwieldy a body to execute anything. And it
is not a legislature, because among other reasons,
it cannot legislate, but only promote and recommend
legislation.

In strict legal theory, the Assembly is a body of representatives of sovereign states, who very seldom have full powers to make any final decision and who cannot even make any valid recommendations except by an unanimous vote. In fact, however, the Assembly is both less and much more than a diet of plenipotentiaries. It is less for the reasons just mentioned. But it is infinitely more also, on account of the peculiar relations it entertains with public opinion. There is no platform in the world from which an eloquent voice may carry as far nor from which a new idea may be launched with greater effect.

The publicity of its proceedings has made of it a very alluring stage for parliamentary prima donnas, but a correspondingly unattractive resort for the professional diplomat. There is no lack of intrigue and of secret parleying in the lobbies of the Assembly, as there is bound to be wherever politicians assemble. But whereas the successful Council member is he who most ingratiates himself with his colleagues, who startles and who offends no one, and who conciliates everybody by aptly suggesting ambiguous and therefore generally acceptable formulae, the successful Assembly delegate is the popular orator who most eloquently, but also most boldly expresses the hopes and the fears, the likes and dislikes, the enthusiasms and the prejudices of the multitude. That is why the popular heroes at the Assembly are never the suave diplomats, rarely the most responsible statesmen, but usually the most gifted orators, the most ardent reformers and those delegates least hampered by official instructions. M. Briand owes his popularity in the Assembly much

more to his eloquence, than to his position and to
his political talent. M. Politis owes his, to his extraordinary intellectual and rhetorical brilliance.
That of Prof. Gilbert Murray, of the late Mr.
Branting, and of Doctor Nansen is due to their well-
known convictions and courage. The case of Lord
Robert Cecil is peculiarly illuminating. He was
eminently successful as long as he represented not
the British Government but South Africa; that is,
his personal friend Smuts; that is, in fact, only himself and his own progressive opinions. When he returned to Geneva as a member of a British conservative cabinet, bound by rigid instructions which
he often resented, he was a much less popular and
influential figure, although officially a much more
important personage.

What we have said explains also why the Assembly always appears more liberal than the Council. Its members, more responsive to the demands
of public opinion and less responsible for the carrying out of the policies they advocate, are apt to be
more internationally minded and less intent upon
securing exclusive advantages for the state on whose
behalf they speak. Thus the Assembly has become
an absolutely essential part of the League machinery. It is the motor that provides the driving power
and that sets the pace for the effective work of the
year, which is naturally intrusted to the Council.
Or rather, the driving power is applied by public
opinion and is transmitted to the Council through
the shaft of the Assembly. It is in this latter body
alone that real leadership on the international plane
can assert itself. Now, for the reasons just evoked,
leadership is more apt to be assumed by a free lance

who happens to be included in some minor delegation by reason of his outstanding personality, than by the official exponent of the foreign policy of a Great Power. But as the latter type predominates in the Council and as the Council must act under the impulsion of the Assembly, if deadlock and paralysis are to be avoided, the problem of the relations between these two organs of the League is of vital importance. The future of the world institution, and therefore of European peace depends in a large measure upon the manner in which this problem can be solved.

4. *The Secretariat.*

The most novel and distinctive organ of the League is its permanent international Secretariat. Every time that, since the Middle Ages, the Great Powers of the day met in concert, they constituted something analogous to the Council and every time that, in the course of the last century, a large number of states were summoned to attend a diplomatic conference, they formed something akin to the Assembly. But, prior to the birth of the League of Nations, there was nowhere to be found a general and common administrative body, such as has always and everywhere proved necessary whenever and wherever independent states have joined to found a confederation.

The Secretariat of the League, as an international administrative body, could conceivably adopt either of two forms. It could be made up of officials paid out of a common treasury and released from all bonds of loyalty to their respective governments. Or it could be constituted by national delegations

salaried and instructed by their respective governments to coöperate toward common ends.

It is impossible from the available material to
discover which of these two conceptions was in the
minds of the framers of the Covenant. It is perhaps
safe to admit that they had not clearly distinguished
them. The precedent to which allusion was most
often made, when the Secretariat was under discussion at Paris in 1919, was that of the permanent
organizations set up to prepare and to execute the
decisions of various interallied bodies during the
War.[11] Now, although the personnel of these organizations no doubt developed a certain interallied
esprit de corps in the course of their common labors,
they always remained under the orders of their
respective Governments who had selected and who
continued to pay them.

On the other hand, Lord Robert Cecil, who seems
to have devoted more thought to this matter than
his colleagues at Paris, obviously realized the importance of securing the independence and impartiality of what was to become the permanent civil
service of the League. He therefore, in his plan of
January 14, 1919, suggested that its head should
bear the dignified title of "Chancellor" and that he
"should be appointed by the Great Powers, if possible choosing a national of some other country."[12]
In the notes to the British draft convention of Janu-

[11] See P. Baker, in *Les origines et l'œuvre de la Société des
Nations,* ed. P. Munch (Copenhagen, 1924), II, 21, 40 *et seq.*
Cf. also General Smuts, *The League of Nations,* quoted in D. H.
Miller, *op. cit.,* II, 43 *et seq.*

[12] D. H. Miller, *op. cit.,* II, 62.

ary 20, 1919, of which Cecil was probably the principal author, it is proposed that

the Chancellor shall appoint ten permanent secretaries at his discretion subject to the following provisions:

He should choose one national of each of the states members of the Council, two nationals of two European states not members of the Council, one national of one of the states of America other than the United States, and two nationals of any states members of the League at his discretion. Before appointing a national of any state, the Chancellor ought, however, to secure the approval of the government of such states, and the Council should have the right to veto any given appointment by unanimous vote.[13]

This proposal is interesting from two points of view. In the first place, it implicitly shows that, in the opinion of its author, the League was to be mainly European, since of the ten permanent secretaries between five and seven were to be chosen from the states of the Old World. This is all the more striking as the contemplated original membership of the League was to make it preponderantly extra-European in its political composition. In the second place, it indicates that the Secretariat was thought of as a truly international body, but still not as entirely independent of the governments represented in the League. Its leading members were to be selected by the Chancellor, and not delegated by their respective governments. They were to be nationals of at least eight and probably of ten different states, but the approval of their governments was to be secured before appointment.

[13] *Ibid.,* p. 115.

The final text of the Covenant contains no provision whatever as to the nationality and status of the members of the Secretariat. It merely states the name of the first Secretary-General[14] and provides that he shall appoint his staff subject to the approval of the Council. It adds that this staff should enjoy diplomatic privileges and immunities when engaged on the business of the League and that its expenses ''shall be borne by the members of the League in a certain proportion.''

As a matter of fact, the Secretary-General, although himself a member of the British diplomatic service, chose most of his first chief subordinates from other, almost exclusively European, countries and from other walks of life than his own. And he appointed them independently of their respective governments. He further asserted his intention of placing the Secretariat on a purely international and impartial basis, by drafting the following statement, which was embodied in a report submitted to and adopted by the Council of the League in May, 1920, by Mr. A. J. Balfour:

By the terms of the Treaty, the duty of selecting the staff falls upon the Secretary-General, just as the duty of approving it falls upon the Council. In making his appointments, he had primarily to secure the best available men and women for the particular duties which had to be performed; but in doing so, it was necessary to have regard to the great importance of selecting the officials from various nations. Evidently no one nation or group of nations ought to have a monopoly in providing the material

[14] This more modest title had been adopted in preference to that of Chancellor by a drafting committee between the first and second readings of the document on February 5, 1919.

for its international institution. I emphasize the word "international," because the members of the Secretariat once appointed are no longer the servants of the country of which they are citizens, but become for the time being the servants only of the League of Nations. Their duties are not national but international. . . . I shall propose that no member of the Secretariat, during his or her term of office, shall accept any honour or decoration except for services rendered prior to the appointment. The reasons for this proposal are fairly clear. . . . The members of the staff carry out, as I have explained, not national but international duties. Nothing should be done to weaken the sense of their international allegiance; the acceptance of special marks of distinction or favour, either from their own or from any other country, militates, in our view, against the general spirit of the Covenant.[15]

In view of all these facts, there is no doubt that, in spite of the silence of the Covenant on this point, the Secretariat was created in accordance with the first of the two above-mentioned conceptions. It was intended to be an international civil service, independent of the governments of its various members.

However, in the course of years, several unmistakable symptoms began to appear of a gradual evolution tending toward the realization of the second conception. The governments of various states,

[15] At a sitting of the Fourth Commission of the last Assembly, Sir Eric Drummond declared that he was "at least a part author" of this statement, which he had already expressly endorsed in 1920 by submitting in his own name a memorandum in which it is said that "the members of the Secretariat act, during their period of office, in an international capacity and are not in any way representatives of their Governments." Cf. League of Nations, *Official Journal*, Special Supplement, No. 68. Records on the Ninth Ordinary Session of the Assembly. Minutes of the Fourth Commission (Geneva, 1928), p. 37.

members of the League, are taking an increasing interest in the selection as League officials of their own nationals. Not only do they tend to insist on being represented by them in an adequate proportion of numbers and rank, but also they tend to favor the selection of individuals chosen from the lists of their own diplomatic services. Rumors have been abroad of high officials informed of their appointments to Geneva by their own governments and ordered by them to the League from the diplomatic post they were holding as to another. Rumors have been abroad also of diplomatic titles and indemnities retained by or even conferred upon League officials during their period of service at Geneva. But even if we disregard such well-accredited rumors, a close examination of the personal composition of the Secretariat will readily reveal its increasingly national and diplomatic character. That, under these circumstances, it should not also tend to become increasingly national in its methods and in its spirit would indeed be surprising.

The reason that I have dwelt on this matter at some length is not only because it has been much discussed in Europe recently before and at the last Assembly, but because it is of very real importance for the past and future evolution of international co-operation.

As an administrative agency, the Secretariat was, from its inception, a very much more vital organ of the League than the language of the Covenant would lead one to suspect and than most of its authors probably anticipated. This is due to two main reasons.

It may be laid down, first, as a general principle

that the relative importance of a civil service stands in inverse ratio to the stability and activity of the political authority it assists. Where governments frequently change and where ministers are more engrossed with extraneous than with departmental duties, as is the case in most parliamentary states, the civil service is the real power behind the throne. Where, on the contrary, as for instance in my own country, the Government is very stable, the actual tenure of office of its members very long, and their duties more administrative than political, the civil service plays only a subordinate part.

Now, if one may compare the Council and the Assembly of the League with national governments on the one hand and the League Secretariat with national civil services on the other, it is quite obvious that the balance of influence was at first in Geneva very heavily weighted in favor of the administrative as against the political organs.

The League, especially during the first three or four years of its existence, was a novel and apparently rather insignificant instrument of international government. The states represented on the Council and in the Assembly at first, as we have seen, were inclined to send to Geneva men of minor importance, who changed from time to time and for whom their intermittent League duties were never their main tasks. The government of the League was therefore a weak government. Its civil service, on the other hand, was correspondingly strong, all the more so as its members were very discriminatingly chosen from an extremely wide field, for their ability and their devotion to the ideals of the League.

In all minor matters, and even in several important ones, the functions of the members of the Council and of the Assembly consisted mainly in delivering speeches, in reading reports, and in voting resolutions which had all been carefully drafted for them by the Secretariat.

During these first years, Council meetings might sometimes have been compared with the harmless pastime of children playing with their toy sailboats on the pond of a city park, the masterful children being the Secretariat and the cardboard admirals on board the boats the dignified and indolent representatives of the powers. As the League grew in importance, a gradual change came about. National governments, recognizing its possibilities, tended to send their most representative men to Geneva, to intrust their national civil services with the preparation of official instructions, and earnestly to discuss these instructions before League meetings. Accordingly, the pond became the high seas of the political world, the toy sailboats the super-dreadnoughts of national policy, and the bemedaled and beplumed, but very passive, admirals the real commanders in action. As a result, the part of the masterful children on the shore naturally became less decisive and more contemplative.

My impertinent and doubly irreverent simile, for which I proffer my humblest apologies to the children no less than to the admirals, is, of course, much overdrawn. It will have served its purpose, however, if it has made clear how the growing importance of the League has affected the functions of the Council on the one hand and of the Secretariat on the other.

What the Secretariat has lost, however, in immediate influence over vital League decisions, it has regained on the other hand, through the increased scope of League action. It has gained also through the development and increased specialization and efficiency of the countless advisory commissions which now coöperate in the preparation of the resolutions of the Council and of the Assembly. The Covenant, it may be remarked, provided for a Secretariat to assist only these two major organs of the League. The advisory committees, except for the permanent Military and Mandates Commissions, are a purely organic product of its evolution, having been provided for not by its constitution, but solely by subsequent decisions.

As a result of this evolution almost every section of the Secretariat of the League has become the special secretariat of one or more advisory committees. Thereby the work of the Secretariat has been increased in technical quality as well as in volume far beyond the expectations to which a mere analysis of the Covenant might give rise.

The fact that certain governments have brought increasing pressure to bear on the Secretariat is a proof of the growing political importance they attach to the League. In so far, it is the symptom, however unwelcome in itself, of a very welcome development. Furthermore it is obviously conducive to prompt and easy international coöperation if the governments called upon to coöperate are represented at Geneva by officials who enjoy their full confidence. This confidence they are, of course, the more likely to enjoy if appointed on their express recommendation. In a certain respect, the change which has come about in the relative importance of the national and international functions of the Secretariat is a tribute paid to what four years ago I called the League to promote international coöperation by what I termed the League to prevent war.

In the field of contentious political debate, the absolute international independence and impartiality of members of the Secretariat are clearly much more important than in that of noncontentious activities. As the latter field has been tilled by the League with far greater success than the former, it is not surprising that there has been a trend in favor of another type of plowman. The sociologically minded historian will readily detect here an example of the function influencing the development of the organ.

It was originally intended by many that the main duty of the League should be to prevent war by settling political conflicts on the basis of justice. If and when the League should, with confidence and energy, again be able to give this item the first place on its program of action, the demand for a Secretariat exclusively composed of officials as unbiased and as purely international in their loyalty as human nature will permit, will doubtless again arise. In the meanwhile it should be noted that in at least one of the very rare cases in which contentious issues vitally involving the political interests of Great Powers have come before the League, the Secretariat officials of the interested nationality have remained in the background. The case to which I refer is the Mosul dispute between Great Britain and Turkey, in the consideration of which the place of the British Secretary-General at the Council table was taken by his French deputy.

COÖPERATION INSIDE THE LEAGUE   221

It should finally be noted also that, as the League grows more universal in membership and the Secretariat more representative in its international composition, the disadvantages and dangers of national bias on the part of the individual officials grow less. To be sure, justice in international relations is not to be defined as the mere mathematical resultant of divergent national claims. There is no doubt, however, that the chances of justice in the world are greater when all divergent claims are presented with equal force than when some alone are urged and others ignored, for lack of advocates to press them. After the perhaps impossible ideal of an international civil service whose members would all be inspired solely by the pure love of international justice, the next best thing is therefore a Secretariat in which all national claims are fairly and freely represented. In this respect, also, the admission of Germany into the League and of a considerable number of Germans into the Secretariat since 1926, has made for greater, if not necessarily for ideal, justice in the consideration of international affairs.

5. *The Advisory Commissions.*

Besides the Council, the Assembly, and the Secretariat, the other major organs of the League are the advisory commissions, the International Labor Organization, and the Permanent Court of International Justice.

Of these I shall say but little, not because there is little to say, but on the contrary because the detailed study of their organization and development would take more time and space than I can spare.

The advisory bodies I regard as the most symptomatic structural product of the League's evolution. As aforesaid, the Covenant itself provided for only two such organs, the permanent Military Commission and the permanent Mandates Commission. The pressure of circumstances, however, has led the Council to surround itself by a whole army of international experts, divided and subdivided into a large number of divisions, brigades, regiments, battalions, companies, squads, and even individual scouts.

The following table showing the number and average duration of meetings held under the auspices of the League for 1920 to 1928 may serve to give an idea of the activity of these consultative commissions.

	Number of Meetings	Average Number of Days in Session
1920	23	10.
1921	37	8.43
1922	47	5.74
1923	67	6.82
1924	86	7.
1925	94	5.77
1926	105	5.54
1927	125	6.1
1928	125	6.3

Although these figures include the sessions of the Council and of the Assembly, they of course relate mainly to meetings of the various advisory bodies which we have mentioned, and they may therefore not irrelevantly be quoted in this connection.

What do all these figures point to? They have but one significance. The League of Nations, created essentially as a political institution to prevent wars between nations, has in fact become the great administrative agency for the promotion of voluntary international coöperation between them in times of peace. The technical advisory committees, which multiply in number and specialize in function from year to year, are the structural expression of a world need.

It should be noted also that, as these technical activities are coming to be less and less limited to states members of the League, these advisory bodies are becoming more and more completely international in membership and more and more autonomous in status. In order to facilitate the coöperation of states outside the League, it has often been found convenient both by the governments of these states and by the Council of the League to appoint nationals of the former to the consultation commissions of the latter. And as these states which might be said to enjoy a sort of associate membership in the League have sometimes expressed the desire not to be drawn into closer intimacy with it, advisory bodies set up by the League have in some cases tended to develop a life of their own. Thus international conventions, initiated by League action, prepared by advisory commissions in which delegates from members and non-member states have sat and labored side by side, have come to be drafted half under the roof of the League and half in its outer courtyard, so to speak. The general tendency in this respect has been in Geneva to subordinate form to substance and author's pride to the real progress of international relations.

6. *The International Labor Organization.*

Of all the numerous technical institutions of the League, the International Labor Organization is the most important, as it is by far the largest. In fact, under the inspiring leadership of the fiery director of the International Labor Office, its independence and its size have become such, that it cannot properly be dealt with as a mere part of the League structure, but calls for a special study. I would here note only that, in its evolution, it has met with the same difficulties as the rest of the League, and that it is struggling to overcome them by resorting to similar methods.

It was intended primarily to improve social conditions the world over by gradually leveling them up to the standards of the most advanced nations. In the drafting, the signing, the ratification, and above all, in the effective application of its labor conventions, it has constantly been battling against the forces of national egotism. Without, of course, abandoning this, its main task, it has tended more and more to enlarge the field of its coöperative and non-coercive activities. It has thus become a great international research institution. By ascertaining the facts of industrial life and progress the world over and by disseminating their knowledge by means of its countless publications, it is attempting to build up a more enlightened public opinion. Thus it hopes that the obstacles which stand in the way of the achievement of its main purpose of international legislation may little by little be overcome.

7. *The Permanent Court of International Justice.*

The Permanent Court of International Justice is the last of the organs of the League to be here considered. It is, in my opinion, in many respects the most important, and would, of course, also demand an independent study. I can here but briefly outline its history and note the evolution of its functions which, perhaps partly unforeseen at the time of the drafting of the Covenant, is doubtless due to the same general causes which have so strongly influenced the development of the other organs of the League.

Article 14 of the Covenant, which called for the creation of the Permanent Court of International Justice, reads as follows:

The Council shall formulate and submit to the Members of the League for adoption plans for the establishment of a Permanent Court of International Justice. The Court shall be competent to hear and determine any dispute of an international character which the parties thereto submit to it. The Court may also give an advisory opinion upon any dispute or question referred to it by the Council or by the Assembly.

The Council, at its second meeting, in February, 1920, decided to appoint a committee of ten jurists for the purpose of preparing the plans mentioned in the first sentence of this article. These jurists met at The Hague in June and July, 1920, and agreed on a draft statute which, amended by the Council in October, 1920, and by the first Assembly, was unanimously approved by the latter body on December 13, 1920. This statute, having come into force before the second Assembly, the Court was elected on September 14 and 16, 1921, and on January 30, 1922, it met for its first session.

The most important change proposed by the Council and reluctantly accepted by the Assembly was the suppression of the compulsory jurisdiction with which the jurists had wished to endow the Court. Although the principle of compulsory jurisdiction seemed to meet with the approval of the majority of the delegates of the Assembly, it was opposed notably by the representatives of France and Great Britain as contrary to the Covenant. It was accordingly sacrificed on the altar of unanimity.

As a concession to the partisans of the extension of the Court's power, its jurisdiction was rendered optionally compulsory, i.e., compulsory in juridical matters as between those states which once for all accepted it as such.

Of this possibility sixteen states have availed themselves up to date: nine[16] in 1921; four[17] in 1922; one[18] in 1923; two[19] in 1926; two renewals[20] in 1928. As China and Lithuania failed temporarily to renew their five-year undertaking, which lapsed in 1927, the number of states bound by the compulsory jurisdiction clause fell to fourteen.

Accordingly it would seem, first, that the principle of compulsory jurisdiction is more popular among the minor states than among the Great Powers and, secondly, that it is not gaining ground very rapidly.[21] It should be noted, however, that its prog-

[16] Bulgaria, Denmark, Haiti, Netherlands, Norway, Portugal, Sweden, Switzerland, Uruguay.

[17] Austria, China, Finland, Lithuania.   [18] Esthonia.

[19] Abyssinia, Belgium.   [20] China, Lithuania.

[21] The recent happenings at the Assembly of 1929 seem to contradict both these statements. Following the lead of Great Britain, fourteen státes, including the whole British Empire, France, and Italy, on that occasion accepted the compulsory jurisdiction of the Court. Their acceptance was subjected, it is true, to various reservations, including, in all but two cases, that of subsequent ratification.

ress cannot be fairly measured by this standard alone, as it may be, and has been, promoted also by other means. Thus, as we shall see in our last chapter, every recent year has witnessed an increase in the number of bilateral and multilateral conventions providing for compulsory recourse to the Court. As a result, a large section in the field of international relations is today already placed under its legal guardianship.

If we consider the scores of international agreements which provide in the last resort for the compulsory jurisdiction of the Court—the Mandates, Minority, Locarno, arbitration treaties, and the host of technical conventions,—if we consider the thousands of possible disputes which may arise over their interpretation and application, we shall note with some surprise that the Court has so far been called upon to decide only sixteen cases in the course of the last eight years. For this apparent anomaly there are at least two excellent reasons.

In the first place, resort to the Court, the *ultima ratio* in peaceful international relations, is provided for only if negotiations and attempts at conciliation have failed. Now in spite of certain glaring failures, one should never overlook the fact that diplomacy almost invariably succeeds in dealing with current international affairs. Secondly, almost any negotiated and therefore—whether willingly or reluctantly—always freely accepted solution is preferable to the costly and uncertain decision of a court. This is true in international relations still more than in private business. Judicial decisions are, or at least should be, imperative. If they seldom give complete satisfaction to the victors, they rarely fail to produce resentment in the vanquished. The Permanent Court of International Justice may therefore very well have assured the negotiated settlement of several disputes by the mere fact of its existence and the consequent threat of its possible intervention.

For both these reasons, friends of peace should not deplore its relative inactivity.

Moreover, this inactivity has not been as marked as it would appear if the rendering of judicial decisions were alone considered. The Court, as is well known, may also be called upon by the Council and the Assembly to give legal advice. As a matter of fact, this consultative function was at first more freely exercised than the other. Up to date the Court has delivered advisory opinions in fifteen different cases.

This predominance of the consultative over the purely judicial functions of the Court, particularly marked in the first years of its existence, is extremely significant. It is still another symptom of what is, in my view, the main characteristic of the League's evolution since its birth. Here, as on every other point on which we have touched in this study, we see the League developing its voluntary and co-operative activities at the expense of its coercive functions.

As the following table shows, there has, however, been a distinct change in the relative importance of the contentious and advisory functions of the Court.

	Judgments	Advisory Opinions
1922	..	3
1923	1	5
1924	2	1
1925	3	3
1926	1	1
1927	4	1
1928	1	1
1929	4	..
	16	15

Whereas, until 1924 the Court rendered but three decisions and handed down nine advisory opinions, the corresponding figures for the five last years are thirteen judgments and only six opinions. This change, however, is not, I believe, due to any modification in the present structure of international society, but rather to technical reasons. The Court itself, which seems not to relish its consultative function, has tended to assimilate its procedure in considering requests for advisory opinions to that of its judicial activity. Besides, the Council has always shown the greatest reluctance to ask for an advisory opinion, except with the concurrence of the interested parties.

Under these conditions and as a result of the recent negotiations with the United States which have placed another difficulty in the way of the free exercise of the consultative functions of the Court, it would not be surprising if it should tend gradually to be abandoned.

8. *The Seat of the League.*

The last point I wish to mention in this hasty sketch of the structure of the League concerns the choice of its permanent seat. I fully realize that the subject is of greater interest to my fellow citizens of Geneva than to the rest of the world. However, the story of how this Swiss town became what some of its ambitious sons like to call the capital of the world, has to my knowledge never been told before. I may therefore be permitted to outline it here.

Before doing so let me declare at once that I take no excessive national pride in this choice.

Whenever the name of Geneva appears in the press of the world, which is almost daily, we, the inhabitants of the ancient city of Calvin, are apt to be flattered in our local patriotism. And whenever the "spirit of Geneva" is hailed as the most precious conquest of the new international statesmanship, we are tempted to see therein the triumph of our own civic traditions. This is, of course, a complete illusion, of which Locarno and Thoiry have done much to cure us. Locarno is a beautiful watering place without any memorable historic past and Thoiry, a tiny little French village, which can boast only of a very hospitable inn, with an estimable wine cellar and a generous cuisine. When, after the famous conferences at these places the "spirit of Locarno" and the "spirit of Thoiry" came to be spoken of as synonymous with the "spirit of Geneva," we Genevese were perhaps a bit mortified but correspondingly enlightened. I trust we all realize today that the unique privilege which we enjoy in being able to witness at first hand the activities of the great peace factory set up by the world within our walls is enviable enough in itself. It need not be enhanced by the ill-founded belief that we have deserved it by any particular civic excellence. I shall be completely satisfied if in future we prove not unworthy of this trust, whose location in Geneva our past may somewhat explain, but which our present merits can certainly not justify.

Long before the War, in fact ever since the days of Calvin, Geneva has had a place in international affairs quite out of proportion with the size and wealth of this diminutive city republic. First, as the chief citadel of French Protestantism, then as a center of free political and scientific thought, and throughout her history as a meeting place of European celebrities and as a refuge for the victims of foreign intolerance, Geneva has been at the intersection of many lines of action and influence. It is doubtless to this curious fact that Thomas Jefferson was referring, when on December 26, 1820, he wrote to his friend Marc Aug. Pictet of Geneva: ''Altho' your Geneva is but a point, as it were, on the globe, yet it has made itself the most interesting one, perhaps, on that globe.'' And the French poet Lamartine lyrically expressed the same idea when, in 1842, he wrote:

Que Genève à nos pieds ouvre son libre port:
La liberté du faible est la gloire du fort.
Que sous les mille esquifs dont ses eaux sont ridées,
Palmyre européenne au confluent d'idées,
Elle voit en ses murs l'Ibère et le Germain
Echanger la pensée en se donnant la main.[22]

In the course of the nineteenth century, under the cover of the neutrality of Switzerland, into which

[22] "Ressouvenir du Léman," *Premières méditations poétiques.*

Geneva had been admitted as a canton after the Napoleonic era, her importance as an international dot on the map steadily increased. The peace movement, the socialist movement, various other humanitarian movements such as that of the International Red Cross, were either started in Geneva or tended toward or gravitated about her, attracted probably by the splendor and charm of her natural surroundings, by her moral and intellectual traditions of freedom, and by the independence and the very insignificance of her political status.

In view of this long past and also in view of all that went on during the World War in the one neutral country which was completely surrounded by belligerents from 1914 to 1918, it is not surprising that Switzerland and Geneva should often have been mentioned after the Armistice as a possible center for the new international institution.

When Colonel House left Washington to arrange for the coming peace conference, President Wilson had agreed that it should be held in Lausanne. On arriving in Paris, Colonel House came to the conclusion that Geneva would be a better place. Mr. Lloyd George had cordially agreed and Signor Orlando had also accepted. M. Clemenceau had, of course, preferred Versailles and the decision in fact remained with President Wilson. To Colonel House's obvious surprise, he received a cable from Washington on November 8, 1918, in which the President, perhaps frightened by the general strike which was brewing in Switzerland and actually broke out a few days later, stated his preference for Versailles and added that the Swiss atmosphere was "saturated with every poisonous element and open to every hostile influence."[23]

Although I was much troubled when I learned of this from Mr. Lippmann in Paris on January 19, 1919, it turned out to be extremely fortunate for the cause I was called upon to defend.

Had the original plan to meet in Geneva been realized, the League of Nations would doubtless never have been established there. The Peace Conference proved to be the graveyard of so many other hopes that no one, in April, 1919, would have dared to suggest that its seat should become that of the great institution which had so narrowly escaped burial there.

As it was, no one at first proposed Geneva. The Phillimore Committee, in its Interim Report of March 20, 1918, had suggested Versailles, if the League was to be confined to the Allies, and "Holland or Switzerland or possibly Belgium" if some neutral states were to be admitted.[24]

Colonel House, in July, 1918, was thinking of The Hague and of Brussels,[25] and President Wilson's first choice seems also to have been the Dutch capital.[26] On December 10, 1918, in the statement he made to his colleagues of the American Peace Delegation on his way to Paris, he declared, according to Dr. Isaiah Bowman, that some capital as The Hague

[23] Charles Seymour, *The Intimate Papers of Colonel House* (London, 1928), IV, 226 *et seq.*

[24] D. H. Miller, *op. cit.*, I, 6.

[25] *Ibid.*, p. 13; II, 6.

[26] That would seem to be the only plausible interpretation of Art. 1 of his first draft of the Covenant. Cf. *Ibid.*, II, 12.

or Berne would be selected for the League of Nations.[27]

The first mention of Geneva to be found in an official document was that made by Lord Robert Cecil in a memorandum circulated to the British Cabinet on December 17, 1918.[28] It was over a month later, on January 19, 1919, that, lunching with some American friends at the Hotel Crillon at Paris, I first learned that the British were favoring Geneva. The news was, of course, very welcome to the Swiss Government, whom I had the honor of representing in an observing capacity at the Peace Conference, but it was as yet far from being decisive. It was known that France was favoring Paris or Versailles and, as a second choice, Brussels, which Belgium was strongly recommending. Holland was very active in Paris in favor of The Hague and, as aforesaid, had some reason to count on the support of President Wilson.

When the question was first broached at the League of Nations Commission at its third session on February 5, 1919, M. Hymans, the Belgian Minister of Foreign Affairs, immediately put forward the candidacy of Brussels, supporting it on moral grounds and invoking in its favor what he said would be "a symbolic decision." President Wilson, who was chairman of the Commission, noted the proposal "with great sympathy" but decided "to reserve this question until a later time."[29]

Although a drafting committee, on which Lord Robert Cecil seems to have played a leading part,

[27] D. H. Miller, *op. cit.*, I, 42.
[28] *Ibid.*, p. 38; II, 63.
[29] *Ibid.*, I, 163–164; II, 260, 427.

inserted the name of Geneva in the blank space
which had been left for the seat after the first reading of the Covenant, the draft tentatively adopted
and published on February 14, 1919, was still silent
on the question.[30] In the meanwhile, on February 12,
1919, I had had the privilege of a long interview
with President Wilson at the Hotel Murat. In this
conversation he informed me that the British were
opposed to The Hague and that, although he could
not judge of their reasons, he himself had certain
objections to the capital of a monarchy. He viewed
the choice of Geneva with favor, ''perhaps,'' he
added laughingly, ''on account of my Presbyterian-
ism.'' He wondered whether the Swiss Government
could make some tempting offer. The cession of a
small area to be made into an international ''District of Columbia'' might, he thought, facilitate
matters.

Plausible as it may have seemed, the suggestion,
if taken literally, could not have been realized. To
make of the Canton of Geneva a world ''District of
Columbia,'' would have meant to separate it from
Switzerland or at least to place it in a position in
which it would have entertained the same relations
with Switzerland as with all the other states members of the League. This was, of course, quite out
of the question.

It was all the more inconceivable since at this date
and for another year it was not at all certain that
Switzerland would join the League at all. The Swiss
people and the Swiss Government were very much
interested in President Wilson's general plans and
very much attached to the ideal of the League of

[30] *Ibid.*, I, 216; II, 305.

Nations. But they were still more attached to the policy of permanent neutrality, which they had practiced for over a century and which had just brought them safely through the World War. It was doubtful whether the Swiss people, who had to be consulted by means of a referendum, would deem it compatible with their conception of neutrality to join a League of Nations from which two of their neighbors were temporarily excluded. And it was equally doubtful whether the League would welcome a state which so clearly manifested its intention of subordinating its new duties under the Covenant to its old obligations of neutrality. These questions were finally settled on May 16, 1920, when the majority of the Swiss people voted to join the League on the distinct understanding, which had been previously secured from the Council, that this step did not imply the abrogation of the previous status of Switzerland as a permanently neutral state.[31]

As, however, Switzerland could not be expected to organize her referendum on the Covenant before it was finally adopted and as the framers of the Covenant could not be expected to await Switzerland's referendum before deciding on the location of the seat of the League of Nations, negotiations were by no means simple. They were carried on informally with Colonel House and his associates and led, on March 22, 1919, to the dispatch of an official letter to President Wilson, as President of the League of Nations Commission, and to M. Clemen-

[31] Those interested in this complicated affair will find it more fully explained in D. H. Miller, *op. cit.*, chap. xxxi, pp. 428 *et seq.*, and in my study on *L'Entrée de la Suisse dans la Société des Nations* (Geneva, 1924).

ceau, as President of the Peace Conference, by M. Calonder, the Swiss Foreign Minister. In this letter it was stated that:

Switzerland would deem it a great honor to be able to offer the hospitality of her territory in case the League of Nations should wish to fix its seat in our country. The Swiss government and people would be happy and proud to show in this way their lively wish to join in the work of world peace undertaken by the originators of the Covenant. The political and humanitarian traditions of the Helvetic Confederation, its democratic institutions and its geographical position seem to recommend it to the choice of the Conference over which you preside. Now and at once I can assure you that the federal, cantonal and municipal authorities will hasten to offer to the League all facilities and all the advantages which it may wish for.[32]

When President Wilson returned to Paris from Washington, Colonel House, in the presence of Lord Robert Cecil, informed him of the steps he had taken during his absence in the matter of the League. Having first considered Lausanne as the best possible location, he had finally come to prefer Geneva. Mr. David Hunter Miller, who has revealed this, as well as much other hitherto unpublished information in his invaluable writings, says about this conversation:

There was also some discussion of Swiss neutrality; Wilson said that neutrality was a part of the Swiss constitution and that the whole Canton in which the seat of the

[32] Cf. Message from the Federal Council of Switzerland to the Federal Assembly of Switzerland concerning the question of the accession of Switzerland to the League of Nations together with the annexes thereto. Official English translation published by the Swiss government in 1919, p. 298.

League was situated would be given to the League for that purpose, and that neutrality of the whole State of Switzerland would be recognized by the League. It was agreed tentatively to put Geneva or Lausanne in the blank in Article 5, so that it might come up for discussion. Cecil said that nearly everybody, for one reason or another, was opposed to having the seat of the League in Belgium.[33]

The discussion took place at the eleventh meeting of the Crillon Commission on March 22, 1919, when President Wilson read the above-mentioned letter from M. Calonder, M. Hymans thereupon eloquently pleaded in favor of Belgium and Brussels. He based his claims on the compensation due to his country for its sufferings, on the importance of its capital as a "great center of intellectual and legal life," and on its convenient geographical position.

M. Hymans was supported by the two French delegates, one of whom, M. Larnaude questioned the possibility of admitting a perpetually neutral state into the League of Nations.[34]

The matter was referred to a subcommittee composed of Messrs. House, Smuts, Orlando, and Makino, all of whom appeared to be favorable to Geneva. This subcommittee, summoned by Colonel House, met on March 29, 1919. They decided to ask for a certain number of assurances from Switzerland for the event of the choice of Geneva.[35] Having received these assurances, Signor Orlando reported on its behalf to the full Commission at its fourteenth session on April 10, 1919, strongly recommending Geneva.

[33] D. H. Miller, *op. cit.*, I, 285.
[34] *Ibid.*, p. 316; II, 339, 505.
[35] C. Seymour, *op. cit.*, IV, 430; D. H. Miller, *op. cit.*, I, 441.

It was on this occasion that the only full debate on the seat of the League took place. M. Hymans, again supported by the two French delegates, spoke at length in favor of Brussels. Other members, such as Messrs. Kramar of Czechoslovakia, Vesnitch of Serbia, and Venizelos of Greece, also spoke, although inconclusively as it would appear from the minutes. Lord Robert Cecil, first, and then President Wilson warmly urged the choice of Geneva. According to the English account of the meeting, Lord Robert Cecil is reported as having said that:

If it were a question of conferring honours or rewards on a city, no one would hesitate between Geneva and Brussels. It would be an impertinence to do so. He implored members to set aside every other consideration, but that of giving this experiment the best chance of success.

He was in favour of Geneva, first because he thought that the seat of the League should not be situated in the capital city of any country. There could be no doubt that the country selected would have a considerable advantage, and it was important that the world should be inspired with a belief in the absolute impartiality of the League. Second, because impartiality and not the preservation of the glorious memories of the war was the object of the League.

Switzerland on the other hand, had not only been a neutral country for a long time, it was also the most cosmopolitan country in the world. Switzerland, and Geneva especially, had international traditions. Switzerland, moreover, was more central than Brussels.

As for President Wilson he added that:

he yielded to none in his admiration for Belgium, but the present question was one not of awarding honours but of finding the best surroundings for international deliberation. The antipathies of the war should be set aside; otherwise it might be thought that the League was a mere coalition of Allies moved by the hatreds born of the war. Our object was to bring about friendly relations between all peoples. We wished to rid the world of the sufferings of war. We should not obtain this result if we chose a town where the memory of this war would prevent impartial discussion. The peace of the world could not be secured by perpetuating international hatreds. Geneva was already the seat of the International Red Cross, which had placed itself at the service of both groups of belligerents, and which, so far as possible, had remained unaffected by the antipathies provoked by the war. Moreover, Switzerland was a people vowed to absolute neutrality by its constitution and its blend of races and languages. It was marked out to be the meeting-place of other peoples desiring to undertake a work of peace and co-operation. The choice of Geneva did not mean that we did not recognize the eminent merits of Belgium and of Brussels. There could be no comparison between the two peoples from the point of view of their conduct during the war. The capitals of other neutral nations might have been proposed, but none had behaved so impartially as Switzerland. Switzerland had always acted with dignity; she had suffered from the war and she had gained the respect of both groups of belligerents.

Twelve out of ninteen members having voted in favor of Geneva and no negative vote having been taken, Geneva was inserted in the blank of what has become Article 7.[36]

As there was no further discussion on this point at the Plenary Conference, it was thus finally settled as far as the drafting of the Covenant was concerned. As a matter of practical politics, however,

[36] D. H. Miller, *op. cit.*, I, 442; II, 365 *et seq.*

the question was reopened in the course of the following year.

After the close of the Peace Conference and before the legal birth of the League on January 10, 1920, the Secretariat had taken up its provisional quarters at London. When the League came into being, the leading members of the Secretariat showed no impatience whatever to leave the British capital and still less to migrate to Geneva. Their official reasons, aside from those relating to their personal tastes, were twofold. On the one hand they feared that the League, already crippled by the abstention of the United States, might be completely paralyzed and forgotten, if its permanent officials withdrew from the principal political center of Europe to a small town which was not even the capital of a small country. And on the other hand the influence of France which, as we have seen, had always been exerted against Geneva and which had been more than neutralized by the combined efforts of Great Britain and of the United States at the Peace Conference, undoubtedly wished to reassert itself. Having become much more potent, after the withdrawal of the American delegation from Europe, it hoped to avenge its defeat on this minor point. In the Secretariat of the League this influence during the first years after 1920 may be said to have been preponderant, thanks to the extremely clever and forceful personality of M. Jean Monnet, the first Deputy Secretary-General, who spared none of his diplomatic talent to prevent what he looked upon as the error of moving to Geneva.

Under these conditions it is not surprising that the Council of the League, at its fifth session in

Rome on May 19, 1920, while calling upon President Wilson to summon the first meeting of the Assembly in accordance with the provisions of Article 5 of the Covenant, suggested that it should meet in Brussels. They did so in the following embarrassed language, which seems to indicate that some previous correspondence had already passed between them on the subject:

The Council are of the opinion that, having regard to all the circumstances, the Assembly should be held in some European city. They are anxious to come to an agreement with you as to the question of the selection of this town, but meanwhile they have expressed the unanimous hope that you will consider whether, without prejudicing the place for future meetings, Brussels should not be chosen in the first instance.[37]

As according to Section 2, Article 3 of the Covenant, "The Assembly shall meet . . . at the seat of the League or at such other place as may be decided upon," the wish not to meet in Geneva clearly betrayed the wish not to establish the League's permanent quarters there.

When the Council's action became known in Berne, it aroused a feeling of aggrieved surprise, to put it mildly. The disappointment was all the keener since three days before, on May 16, the majority of the Swiss people, under unprecedented pressure by the Government had decided to join the League. President Wilson was not left uninformed of this state of affairs, so the joy was greater than the astonishment in Switzerland when it became known that, on July 17, 1920, President Wilson had sent the

[37] League of Nations, *Official Journal,* No. 4 (June, 1920), p. 127.

following cable to the Secretary-General of the League of Nations:

At the request of the Council of the League of Nations that I summon a meeting of the Assembly of the League of Nations, I have the honor, in accordance with the provisions of Article 5 of the Covenant of the League of Nations to summon the Assembly of the League to convene in the city of Geneva, the seat of the League, on the 15th of November, 1920, at eleven o'clock.

Woodrow Wilson.[38]

Thus President Wilson, who was already more responsible than anyone else, except Lord Robert Cecil and Colonel House, for the choice of Geneva in the spring of 1919, was again immediately and alone responsible for the defeat of the plan to escape Geneva, which was not yet abandoned in certain quarters over a year later.

After this, the Secretary-General still proposed to return to London after the Assembly, but as there was no trouble in finding convenient temporary lodgings for the Secretariat in Geneva, it moved there at the beginning of November, 1920, and thus rejoined the International Labor Office, which had already settled there several months sooner.

There is no doubt that President Motta of Switzerland was expressing the sincere feelings of the whole Swiss people when, welcoming the first Assembly at its first meeting on November 15, 1920, at the Salle de la Reformation in Geneva, he said:

I would ask you to allow me to send an especially hearty expression of gratitude to President Wilson for having,

[38] *Ibid.*, No. 6 (September, 1920), p. 351.

by a friendly and spontaneous act, convoked the first meeting of the Assembly of Nations at the seat of the League as laid down by the Covenant.

The competition between Brussels and Geneva, which thus most peacefully ended, was in no way a struggle between two cities or between two countries. It was in reality a conflict between two conceptions of the League of Nations. Those who believed that the League should as soon as possible forget the bitter memories of the war and seek to reëstablish peace in a spirit of impartiality and universality, naturally favored the neutral Swiss town. And those who looked upon the League primarily as a weapon in the hands of the victors for the punitive control of the defeated aggressors, were not unnaturally in favor of the capital of the country which had witnessed the latter's greatest crime.

As in 1926 Germany was sincerely and unanimously welcomed to the League even by those who had most violently resented the very thought of her entry six years earlier, so today even those who had most ardently opposed the establishment of the League in Geneva in 1920, are quite generally reconciled with the results of President Wilson's choice.

The people of Switzerland, of course, were, are, and will ever remain deeply grateful to their great American champion. They look upon him as their champion, not only, nor primarily, because he was led indirectly to defend their national interest, but mainly because they share his conception of the League of Nations as a serene and impartial tribunal for the pacification of the world on the basis of justice.

CHAPTER V

COÖPERATION INSIDE THE FRAMEWORK OF
THE LEAGUE OF NATIONS—*Concluded*

II

The Changing Activities of the League.

IN our last chapter we have seen what the League of
Nations was intended to be and how it became what
it is today. We have now to consider what it was intended to do and how it has by its deeds tended to
fulfil the intentions of its founders.

The two topics are very closely related to one
another. The structure of the League was not the
casual product of a historical accident. Both in its
original design and in its subsequent evolution it
was determined by the functions which the League
was destined and has been called upon to perform.
Thus it was set up as a world organism because its
tasks were world tasks. Thus it has become more
European in its memberships because its principal
activities have centered around the Old World. Thus
the Council became larger, the Assembly more parliamentary and its sessions longer, periodic, and
more frequent, the Secretariat more national and
the Advisory Commissions more numerous, because
the activity of the League proved to be less executive
and more consultative, less political and more technical in character than had first been anticipated.

In my former Williamstown lectures, I spoke of
the League of Nations as of three leagues in one,
each distinguished by its special order of func-

tions.[1] I recognized a league to enforce the peace treaties, composed of the states represented on the Council, a league to promote international coöperation, whose membership extended beyond the signatories of the Covenant, and a league to outlaw war, restricted to the latter. This mode of presentation, adopted for reasons of clarity and in order to call attention to the variety of heterogeneous members and activities of the League, did, I believe, serve its purpose. But while it was intended to stress, by deliberate and admitted overemphasis, the pluralistic character of the nascent Geneva institution, it would hardly, were it retained today, do justice to the evolution which has taken place since 1925.

The extension of the Council, the election into it of more ex-neutral states and especially the admission of Germany, the interest shown by the Assembly in the problem of minorities, as well as the changed spirit of what I had termed the League to enforce the peace treaties have all tended to deprive it of its peculiar characteristics. And likewise, although what I called the league to promote coöperation has not ceased to extend its activities as well as its membership far beyond the scope of the Covenant, the participation of leading nonsignatory powers in important parts of the work of my former league to outlaw war has tended to erase what was a clear distinction in 1925.

Today therefore I shall no longer speak of three leagues in one, but rather of the three main functions of the one League of Nations. These functions, however, are essentially the same as those distinguished both in my previous book and in our present

[1] Cf. Rappard, *op. cit.*, pp. 9 *et seq.*

discussion of international coöperation outside the framework of the League. Today, as formerly, and within as without the League of Nations, international coöperation in Europe tends toward three distinct goals: the execution of the peace settlement, the promotion of prosperity and welfare, and the achievement of peace and security. Let us in this concluding chapter consider in turn the efforts of the League in pursuit of these three objects.

1. *The Execution of the Peace Treaties.*

As we have seen above, the principal authority for the execution of the European peace treaties was the Supreme Council and its subsidiary interallied bodies. Why and how should the League of Nations have been called upon to coöperate in this task? To be sure it had been set up by the victors of the World War, and its Constitution is part of all the principal treaties of peace except that concluded with Turkey at Lausanne in 1923. But had not thirteen ex-neutral states joined as original members at its very birth and four ex-enemy states been admitted since? Why and how should the decisions of the victors imposed on the defeated be carried out in peaceful coöperation by victors, defeated, and neutrals alike? This question may well be asked, especially in view of the peculiarly dictatorial character of the treaties of 1919, which were more truly imposed and less really negotiated than most previous multilateral treaties of peace in history.

To this question there is no one answer, both simple and true.

The cynics, when they attempt to reply to it, are prompt to display a great wealth of literary imagination. They like to compare the League of Nations in this rôle either to a transparent screen, behind which the victors vainly seek to hide their annexations, or, more bluntly, to the classical fig leaf, or, more dramatically, to an obscure cavern in which the successful robbers take refuge when they disagree among themselves over the division of their booty, or, more subtly, to a police force in which the crafty masters of the post-war world have conscripted the naïve neutrals to watch over their spoils.

This view, which was commonly held in the defeated countries and notably in Germany in the first years after the War, is today less frequently and less boldly put forward.

On the opposite pole of political philosophy we find the Wilsonian conception. If more profound and less susceptible of metaphorical formulation, it is none the less clearly expressed in the following extracts drawn from the great speech President Wilson delivered at the Plenary Session of the Peace Conference on January 25, 1919, when it was decided to appoint the League of Nations Commission:

We have assembled for two purposes—to make the present settlements which have been rendered necessary by the war, and also to secure the peace of the world, not only by the present settlement but by the arrangements we shall make in the Conference for its maintenance. The League of Nations seems to me to be necessary for both of these purposes. There are complicated questions connected with the present settlements which perhaps cannot be successfully worked out to an ultimate issue by the decisions we shall arrive at here. I can easily conceive that many of these settlements will need subsequent reconsideration;

that many of the decisions we shall make will need subsequent alterations in some degree, for if I may judge by my own study of some of these questions they are not susceptible of confident judgment at present. It is, therefore, necessary that we should set up some machinery by which the work of the Conference should be rendered complete. We have assembled here for the purpose of doing very much more than making the present settlement. . . . It is a solemn obligation on our part . . . to make permanent arrangements that justice shall be rendered and peace maintained. This is the central object of our meeting. Settlements may be temporary, but the actions of the nations in the interests of peace and justice must be permanent. We can set up permanent processes. We may not be able to set up permanent decisions . . . The United States would feel that her part in this war had been played in vain if there ensued upon it merely a body of European settlements. She would feel that she could not take part in guaranteeing those European settlements unless that guarantee involved the continuous superintendence of the peace of the world by the associated nations of the world.[2]

If we analyze this passage closely, in order to discover the exact relation which the League of Nations was to bear to the peace settlement in President Wilson's mind, I think we may note two distinct ideas. In the first place, the problems of the immediate peace settlement are so numerous and so difficult that the decisions reached may be incomplete and imperfect. We therefore need a League of Nations as a permanent international organization to continue our present labors and, if necessary, to correct our present errors. We need it also—and this is the second idea—because we cannot have permanent peace without an international guaranty of

[2] D. H. Miller, *op. cit.*, II, pp. 155 *et seq.*

the present European settlement. And we cannot hope to enlist the coöperation of the United States in guaranteeing this settlement, which may be or become unjust, without a permanent organization for the continuous superintendence of peace.

For President Wilson, then, the League of Nations was to supplement, to correct, to guarantee, in a word, to serve the peace settlement. For General Smuts, who with Wilson did most to tie up the League and the peace, it was the immediate settlement which was to serve the League of Nations. In his famous pamphlet of December, 1918, he wrote:

If the League of Nations is ever to be a success, it will have to occupy a much greater position and perform many other functions besides those ordinarily assigned to it. The League will have to occupy the great position which has been rendered vacant by the destruction of so many of the old European empires and the passing away of the old European order. And the League should be put in the very forefront of the programme of the peace conference, and be made the point of departure for the solution of many of the grave problems with which it will be confronted.[3]

In order further to give the League of Nations the necessary vitality and potency for the accomplishment of its general peace mission, General Smuts deliberately proposed to intrust it with political and other tasks which would oblige the world to reckon with it.

Between the cynical, German, and the idealist, Wilsonian, view, General Smuts, with his constructive realism, occupies an intermediate position.

If we now examine briefly how and why the

[3] Reprinted in D. H. Miller, *op. cit.*, II, 23.

League of Nations has actually participated in the
execution of the peace settlement, we shall find that,
as usual in the case of conflicting prophecies and
generalizations concerning political events, all three
of these views have been partly confirmed and partly
contradicted by the course of subsequent events.

Let us observe, first of all, that the League has
received its mission for the liquidation of the War
from three different sources.

The Covenant itself, although inserted as Chapter
I in all the four main treaties of 1919 and although
obviously inspired in many of its essential provisions by the experience of the World War, is singularly reticent about the tasks of the League in this
connection. According to its Preamble, its objects
are confined to the promotion of international co-
operation and the achievement of peace and security. And, with only two exceptions, none of its
twenty-six Articles contains any express reference
to the execution of any part of the peace settlement.
These two exceptions are Article 22, in which the
principles of the Mandate system are defined, and
section (e) of Article 23 in which an incidental
allusion is made to the "special necessities of the
regions devasted during the war of 1914–1918,"
which are to be "borne in mind" in the establishment of freedom of communications and transit and
of equitable commercial relations.

The second source from which the League of Nations derives rights and duties in connection with
the execution of the peace settlement is that constituted by the peace treaties themselves and by their
subsidiary conventions. The number of matters referred to the League of Nations or to its Council in

these various instruments, beginning with the Treaty
of Versailles of June 28, 1919, and ending with that
of Lausanne of July 24, 1923, is so great that they
cannot even be enumerated here. Sometimes the
League is merely asked to make an appointment,
as in the case of chairmen of mixed arbitral tribunals, of members of the commission intrusted with
the execution of the Greco-Bulgarian reciprocal exchange, or of the High Commissioner of Danzig.
Sometimes it is called upon to organize a plebiscite,
as in the Saar Basin in 1935, or to decide on the
sovereignty of a given area, as for Eupen and Malmedy. Sometimes the Council is referred to as the
authority which may revise certain clauses of the
treaties, as those dealing with international means
of communication in the Treaty of Versailles, which
may conduct enquiries into the state of disarmament
of the defeated nations, or which may decide on the
alienation of their independence, as in the famous
question of the Austro-German *Anschluss*. Sometimes the League is called upon to guarantee a constitution, as in Danzig, or the stipulations of certain
treaties, as those concerning the protection of minorities. Sometimes certain activities, as those of
the Commission of the Straits or of the Mixed Commission for the exchange of populations, provided
for under the Treaty of Lausanne, are placed ''under
the auspices'' of the League, whatever that may
mean. Sometimes the Council is called upon to settle,
in case of disagreement between the parties, the
terms of bilateral conventions, as those relating to
questions of communication between Germany or
Poland or those relating to the frontiers of Iraq between Great Britain and Turkey. Sometimes the

League is intrusted with the protection of a given
area, as in the case of the Free City of Danzig, or
even with its trusteeship, as in that of the Saar
Basin.

The League has thirdly and finally been invited
to coöperate in the execution of the peace treaties
by constant appeals from the Supreme Council and
the Conference of Ambassadors. In the first years
after the War it seems to have become a regular
habit with the principal Allied Powers to call upon
the League to overcome the difficulties encountered
in the application of the treaties they had framed.
This was especially the case when such difficulties
appeared insurmountable. Thus in 1920, when nobody was prepared to sacrifice the necessary blood
and treasure to protect Armenia against the Russians and the Turks, they suggested that that unfortunate country should be placed under the protection
or even under the mandate of the League. In the
same year, when Turkey proved unwilling to ratify
the ill-starred Treaty of Sèvres, the Supreme Council requested the League to guarantee the minority
clauses contained in that instrument and to coöperate in their execution. In the following year, when
France and Great Britain had reached a deadlock
over the settlement of the Upper Silesian question,
the Supreme Council reverted to the League, hoping,
and curiously enough, as subsequent events proved,
hoping rightly, that the fog of Franco-British disagreement would not resist the dissolving influence
of the Geneva sun. In 1922 when Austria, territorially mutilated, economically exhausted, and legally
deprived of the right of linking up her destiny with
Germany, all by the will of the principal Allied

Powers—when this starving and prostrate Austria
appealed in despair to the Supreme Council, she also
was referred to Geneva. And again this problem,
which seemed still more insoluble than that of
reconciling the French and the British views about
Upper Silesia, was solved to general satisfaction in
the course of a few weeks' negotiation in the Secretariat of the League. In 1923 a Polish-Czechoslovakian frontier difficulty and the vexed Memel question
were likewise referred to Geneva by the Supreme
Council and settled there after Paris, London, Warsaw, and Prague had vainly struggled to reach a
settlement.

Many other political problems arising out of European frontiers, such as those of the Aaland Islands, Poland, Lithuania, Albania, Eastern Carelia,
and Persia, were discussed by the League. As they
were, however, brought before the tribunal of the
Council not by the Supreme Council, but by states
members of the League, acting under the provisions
of the Covenant, they are not to be considered here.
It was not to execute the peace treaties but, in the
language of the relevant Article 11 of the Covenant,
to take "any action that may be deemed wise and
effectual to safeguard the peace of nations" that the
League intervened. The ultimate causes as well as
the ultimate results of its intervention may have
been the same as in the above-mentioned class of
cases. But the starting point of its action was somewhat different.

If we now cast a glance over the whole course of
events of the last decade, we cannot fail to discern
the great change which has gradually come over the
spirit and the results of the League's deliberations

and decisions relating to the execution of the peace treaties. Viewed in the light of the three political philosophies we have outlined above, this evolution is particularly interesting.

During the first years after 1919 the cynics had every reason to be confirmed in their pessimism. The allocation of the mandated territories by the Supreme Council, in strict accordance with the provisions of the secret treaties concluded between the victors during the War on the basis of military conquest, was ratified without a question by the Council of the League. After the ludicrous caricature of a plebiscite in the former German districts of Eupen and Malmedy, these territories were without any hesitation solemnly turned over to Belgium by the League. The Governing Commission of the Saar Basin was by the Council of the League placed under the chairmanship of a French prefect and composed of members four out of five of whom were known to be devoted to French interests and seem to have owed their choice to that reason. The radical, linguistic, and religious minorities, whose protection was formally guaranteed by the League, were abandoned to the tender mercies of their new masters. When they looked and appealed to Geneva for redress against the discriminatory and oppressive treatment which they claimed was their common lot, Geneva remained ominously silent.

In view of these and many similar facts, one is forced to admit that there was not a little justification for the "screen," the "fig leaf," and the other flattering metaphors jeeringly used by the cynics to describe the part played by the League in disguising the annexationist policies of its victorious masters.

But even in this first, admittedly nauseous stage of the League's evolution—which was not rendered less unpalatable, either to its foes or to its sincerest friends by the constant use of distorted Wilsonian phraseology in which its spokesmen often indulged —the wisdom and soundness of General Smuts' views soon became apparent. The League, as the faithful protector of the weak and as the just pacificator of a distracted and embittered Europe, was still mute. But all the leading foreign offices of Europe were actively engaged in negotiations with it about the execution of the peace treaties. As a result the League, which might have succumbed under the weight of official ridicule and might soon have fallen into oblivion had it had only its ideal program to advertise and to support it, came to be known and reckoned with as a positive factor of political life, even by those who were least able and disposed to appreciate its reforming possibilities.

Little by little, however, the clouds began to break. The Mandates Commission, set up in 1921, promptly showed a measure of independence and of real impartiality which surprised its critics perhaps no less than it alarmed some of its originators. The supervision and control of the administration of the former German colonies by public opinion focused upon it by the discussions in the Commission and in the Assembly, were soon recognized as being a reality. Presently, the mandatory powers were seen to coöperate with the Commission by accrediting with it some of their most important administrators. When later on a German member was appointed to it and began to take an active part in its debates, it was no longer possible even for the most cynically minded, to dispose of the institution as a mere "screen" or "fig leaf."

The same change came over the composition and the activities of the Saar Governing Commission. A German inhabitant of the territory itself, truly representative of his fellow countrymen, was selected in place of the dubious personage who had owed his appointment to his questionable relations with the Quai d'Orsay more than to the confidence of his local neighbors. The French troops, which, for the first years, had been garrisoned in the Saar, were step by step withdrawn, and a local police force was recruited and substituted for them. Under the pressure of public opinion, aroused by independent critics and notably by M. Branting of Sweden, at the Council table at Geneva, dictatorial measures taken by the Governing Commission were revoked and finally the French chairman was replaced by an Englishman.

As for the protection of minorities, the League also began to assert itself. After a long silence, hardly interrupted by the very discreet measures taken by the Secretariat, the 1928 Assembly called attention to the necessity of reforming the adopted procedure dealing with petitions. The wishes of the Assembly were reëchoed not only by a large portion of the world press, but also at the Council itself by Messrs. Stresemann of Germany, Dandurand of Canada, and Procopé of Finland.

The same general trend toward greater fairness would be revealed by a close study of the League's action in several other minor matters connected with the execution of the peace treaties. Little by little and even as yet often timidly, it is nevertheless beginning to vindicate President Wilson's hopes that the League may, while executing the treaties, tend to improve them and by exercising "the continuous superintendence of the peace of the world" he had spoken of, tend to consolidate it.

The reasons for this evolution are not difficult to discover. They may, I believe, be summarized under four general headings.

In the first place, the healing effects of time are making themselves felt. The memories of the War, its resentments, and its disappointments are gradually fading away, and with them the vindictive dispositions which they engendered and sustained in the victors.

Secondly, the solid interallied front, which the War had created, was soon broken after the peace and new political alignments came to be made. Now the League could carry out the provisions of the treaties in the sole interest of the victors and irrespective of all considerations of fairness only so long as these victors were unanimous. As soon as they began to criticize and to control each other the chances of justice were immediately increased.

Thirdly, the modified composition of the League and of its organs also tended to prevent unfair dealing and to promote equity. Not that the ex-neutrals and especially the ex-defeated are in my estimation inherently more amorous of justice than the victorious ex-allies. But the love of justice, which is an altruistic virtue in the strong, who can afford to do without justice, is imposed on the weak as a selfish necessity by their very weakness. And, sad as it is, it is certain that selfishness is a more potent motor, in the political world as elsewhere, than altruism. Therefore it is not surprising that the League is showing more fairness in the execution of the peace treaties since the weak, that is the victims of the treaties, and the disinterested neutrals are more closely associated with its activities in this respect.

Fourthly and finally, the very mechanism of the League, thanks to the complexity of its collective structure and to the publicity of its debates, naturally makes for moderation and for fairness. For saints as for sinners, solitude and darkness are dangerous companions. A sinner knows no restraint when he is alone in the midst of night, and even a saint may be tempted under those conditions. A saint is likely to be more saintly and a sinner more careful, even in the dark, when they are in the society of their fellows. But on the market place, in the broad light of day, the outward behavior of the most sinful of sinners is apt to resemble that of the saintliest of saints. Nations, as a rule, are neither saints nor sinners. They are very much like the average citizens who compose them. And like the average citizens, they behave much better when they meet together in public, as they do in Geneva, than when they plot together in secret or brood alone. That is why the League of Nations, without being in any sense the miracle-machine which some of its enthusiastic friends are inclined to see in it, does possess, by the very fact of its existence and continued public functioning, the ability to improve international morality.

The last war was a world war, but still essentially

a European war. The peace settlement was a world settlement, but still essentially a European settlement. Therefore the League of Nations, in the execution of the peace treaties has, with the sole exception of the Mandates and a few Turkish matters, dealt exclusively with European affairs. In its second function, the promotion of prosperity and welfare, which we are now to consider, it has more frequently been led to overstep continental boundaries.

2. *The Promotion of Prosperity and Welfare.*

Before enumerating the countless tasks which the League has successfully or still gropingly performed in this field, let us pause for a moment to enquire into the relations between international coöperation on the one hand and the pursuit of national prosperity on the other. That the pursuit of national prosperity is primarily a national matter is obvious. But that, under modern world conditions, the greatest possible national prosperity cannot be achieved by national means alone is hardly less obvious. Even if we were to consider only these United States, we should soon be convinced of it. To be sure, they are almost a world unto themselves and of all advanced nations the most self-sufficient. And still the proportion of the American people who are in no way and in no measure directly or indirectly affected in their prosperity by the welfare of the rest of the globe is infinitely small. How many Americans are there who in the course of the year, nay in the course of a single day, consume no foreign products? How many are there who in their professional, productive life are entirely independent of foreign sources of supply, of foreign markets, of foreign competi-

tion, of foreign fashions, and of foreign examples?
To put the question is to reply to it: hardly one.

If this is so of the United States of America, how
much more true must it not be of Europe—Europe,
which on an approximately equal area possesses appreciably less natural resources, a population over
four times greater, and a score and a half of so-
called independent states, instead of one only?

Now, as soon as the material life of one nation is
in any degree dependent upon that of another, it
cannot hope to achieve its maximum of prosperity
by national means alone. It must either engage in
international coöperation or suffer. The human sufferings of the World War were due in a far smaller
measure to the unspeakable cruelties and frightful
destructions on the battle front than to the priva-
tions caused by the interruption of normal international relations. In the midst of the struggle we, in
Switzerland, witnessed a certain amount of Franco-
German trade, carried on with the full consent of
the two governments concerned. This was due to the
simple fact that, even while the two peoples were
straining every nerve to exterminate each other,
they could not live without each other. They needed
each other's coöperation, were it only in order to be
able to exterminate each other. Could anything more
drastically and more tragically illustrate the fundamental solidarity of the nations of Europe, a solidarity which progress in population, wealth, and
civilization renders ever more intimate and more
compelling?

As long as population was sparse, wealth incon-
siderable, and civilization rudimentary, bilateral,
occasional agreements were sufficient between gov-

ernments to allow progress to continue. But ever since the nineteenth century and especially toward its close and at the beginning of the twentieth, such agreements proved lamentably insufficient. Hence all the pre-war international conferences, organizations, and conventions. Hence also, at the close of the War, the League of Nations.

The League of Nations was in reality the child of this growing need for closer international and principally European coöperation. The World War, which is often looked upon as its parent, might, more fitly if not too boldly, be described as the midwife who brutally wrenched it into life.

The League became all the more indispensable for Europe since the War, as a movement of extreme nationalism set in which rendered spontaneous international coöperation more difficult. Divided into separate units for purposes of political self-assertion, humanity is, economically and socially, one great organism. As its component parts become more conscious of their interdependence, this organism tends to express its unity by means of other than political institutions.

In the present state of civilization, there is in this respect a fundamental contradiction. Politically, nations seem to be striving apart and never have they been more insistent on their sovereign rights as independent entities. Economically and socially, however, they are being drawn closer and closer together by forces which are ever growing more irresistible and of which they are growing ever more conscious. Through its technical organizations and activities, the League is seeking to reconcile these otherwise irreconcilable tendencies. It is striving to overcome the obstacles which the dogma of national sovereignty has placed along the road of human evolution. It is thus promoting voluntary coöperation between those whom frontiers divide, but whom common aims and needs unite.

The higher the political barriers, the more imperious the necessity of international coöperation. But the closer and more continuous international coöperation becomes, the more irksome and the less indispensable the high political barriers will doubtless in time grow to be. Thus checked in its frontal attack on the citadel of war by the as yet invincible forces of national sovereignty, the League is by means of its technical bodies executing a vast flanking movement around and against it. This movement is slow and its achievements are undramatic, but its eventual success seems assured, unless mankind would deliberately prefer poverty and stagnation in a state of potential war, to well-being, fraternity, and progress in international security.

International coöperation, organized by and under the League in the course of the last decade, has not at all always been consciously undertaken to combat war, but much more often to overcome an immediate difficulty encountered during peace. Whenever it has succeeded, however, it may be said to have reduced the danger of international conflict.

This possibility had not been provided for in the early drafts of the Covenant. The Phillimore Commission, as well as Colonel House and President Wilson before 1919, seem to have held that the functions of the League should be confined to those of an international judge and policeman, appointed to prevent disputes from being settled by warlike means.

It was again due to General Smuts that a broader view of its rôle was finally taken. In his famous pamphlet, which can never be too often consulted by those who would understand the origin and development of the League, he expressly declared:

An attempt will be made in this sketch to give an essential extension to the functions of the League; indeed to look upon the League from a very different point of view, to view it not only as a possible means for preventing future wars, but much more as a great organ of the ordinary peaceful life of civilization, as the foundation of the new international system which will be erected on the ruins of this war, and as the starting point from which the peace arrangements of the forthcoming conference should be made. Such an orientation of the idea seems to me necessary if the league is to become a permanent part of our international machinery. It is not sufficient for the league merely to be a sort of *deus ex machina,* called in in very grave emergencies when the spectre of war appears; if it is to last, it must be much more. It must become part and parcel of the common international life of states, it must be an ever visible, living, working organ of the polity of civilization. It must function so strongly in the ordinary peaceful intercourse of states that it becomes irresistible in their disputes; its peace activity must be the foundation and guarantee of its war power.[4]

This conception of the League as an agency of peaceful coöperation, which was generally supported by Lord Robert Cecil from the start, came step by step to be shared also by the other members of the Crillon Commission. Its gradual emergence into favor and prominence is clearly shown by the evolution of the Preamble of the Covenant. According to

[4] D. H. Miller, *op. cit.,* II, 24–25.

the Phillimore plan of March, 1918, this Preamble
was to define the purpose of the League as being,
"if possible," to "prevent all wars in the future."
In his draft of July, 1918, Colonel House had defined
it as "the maintenance . . . of peace, security, progress and orderly government." Of this enumeration
President Wilson had omitted "progress" in his
first draft and "orderly government" in the second.
The latter modification seems to have been suggested
by General Bliss, who feared that it might evoke unpleasant recollections of the Holy Alliance.

In President Wilson's third draft of January
twentieth there remained therefore in the first
phrase of the Preamble, only the words "in order
to secure international peace and security." But a
second phrase was added, indicating that the purpose of the signatory powers was also "to promote
international coöperation." Finally, at the second
meeting of the Crillon Commission on February 4,
1919, it was decided, on the proposal of Lord Robert
Cecil, to transfer the latter words to the beginning
of the Preamble, which now reads: "in order to promote international coöperation and to achieve international peace and security."[5]

The evolution thus started before the birth of the
Covenant has continued ever since in the life of the
League, whose coöperative activities have today
completely eclipsed its coercive functions. The activities for the promotion of prosperity and welfare
have been pursued in so many different fields and
according to so many different methods that it is
not easy to devise a system of classification that will

[5] Cf. *Ibid.*, pp. 3, 7, 12, 65, 94, 98, 256.

show them in their true perspective and real significance.

Classified according to their ultimate purpose we may distinguish:

1. Activities for the removal of international friction.

2. Activities for the achievement of a common purpose external to the coöperating states.

3. Activities for the improvement of national conditions by international action.

An example of the first type of coöperation is that by which the states signatory to an especial convention concluded at Geneva in 1923 agree to simplify their customs formalities. Here is an obstacle on the road to prosperity which can be removed only by international action, if the states concerned refuse to grant the benefits of a simplified procedure only on condition of guaranteed reciprocity. The reconstruction of Austria by the combined efforts of her neighbors and of the great European Powers, undertaken in 1922, is an example of the second type of coöperation. As for the third type, it is represented, for instance, by international labor conventions or common action to regulate the opium traffic. The original idea on which these labor conventions are based is that social progress, impeded by considerations of international economic competition, can be realized in one state only if it be realized simultaneously in all competing states. Besides, international action is being ever more frequently resorted to as a means of improving national conditions in fields quite unaffected by competition, such as those of child welfare, for example. The lever in those cases is mutual information and mutual emulation and not, as in labor conventions, the desire to equalize the social conditions of economic competition or, as in the opium agreements, to protect national welfare by international police measures.

The various types of international coöperation may be classified also according to the means employed for the attainment of these various aims. Thus we may distinguish: first, the drafting and conclusion of conventions and agreements by which the signatory states bind themselves to adopt certain common standards and to follow certain definite practices; secondly, the discussion and adoption of resolutions by which certain policies are recommended by selected international experts; and thirdly, the establishment of some temporary or permanent machinery for international study, investigation, and action.

In the limited space at our disposal, we cannot attempt to enumerate, much less to describe, all the coöperative enterprises launched, conducted, and carried out by the League of Nations in the last decade. We must refer the reader on this point to the mass of official and semiofficial material produced by the League itself and to the many excellent monographs and general surveys which have been published on the subject in all countries, in the United States perhaps more than elsewhere. In the following summary table, in which these activities are classified both according to their main purposes and to the means adopted to achieve them, we have sought to do no more than to indicate their character and to give at least a general idea of their scope.

ACTIVITIES FOR THE REMOVAL OF INTER-
NATIONAL FRICTION

By means of conventions and agreements:

1921 Conventions on freedom of transit and on the *régime* of navigable waterways of international concern.

1923 Protocol concerning arbitration of commercial disputes.

1923 Convention for the simplification of customs formalities.

1923 Convention on the international *régime* of railways.

1923 Convention relating to the transmission in transit of electric power.

1923 Convention relating to the development of hydraulic power.

1925 Convention on inland navigation.

1926 Convention on road traffic.

1927 Convention for the abolition of import and export prohibitions and restrictions.

1927 Convention on the execution of foreign arbitral awards.

1928 Agreements for the abolition of export prohibitions on hides, skins, and bones.

By means of recommendations:

1920 Conference of experts on passports, customs, and transit facilities for travelers.

1921 Barcelona conference on railways and ports.

1926 Second passport conference.

1927 World economic conference.

1927 Conference of press experts.

By the establishment of administrative machinery:

1921 General conference on freedom of communications and transit.

1921 Advisory and technical committee on communications and transit.

1922 Commission on intellectual coöperation.

1924 International institute for the unification of private law.

1926 International institute of intellectual coöperation.

ACTIVITIES FOR THE ACHIEVEMENT OF A COMMON PURPOSE OUTSIDE THE COÖPERATING STATES

By means of conventions and agreements:

1922 Protocols relating to the reconstruction of Austria.

1923 Protocols relating to the financial rehabilitation of Hungary.

1926 Esthonian bank protocol.

1927 Protocols relating to Greek stabilization.

1928 Protocols relating to Bulgarian stabilization.

By means of recommendations:

1922 Warsaw health conference.

By the establishment of administrative machinery:

1920 Campaign against typhus in Poland.

1920 Repatriation of war prisoners.

1921 Relief of Russian refugees.

1922 Reconstruction of Austria.

1923 Financial rehabilitation of Hungary.

1923 Greek refugee settlement commission.

1924 Greek refugee loan.

1925 Danzig loan.

1926 Esthonian loan.

1927 Danzig loan.

1928 Bulgarian stabilization loan.

ACTIVITIES FOR THE IMPROVEMENT OF INTERNAL CONDITIONS BY INTERNATIONAL ACTION

By means of conventions and agreements:

1919 Labor conventions.

1920 Convention on the traffic in women and children.

1920 Labor conventions.
1921 International opium convention.
1921 Labor convention.
1922 Convention on obscene publications.
1925 Opium convention.
1927 International relief union convention.
1928 Convention on economic statistics.
1929 Convention for the suppression of counterfeit currency.

By means of recommendations:

1920 Brussels financial conference.
1921 Conference on the traffic in women and children.
1924 Conference on unfair competition.
1925 Conference for the unification of the formulae of powerful Drugs.
1927 Conference of press experts.
1927 World economic conference.
1927 International relief conference.
1928 Conference on central bank statistics.

By the establishment of administrative machinery:

1920 Provisional Economic and Financial Committee.
1921 Advisory Committee on the traffic in opium.
1923 Economic and Financial Commission.
1923 Interchange of sanitary personnel organized.
1925 Eastern Bureau of the Health Organization.
1924 Malaria Commission.
1925 Legal aid for the poor.
1924 Cancer Commission.
1924 Economic Consultative Committee.
1928 Permanent Central Opium Board.

This table is incomplete and its arrangement may well be criticized as arbitrary on many points. If it convinces the reader, however, of the extraordinary and growing variety of forms of international co-operation initiated or developed by the League, it will have served its only purpose.

That much of the agitation caused by these efforts at international organization is sterile, that many conventions remain unsigned, unratified, and unapplied, and perhaps most recommendations unheeded by those to whom they are addressed, may well be admitted. But if all these efforts were really useless it would be impossible to understand why, as is the case, more and more states should wish to be associated with them even without formally joining the League.

The fact is that they represent the often still unsuccessful but increasingly necessary attempt to organize the world and particularly the European continent into a true economic and social community. Were Europe politically centralized, most of these attempts might be dispensed with, because their objects could and would be achieved more promptly and more fully by national legislation. But as long as states retain their complete political independence, while becoming increasingly interdependent economically and intellectually, international coöperation, wasteful and inefficient as it often is from the administrative point of view, will continue to be and ever more to become a vital necessity for all. The experience reaped in Geneva in the course of all these endeavors is invaluable. Little by little a technique of voluntary intergovernmental coöperation is being devised and perfected, which although unforeseen by the founders of the League, may well become the greatest historical achievement of their successors.

Although, as above remarked, this part of the

League's work also is still primarily European, it is becoming more and more intercontinental. Today already it is no longer an exaggeration to say that no government, be it that of a member or not of the League of Nations, is taking a more active and a more helpful part in the labors of all the conferences, committees, and subcommittees summoned to Geneva than the American Government. And this is after all not surprising. It is merely the inevitable result and indeed the natural expression of the fact that the United States is today one of the greatest World Powers, that is, one of the powers whose association with, interest in, and influence on the rest of the world is greatest.

3. *The Promotion of Peace and Security.*

The execution of the peace treaties is a secondary, an almost accidental, and essentially a transient function of the League. Its relative importance has already appreciably diminished since 1920. The promotion of prosperity and welfare by means of international coöperation, on the contrary, is, as we have just seen, a primary and essential function which is from year to year increasing in scope and variety. As for the prevention of war it remains, of course, the most essential duty of the League.

It was neither in order that a particular piece of administrative machinery be set up to execute the peace treaties, nor even in order that new methods of international coöperation be devised, that men bled and died in millions on the battlefields of Europe for over four terrible years. It was, for the noblest of them, in order that their children might be spared a like catastrophe. And it was to this hope

that the leading statesmen in the belligerent countries and particularly in Great Britain and in the
United States, continually appealed to maintain the
morale of their peoples throughout the struggle.

The League of Nations was created in order that
the solemn pledges then given be not broken. And
fully as it may justify its existence in other fields,
it is on its ability to redeem those pacific pledges
that its fate in history will ultimately depend.

Now, what has the League done, since its foundation, to redeem those pledges? What has been its
contribution to the promotion of peace and security
in Europe and in the world?

The answer to this question of questions, to which
we shall seek briefly to reply in the last part of this
closing chapter, must be given under two headings.
On the one hand, the League of Nations has sought
to prevent the immediate outbreak of hostilities, as
they have threatened mankind from year to year
since 1920, by making full use of its limited present
resources. And on the other hand, it has sought to
enhance these resources in view of future emergencies, by building up new dikes to withstand the flood
of war and by perfecting existing mechanisms for
the peaceful settlement of international disputes.
Let us hastily survey its record in both these fields.

The list of international disputes handled and for
the most part peacefully settled by the League is
extremely long and for the historical student embarrassingly elastic. It is much longer than is generally realized. Even disregarding the legal controversies submitted to the Permanent Court at The
Hague and countless minor difficulties, such as those
occasioned by the execution of the peace treaties, the

Council has been called upon to intervene in one to two more or less serious political disputes every year for the last decade. And this list is elastic, because it is as difficult to define a political dispute worthy of notice as it is to define a fire or a motor accident worthy of headlines in the papers. In all these three cases the loss of life is no decisive criterion. The most dangerous political crisis may be averted, as the most threatening fire extinguished, and the most terrible motor accident avoided, by the prompt and effective intervention of some saving agency. Thus the absence of human or material losses may be the proof of the potency of this agency much more than of the insignificance of the occurrence. No one can assert or deny with certainty that the League has as yet prevented any war which would have broken out, were it not for its intervention. All that can be said is that it has been called upon to settle several disputes which apparently offered at least as grave possibilities of danger as many disputes that have degenerated into wars in the past, and that in all these cases peace has been maintained.

The following summary of thirteen of the most serious conflicts which have been considered by the Council of the League, presented in chronological order, may give an idea of the nature of post-war international difficulties and of the mode of settlement adopted.

In 1920 the British Government, invoking Article 11 of the Covenant according to which it is "the friendly right of each Member of the League to bring to the attention . . . of the Council any circumstance whatever . . . which threatens to disturb international peace, or the good understanding

between nations upon which peace depends . . ."
called the matter of the Aaland Islands to the notice
of the Council. These Baltic Islands, formerly under
the sovereignty of Russia, inhabited by a population of Swedish tongue, were administrated by Finland but claimed by Sweden. Finland was not yet a
member of the League nor Sweden of the Council.
Both states, however, accepted the invitation to
send representatives to the Council to consider the
dispute. After a report by independent legal experts, who refused to allow Finland's contention
that the matter was one of purely domestic concern,
the Council proposed a settlement which was accepted by both parties. The Islands remained with
Finland, but they were demilitarized and their inhabitants assured of a large measure of cultural
autonomy.

In 1920 also, the famous Polish-Lithuanian dispute was for the first time brought before the Council. Poland complained that Lithuanian troops had
crossed the provisional frontier which had been
proposed to, but not yet finally accepted by, both
these two new states. The dispute has gone through
many varied phrases, given rise to many conflicting
claims and counterclaims on the part of the litigants
and to many conciliatory proposals by the Council,
which have invariably been rejected by one of the
two parties or both. The matter is still unsettled but
peace has so far been maintained.

In 1921 the Supreme Council, also acting under
Article 11 of the Covenant, referred the problem of
Upper Silesia to the Council of the League. It
had added that the recommendation of the Council
would be considered binding by the states repre-

sented on the Supreme Council. Here was a dispute
over the execution of a provision of the Treaty of
Versailles which opposed Polish interests, backed by
France, and German interests, supported by Great
Britain. The Council proposed a frontier line to
separate Polish from German Upper Silesia and
established a temporary economic and social *régime*
in the contested area. The Supreme Council accepted the solution and a very detailed convention
was negotiated under the auspices of the League and
accepted by Poland and Germany.

In the same year, the as yet unsettled frontiers
of Albania gave rise to two successive appeals from
that country, which had just been admitted to the
League against alleged encroachments on the part
of her Greek and Yugoslav neighbors, and later to a
request, under Article 11, by the British Government to the Council for intervention in the interest
of peace. The Council, to which Albania and Yugoslavia had been invited to send representatives, met
and reached an agreement as to the common recognition of frontiers and as to the evacuation of the
hitherto contested area by the Yugoslavian troops
which had occupied it.

In 1921 also, another territorial matter was
brought before the Council. Finland requested that
a final decision be reached concerning the status of
Eastern Carelia, a neighboring district of the Soviet
Union, inhabited by a population akin to the Finns,
to which a measure of autonomy had been promised
under the Finno-Russian treaties of peace. The
Soviet Government, declaring the matter to be of
purely Russian concern, refused to discuss it either
at Geneva or at The Hague, to which the Council

had reverted for an advisory opinion. The Court, thereupon, declined to consider the question and the Council refrained from taking any further action.

In 1922 Great Britain brought before the Council a question relating to the promulgation by France in Tunis and in the French zone of Morocco of nationality decrees which, applied to persons in Tunis of Maltese origin and of British allegiance, conflicted with British nationality legislation. The British and French representatives agreed to request the Council to apply to the Permanent Court of International Justice for an advisory opinion as to whether the matter at issue was or was not exclusively a question of domestic jurisdiction. The Court having replied in the negative, a friendly agreement was reached between the two governments.

In 1923 the Council was called upon by the powers represented on the Conference of Ambassadors to settle a Polish-Czechoslovakian frontier delimitation difficulty relating to the Jaworzina district in the Carpathians. After an advisory opinion on a point of law had been sought for by the Council of the Court at The Hague, given by the Court and accepted by the parties, the Council fixed a frontier line on the basis of proposals made by a special boundary commission and urged the parties to negotiate agreements relating to the economic interests of the local population. The parties accepted both the decision regarding the frontier and the additional recommendations and nothing more has been heard of the matter since.

Another question was referred to the Council of the League by the Conference of Ambassadors in

1923. Invoking Article 11 of the Covenant, the Principal Allied Powers, to whom the territory of Memel had been intrusted for final disposition by the Treaty of Versailles, requested the Council to settle the dispute which had arisen between them and Lithuania. This dispute concerned the conditions under which this territory was to be administered by the latter state, to whom the Principal Allied Powers were prepared to cede it. The question, which was of indirect interest to Poland, on account of the Nieman, which flowed through the district, and to Germany, on account of the preponderantly German population of the city of Memel, was settled by an impartial commission set up by the Council under the able chairmanship of Mr. Norman H. Davis, former Undersecretary of State of the United States.

On September 12 of the same year, Greece appealed to the Council in a serious conflict which had broken out between her and Italy. Basing her action on Article 12 to 15 of the Covenant relating to "disputes likely to lead to a rupture," Greece, whose territorial integrity had been violated by the temporary occupation of the Island of Corfu, declared that she was prepared to accept any peaceful settlement proposed either by the League of Nations or by the Conference of Ambassadors. Italy, however, questioned the competence of the Council in the matter and argued that it should be left in her hands and in those of the Conference of Ambassadors. The conflict, as will be remembered, had arisen out of the murder on Greek soil of some Italian officers engaged in fixing the frontier line between Greece and Albania on behalf of the Conference of Ambassadors. Italy had demanded prompt apologies and reparations from Greece and had bombarded and occupied Corfu as a guaranty. The Council, with the moral support of the Assembly, which happened to be sitting at the same time, while refusing to share the Italian views as to the competence of the League, agreed to allow the action undertaken by the Conference of Ambassadors to follow its course. A settlement was soon proposed by the latter body and accepted by the parties. Greece paid the indemnity and submitted to the moral reparations demanded of her, while Italy evacuated Corfu.

In August, 1924, the Council was requested by the British Government to take up the question of the frontier of Iraq under the provisions of the Treaty of Lausanne. This treaty had provided that the said frontier was to be fixed by friendly agreement between Turkey and Great Britain, but that, in case of disagreement, the matter was to be referred to the Council of the League. The Council's action, after much legal and political controversy involving an advisory opinion by the Court, finally led to a negotiated agreement between the two parties. As this action, however, was clearly taken in execution of a peace treaty and not under the provisions of the Covenant dealing with political disputes, its discussion need not detain us here.

The Greco-Bulgarian conflict of October, 1925, on the other hand, was considered and settled by the Council in accordance with Articles 10 and 11 of the Covenant, under which Bulgaria had appealed to the League. The occasion for the conflict was a series of frontier incidents northeast of Salonica, culminating in the invasion of Bulgarian territory by Greek

forces. On the request of the invaded state, the
Council was immediately summoned by the Secretary-General. Even before it assembled three days
later, its Acting President, M. Briand, wired to the
two prospectively belligerent governments remind-
ing them of their solemn obligation under the Covenant not to resort to war and exhorting them to
withdraw their troops behind their respective frontiers. When the Council met, Bulgaria and Greece
being represented, this recommendation was repeated in a more imperative form and a time limit
of sixty hours fixed within which its execution was
to be certified by the two governments concerned.
Both parties complied with the instructions of the
Council and later on accepted its decision relating
to the reparations to be paid and to the measures to
be taken to avoid the renewal of similar incidents.

At the beginning of 1927, the Rumanian Government, having withdrawn the Rumanian member of
the Mixed Arbitral Tribunal set up under the Treaty
of the Trianon for the settlement of the claims of
Hungarian and Rumanian nationals, requested the
Council under Article 11 of the Covenant to allow it
to explain its reasons for so doing. The vexed question of the so-called "Hungarian optants," which
had been before the Council ever since 1923, as an
administrative matter, was thus formally changed
into a political dispute. Since 1927 it has not disappeared from the agenda of the Council. The question involves the rights and interests of Hungarian
landholders in those parts of Rumania which were
formerly Hungarian territory. As rights, Hungary
claims they are entitled to legal protection under the
Treaty of the Trianon, and as interests, they have

been seriously injured by the application of the
Rumanian agrarian law, which has deprived the
claimants both of their property and of a fair indemnity. The Council, whose various conciliatory proposals have heretofore always been rejected by one
of the two parties, seems to have almost exhausted
the possibilities of its action as a mediator. It is now
still awaiting the conclusion of direct negotiations
between the two governments, by means of which it
has urged them repeatedly to reach a mutually acceptable arrangement.

The last political dispute here to be mentioned
was that which broke out in December last between
Bolivia and Paraguay over the Chaco frontier. All
circumstances but one were unfavorable to an ener-
getic action by the League in this case.

Although both states were formally members of
the League and although the military measures reported as having been taken on both sides were
hard to reconcile with the provisions of the Covenant, neither Bolivia nor Paraguay appealed to the
League for intervention. Besides, neither had ever
shown much active interest in the Geneva institution. Moreover, their landlocked, far distant territories bordered on two large countries, one of which
had seceded from the League while the other only
nominally belonged to it. Finally, the specter of the
Monroe Doctrine and the fear of offending American susceptibilities further tended to weaken the
position of the League. However—and that was the
slightly counterbalancing favorable circumstance—
the Council happened to be in session when the news
of the conflict became known; and in the Council
were sitting, beside three Latin-American diplomats,

three foreign ministers representing three of the
Great Powers of Europe.

After some hesitation, the Council decided to take
at least telegraphic action. It cabled to the two
governments, expressing "its full conviction that
the incidents which have occurred between two members of the League of Nations will not become more
serious." It added:

It does not doubt that the two States which, by signing
the Covenant, have solemnly pledged themselves to seek by
pacific means the solution of disputes arising between them,
will have recourse to such methods as would be in conformity with their international agreements and would
appear in the actual circumstances to be the most likely to
ensure, together with the maintenance of peace, the settlement of their dispute.

After much further correspondence with the Bo-
livian and Paraguayan Governments, in which both
states unreservedly accepted the legal premises upon
which the Council's action was based, and not without official contact with Washington, where a Pan-
American Conference happened to be sitting, war
was averted, both prospective belligerents having
accepted the good offices of that Conference. The
satisfaction felt in Geneva over this issue was not
lessened by the competition of the American agency
to which it was primarily due, but on the contrary
enhanced by what was felt to be a most useful and
promising precedent of intercontinental coöperation
in the interests of peace.

Of the thirteen conflicts dealt with by the Council
of the League, eleven arose as a direct or indirect
consequence of the World War; ten were of purely

European origin; and of the three others, only one was entirely foreign to the Old World; nine were frontier disputes.

We may say, therefore, that the Council, in its rôle as an international peacemaker, has in the past been called upon to settle disputes which were mainly, although not exclusively, of a European, territorial, and post-war character. In most of the cases in which a positive solution was found, the Council enjoyed the coöperation of other agencies such as the Supreme Council, the Conference of Ambassadors, or the Pan-American Conference, and in all of them it enjoyed that of both litigant parties themselves. In the only case in which no such co-operation was forthcoming—that of Eastern Carelia —the difficulty remained unsettled. In only one case was coercion threatened, and in none was it found necessary or practicable to apply it. In other words, the Council has throughout acted as a somewhat modest and timid international conciliator, mediator, and arbiter, but never as a world magistrate, majestically enforcing the dictates of justice.

Who could deny, however, that such as it has been its action has been useful? If it has not always been able to prevent violence or to secure the complete triumph of right over might, it has certainly, indisputably, been instrumental in the maintenance of peace. Thus in the most trying times, on the morrow of the greatest war in history, and under the most difficult psychological and political circumstances, it has sought faithfully to fulfil the intentions of the framers of the Covenant. It has done so without the support of the state which had been expected to be its mainstay, both because its head had done most to set up the League and because it was and is the most powerful of the disinterested and the most disinterested of the Great Powers of the world. On this score there is no recrimination but only deep regret in Geneva.

We know that in this country this regret is shared by many and that the measure of success which the League has achieved in its pacificatory mission is begrudged by none. May we not be permitted to look forward to the glorious day on which this regret will be dispelled and on which the League of all Nations will be able, with the full help and for the benefit of all, to build up the temple of lasting peace on the secure foundations of true and uncompromising justice?

In the meanwhile, the League of fifty-four Nations has not been content with settling, as best it could with the instruments at its present disposal, the disputes which have from year to year been brought before it. With a view to the future, it has also been insistently occupied in improving these instruments.

In other words, it has constantly sought to implement and to perfect the machinery which had been somewhat tentatively and loosely set up by the framers of the Covenant in 1919. Let us, before closing, briefly survey these efforts in order to note the points on which progress has been achieved or at least initiated.

The peace-maintaining machinery of the Covenant may be said to be made up of five essential parts:

First, under Articles 10, 11, 12, 13, and 15, the states members of the League bind themselves not to go to war except in certain defined circumstances;

Secondly, under the same Articles they bind themselves to submit their disputes to various impartial authorities of which one, the Permanent Court of International Justice, is expressly provided for under Article 14;

Thirdly, as disputes can only be peacefully and justly settled on the basis of generally recognized rules, as these rules, which form the substance of international law rest largely on treaties, and as treaties may be secret and may be or become unjust, Articles 18, 19, and 20 provided the publicity of all treaties and the abrogation and revision of dangerous treaties;

Fourthly, as even the most sacred pledges may be broken, sanctions for their enforcement are set up under Articles 16 and 17;

Fifthly and finally, as the "Members of the League recognize that the maintenance of Peace requires the reduction of national armaments," plans for such reduction are contemplated under Article 8.

Thus the five essential parts of the Covenant peace machinery may be referred to by the five catchwords of renunciation of war, arbitration, progress of international law, sanctions, and disarmament. Now let us see how each of these five parts have been, in the course of the last decade, carefully examined by the League with a view to their possible application and improvement.

First, as to the renunciation of war: When under Article 10 of the Covenant the members of the League undertook mutually "to respect . . . the territorial integrity and existing political independence" one of another, they very clearly put a ban upon aggressive war in their reciprocal relations. Furthermore, they still more expressly renounced war under Articles 12, 13, and 15. Under Article 12 they agreed "in no case to resort to war until three months" after the decisions of the arbitrators or of the Council to whom they undertook to submit "every dispute likely to lead to a rupture." Under Article 13 they agreed never "to resort to war against the Members of the League which" had complied with the award of a court of arbitration. And finally, under Article 15, section 6, they agreed "not to go to war with any party" which complied with the unanimous recommendations of the Council on the merits of a dispute.

Under these provisions, war and even aggressive war, it is true, remained legitimate, as between members of the League, in a few hypothetical cases. Even then, however, Article 10 still bound the aggressor to respect the territorial integrity of his victim. We may conclude, therefore, that already under the Covenant aggressive war was more than partly outlawed by and for its signatories.

Since 1919 successive Assemblies of the League have repeatedly sought to narrow down these already restrictive provisions. The first Article of the Draft Treaty of Mutual Guarantee of 1923 reads as follows:

The High Contracting Parties solemnly declare that aggressive war is an international crime and severally undertake that no one of them will be guilty of its commission.

In the famous Geneva Protocol of 1924 the signatory states:

. . . asserting that a war of aggression constitutes . . . an international crime . . . agree in no case to resort to war either with one another or against a state which, if occasion arises, accepts all the obligation hereinafter set out, except in case of resistance to acts of aggression or when acting in agreement with the Council or the Assembly of the League of Nations in accordance with the provisions of the Covenant and of the present Protocol.

The Protocol went still farther since, under the provisions of its Article 8, the signatory states undertook to "abstain from any act which might constitute a threat of aggression against another state."

As neither the Draft Treaty of 1923 nor the Protocol of 1924 ever came into force, the Assembly of 1925 unanimously passed a resolution "declaring afresh that a war of aggression should be regarded as an international crime."

In 1927 the following, still more explicit, resolution was adopted by the Assembly at its eighth ordinary session:

The Assembly,

Recognising the solidarity which unites the community of nations;

Being inspired by a firm desire for the maintenance of peace;

Being convinced that a war of aggression can never serve as a means of settling international disputes and is, in consequence, an international crime;

Considering that a solemn renunciation of all wars of aggression would tend to create an atmosphere of general confidence calculated to facilitate the progress of the work undertaken with a view to disarmament;

Declares:
1. That all wars of aggression are, and shall always be, prohibited;
2. That every pacific means must be employed to settle disputes, of every description, which may arise between States.

The Assembly declares that the States Members of the League are under an obligation to conform to these principles.

Finally on September 26, 1928, the Ninth Assembly recommended to the consideration of all states, members or not of the League of Nations, three model treaties of non-aggression. Under Article 1 of all these treaties the High Contracting Parties "mutually undertake that they will in no case attack or invade each other or resort to war against each other," except in the case, first, of legitimate defense; secondly, action in pursuance of Article 16 of the Covenant; and thirdly, action as the result of a decision of the League itself.

These quotations clearly show that Geneva has done her full part in urging the renunciation of war. They show also that, if what we have called the total abstinence pledge method or what might also be called the Coué method of maintaining peace was a sufficient safeguard against war, even the Kellogg Pact might have been held to be superfluous.

The second part of the peace machinery of the Covenant is that which we have referred to as arbitration, in the broadest sense of that elastic term, that is, all methods for the pacific settlement of international disputes.

The Covenant already provided for arbitration proper under Article 13, for the establishment of a

Permanent Court of International Justice under Article 14, and for mediation and report by the Council under Article 15. On this point also, the work of implementing and perfecting the Covenant set in as soon as the League came into existence.

The Statute of the Court was drafted in 1920 and ratified in 1921. The second Assembly having elected the judges, the Court was set up in 1922. In view of its activities the Covenant was amended so as to provide for judicial settlement besides arbitration in the narrow sense as an alternative method for the pacific settlement of international disputes.

Another series of draft amendments to the Covenant had been presented at the first Assembly by the three Scandinavian states to provide for a system of impartial compulsory conciliation. These amendments were not adopted. But ever since 1921, when the second Assembly expressed "its approval of the procedure of conciliation in conformity with the spirit of the Covenant" the League has shown itself increasingly convinced of the importance of perfecting and completing this part of its machinery. In 1922 the Assembly, "with a view to promoting the development of the procedure of conciliation in the case of international disputes," recommended the conclusion of bilateral treaties to that effect. It drafted a model convention relating to the constitution and procedure of conciliation commissions and expressed the hope that their competence "will extend to the greatest number of disputes and that practical application of particular conventions between States . . . will, in the near future, make possible the establishment of a general convention open to the adhesion of all States."

In 1924 a proposal was drafted, which introduced the principle of complete compulsory arbitration. After its rejection, the Assembly of 1925, less ambitious than its predecessors, cautiously called the "attention of States members of the League to the desirability, from the point of view of security, of concluding particular conventions for arbitration or for the judicial settlement of disputes."

As we have seen when dealing with the efforts of Europe to promote national security without the framework of the League, these recommendations to conclude bilateral conciliation and arbitration treaties did not pass unheeded. In 1926 the Assembly, encouraged by the conclusion of the Locarno Treaties, the most precious part of the cargo saved from the shipwreck of the Protocol of 1924, asserted "its conviction that the general ideas embodied in the clauses of the Treaties of Locarno, whereby provision is made for conciliation and arbitration and for security by the mutual guaranteeing of states against any unprovoked aggression, may well be accepted amongst the fundamental rules which should govern the foreign policy of every civilized nation."

Thus, the work of perfecting and multiplying the methods of pacific settlement was pursued by every successive Assembly, until at last, in 1928, a whole code of conciliation, judicial settlement, and arbitration treaties was produced.

In this code there is, on the one hand, the so-called general act open to the signature of any state, whether a member of the League or not, and, on the other, three types of bilateral conventions which are proposed as models to any two states wishing to accept one with respect to another, obligations of conciliation or arbitration and judicial settlement, with or without preliminary conciliation. Under these various instruments every conceivable possibility is offered to states wishing to conclude multilateral or bilateral, complete or only partial, agreements for the pacific settlement of all or only of certain categories of disputes.

By resolution of September 26, 1928, the Assembly

1. Firmly convinced that effective machinery for ensuring the peaceful settlement of international disputes is an essential element in the cause of security and disarmament;

2. Considering that the faithful observance, under the auspices of the League of Nations, of methods of pacific settlement renders possible the settlement of all disputes;

. . . .

8. Invites all States, whether Members of the League or not, and in so far as their existing agreements do not already achieve this end, to accept obligations in pursuance of the above purpose either by becoming parties to the annexed General Act or by concluding particular conventions with individual States in accordance with the model bilateral convention annexed hereto or in such terms as may be deemed appropriate.

Without any attempt at coercion or at forced uniformity, the League of Nations has thus evened the road leading up to the ultimate goal of agreed pacific settlement of all disputes. Toward this goal all states who sincerely wish to renounce war as an instrument of national policy must strive and not before they have all reached it can their resolution bring promise of lasting peace. Thus the ideal of the framers of the Protocol of 1924 may gradually be realized by a process resembling organic growth instead, as they had suggested, of being suddenly imposed by the simultaneous acceptance by all of one and the same system of hard and fast rules.

The more the procedure of arbitral and judicial settlement is perfected and the more generally it is accepted as a method of settling international disputes, the more the need of some universally recognized principles of international law becomes imperative. How can tribunals and courts be expected to insure the reign of justice and peace if there are no laws and no precedents, or worse still, only conflicting laws and precedents to guide them in their decisions?

What little the Covenant contains concerning international agreements was obviously insufficient to meet this growing demand. The League, however, by promoting the negotiation of treaties in the most varied fields soon began to build up a whole series of new legal edifices. But this work of construction was necessarily sporadic and concerned only those states who coöperated in it. Therefore, we are not surprised to find the fifth Assembly calling upon the Council to convene a Committee of Experts "to prepare a provisional list of these subjects of international law, the regulation of which by international agreement would seem to be most desirable and realizable at the present moment." The preamble of the resolution adopted on September 22, 1924 is so significant that I may be allowed to quote it here. It reads as follows:

The Assembly,
Considering that the experience of five years has demonstrated the valuable services which the League of Nations

can render towards rapidly meeting the legislative needs of international relations, and recalling particularly the important conventions already drawn up with respect to international conciliation, communications and transit, the simplification of customs formalities, the recognition of arbitration clauses in commercial contracts, international labor legislation, the suppression of the traffic in women and children, the protection of minorities, as well as the recent resolutions concerning legal assistance for the poor;

Desirous of increasing the contribution of the League of Nations to the progressive codification of international law . . .

requested the Council to promote the preliminary study of this problem.

The Council, as always, acceded to the wish of the Assembly. A committee of legal experts was convened and, after several sessions, many reports, and much discussion, so far proceeded in its delicate task that the Eighth Assembly of 1927 could recommend a further step. On September 27, 1927, it adopted a long resolution on the Codification of International Law from which I shall quote but a few lines:

The Assembly,
. . . .
Considering that it is material for the progress of justice and the maintenance of peace to define, improve and develop international law;

Convinced that it is therefore the duty of the League to make every effort to contribute to the progressive codification of international law;

Observing that, on the basis of the work of the Committee of Experts . . . systematic preparations can be made for a first Codification Conference, the holding of which in 1929 can already be contemplated;

Decides:

1. To submit the following questions for examination by
   a first Conference:
   (a) Nationality,
   (b) Territorial Waters, and
   (c) Responsibility of States for Damage Done in Their
       Territory to the Person or Property of For-
       eigners.

These plans aroused the greatest interest all over
the legal world and nowhere more than in the United
States, where a body of jurists, under the able
leadership of my friend Professor Manley O. Hudson of Harvard University, has already produced
a most useful volume of preliminary suggestions.[7]
When the first Codification Conference meets—it is
now scheduled to assemble at The Hague in March
1930—a very important step toward the organization of peace will have been taken.

Thus, the League, by contribution to the development of international law, is building up and perfecting the third part of its peace machinery.

In the two remaining fields of sanctions and disarmament, its efforts, though not less strenuous,
have so far been appreciably less fruitful.

In the Covenant, sanctions, that is common action
in certain cases to enforce peace against a recalci-
trant state, are provided for under Articles 10 and
16. The origin of Article 10 is distinctly and exclusively Wilsonian, while Article 16 embodies the
original conception of the authors of the British
Phillimore Plan.

[7] Nationality, Responsibility of States, Territorial Waters,
Drafts of Conventions prepared in anticipation of the first Conference on the Codification of International Law (Cambridge,
1929).

During the whole discussion of these Articles in Paris, in 1919, everyone realized both their crucial importance and the extremely delicate character of the problem they were intended to solve. Deprived of all provisions for the enforcement of its fundamental undertakings, the Covenant would not have been accepted by the states of Europe most threatened in their security, as offering a sufficient safeguard against war, nor as a possible basis for disarmament. But, on the other hand, the governments of many other states particularly in America and among the former European neutrals were very reluctant to accept obligations to go to war under any conditions.

The result of these divergent national views and interests was a compromise which completely satisfied no one. As a consequence, we have seen that France and her continental allies, finding no sufficient protection in Articles 10 and 16 of the Covenant, as they were finally adopted, initiated and have pursued a policy of special defensive conventions among themselves. But, as a consequence also, the Senate of the United States, fearful lest the obligations defined under Articles 10 and 16 might carry their country too far into the realm of undesirable entanglements, repudiated the whole scheme.

When the first Assembly met in 1920, France and her continental allies had already decided to look beyond the bounds of the Covenant for protection. Among the other members of the League, the dominant feeling was that Articles 10 and 16, if literally interpreted, imposed obligations which they were unwilling and unable to assume. They were the more anxious to escape such obligations, as they were neither enthusiastic about the terms of the peace which was to be guaranteed, nor indifferent to the dangers which such a guaranty might constitute for the friendly relations they wished in all cases to maintain with the United States. Accordingly they set out to whittle down these obligations. Canada, whose eminent statesman, Sir Robert Borden, had already severely questioned the wisdom of Article 10 at the Peace Conference,[8] proposed in 1920 to delete it altogether. After this attempt had failed, the Canadian delegation endeavored to have its provisions interpreted into harmless insignificance, which was done in 1923.

Although the vote on the resolution thus to interpret Article 10 was not legally binding, Persia having by her veto prevented the necessary unanimity, it was so overwhelming as to be politically decisive.

As for Article 16, it received at the hands of the second Assembly, in 1921, an interpretation so emollient that it reassured the least enterprising of the prospective guarantors but, of course, correspondingly depressed the most threatened of those states who had looked to it for their protection.

This evolution tended to transform the fundamental character of the League. While it had been conceived of originally as primarily a society for the mutual protection of its members against the dangers of aggression, it now seemed to become an association for conference only.

A reaction, however, was not long in setting in. It was soon realized that if the League wished ever to carry out its disarmament program, it could not

[8] D. H. Miller, *op. cit.*, I, 358.

entirely abandon its member states in case of danger. Even the most militaristically inclined governments were prepared to consider the reduction of their national armaments, were it only to relieve their peoples of a crushing financial burden. But, they added, they could consider such a reduction only as the framers of the Covenant themselves, that is, "to the lowest point consistent with national safety and the enforcement by common action of international obligations." If, they argued, the League would or could do nothing to enhance their national safety by common action, they would have to look out for themselves and could not expose their countries to aggression by disarming. And still the Covenant declared that "the maintenance of peace" required "the reduction of armaments." Thus, sanctions having been expelled from Geneva by the rear door, again presented themselves at the front entrance and insistently demanded admittance.

This demand could not remain unheeded, if the League was not to forfeit the confidence of the masses, who, very naturally, have always shown more interest in disarmament than in any other part of its program. Successive attempts were made to meet it, in 1923 by the Draft Treaty of Mutual Guarantee, and in 1924 by the famous Protocol. But these attempts were unsuccessful, for the same reasons as had been those to defend Articles 10 and 16 of the Covenant against the dissolving interpretations which they had received at the hands of the first Assemblies. The states who did not consider themselves particularly threatened from without refused to sacrifice their own peace and security to those of their less fortunate and more heavily armed neighbors. They were the less inclined to do so as they were apt to attribute the latters' insecurity in part at least to what they held to be their unreasonable and provocative policies, which they were reluctant to encourage, but powerless to alter.

Thus armaments and policies based on armaments have in part prevented the development of international sanctions, while the absence of international sanctions, that could be relied on for national security, has in turn been the main obstacle on the road to disarmament.

Several recent circumstances have, however, broken into this vicious circle. The Dawes plan, Locarno, the admission of Germany into the League, the rapid progress of conciliation and arbitration, the general trend of European evolution toward somewhat greater confidence and, last but not least, the increasing coöperation of the United States have appreciably lessened the tension in international relations. Accordingly the prospects for disarmament and for mutual assistance within the League in case of crisis are not quite as gloomy as they were ten and five years ago. It would take more optimism than I can command, however, to say that these prospects are bright today.

Real disarmament will come about only as a result of enhanced national security based on far greater international confidence than as yet obtains in Europe. No Great Power and few minor states will ever willingly reduce their military establishments as long as they have reason to fear that they will be attacked, if weak, and as long as they have no reason confidently to hope that they will be protected, if attacked. The progress of the ideals behind non-aggression treaties such as the Kellogg Pact, the spread of arbitration, and the development of international law which we have noted, are promising symptoms of a wholesome evolution. But that evolution is still in its first stages, which, after all, is not surprising only ten years after the end of the War and less than ten years since the birth of the League of Nations.

CONCLUSION

How Europe Made Peace without America, is
the title of a brilliant book published in 1927 by
that extraordinarily clever American journalist, Mr.
Frank Simonds. "How Europe made peace without
America"— such might also have been the title of
the story which I have sought to tell here. The trend
of events I have recalled is assuredly not such as to
fill Europeans with pride and satisfaction. But on the
other hand I cannot frankly say that it is a record of
which they should feel ashamed.

America is apt to look upon Europe as, in Europe
no less than in America, I am afraid, the younger
generation is apt to look upon the elder. Some interest in their quaintness, some impatience with
their trying inefficiency, perhaps a little condescend-
ing affection, as one remembers childhood days, and
a large measure of compassionate contempt or contemptuous compassion for their inability to adapt
themselves to the exigencies of the day and especially for their blindness to the superiority of their
offspring! Such would seem to be the general attitude of the younger toward the older generation and
of the New toward the Old World.

I am here to defend neither my generation nor my
continent. But as a student of history, it seems to me
that, in all fairness, the spectacle of Europe emerg-
ing from the War and struggling through a morass
of unheard of difficulties made of political prejudices,
economic follies, social aberrations, and ethnical
animosities, toward new forms of national life and
of international coöperation, that this impressive

spectacle, I say, can leave no one indifferent. It should inspire not only pity for the all too numerous failures, nor, of course, any envy for the all too rare successes, but real respect for the tremendous and truly virile efforts that have been made, on the morrow of the most demoralizing and devastating revolution, to restore order and to promote prosperity and progress.

The peace which Europe has made without America is neither as just nor as secure as it might have been. But it is peace and, as such, a sufficient foundation for the further advance of civilization.

In ten years perhaps another European lecturer will again, on this platform, attempt to interest another American audience in the recent evolution of the Old World. May coming events be such as to allow him then to entitle his lectures "How Europe has completed, perfected, and ennobled peace with the help of America!"

That help has, to be sure, never been completely withheld. It was granted generously during the War both on the battlefields and in the rear. It was granted magnificently at the Peace Conference, where it may be said that the name of President Wilson is associated not only with the greatest piece of constructive statesmanship that history has witnessed—I refer to the creation of the League of Nations—but also with every wise and moderate decision that was taken. And since then American help, economic and even political, has ever been forthcoming. It is from year to year forthcoming more boldly and more promisingly, so that I already envy my European successor on this platform his peroration in 1939!

It would be unreasonable for Europe, however, to expect more intimate American coöperation from a progress of altruistic philanthropy. No. Every state has the right to consult primarily its national interest in the formulation of its national policies. But the fundamental unity of mankind is ever becoming more real and more obvious, and mankind is ever becoming more conscious of it. Therefore it is from the progressive realization of the inevitably increasing interdependence of all nations that we must expect the progress of international coöperation.

The evolution of humanity, in spite of all protectionisms and restrictions of migration, tends toward ever closer international solidarity. Of the possibly ensuing entanglements, war is by far the most threatening and the most dangerous. But of them all, war alone perhaps is avoidable. That it is not avoidable by policies of national isolation, recent history should have made abundantly clear. The world policy of the future cannot therefore be a policy of impossible non-entanglement. It will rather be a policy of rational regulation and of peaceful coordination of the inevitable and beneficial entanglements of history. To quote President Wilson once more, in closing these lectures on the trend of international coöperation in a continent which will forever remain his debtor, I would say that for all nations the policy of the future is one of universal, vigilant, constructive, and "continuous superintendence of peace."

INDEX

Aaland Islands, 275

Abyssinia, 193, 226 n.

Africa, 63, 88, 90, 91, 193

Agrarian reform, 81–82, 96, 281

Agricultural populations, and birth rate, 67, 76; and dictatorship, 39–42

Albania, 7, 8, 38, 40, 42, 184, 193, 276

Alliances, 151, 152, 155, 169–170, 175–185, 295; and avoidance of war, 170, 170–171, 172, 185; League and, 170, 171, 172–174, 175–177, 179, 185

Allied and Associated Powers, contrary aims of, 118, 123–124, 126–127, 258; decisions of, 114–115, 116–118; and League, 131

Americas, the, 193

Andrassy, Julius, Count, 30; quoted, 30

Arbitration. *See* Peaceful settlement of disputes

Argentine Republic, 169, 193, 199

Armament, 150–151, 161, 180, 186; of defeated nations, 112, 113, 115, 150, 151; limitation of, 130, 151, 187, 285, 291, 296–299

Asia, 63, 90, 91, 193

Assistance, treaties of mutual. *See* Alliances

Austria, 66, 101, 125, 180, 183, 194; and pacific settlement, 169, 226 n.; republicanization of, 8, 9–10, 16, 22–23, 28–29

See also Austria-Hungary

Austria-Hungary, 18, 22, 85; re-

publicanization of, 8, 9–10, 16, 22–23, 27–30

See also Austria; Hungary

Baldwin, Stanley, 127

Balfour, A. J., 214

Baltic Entente, 183–184

Bauer, Otto, 29 n.

Belgium, 37, 38, 85, 180, 190; alliance of, with France, 177; occupational distribution in, 40, 74; and peaceful settlement, 155, 169, 226 n.; and Ruhr, 118; vital statistics of, 66, 68

Benes, E., 31, 31 n., 180–181, 182

Birth rate, 64–70, 76

Bismarck, O. E. L. von, quoted, 24

Bolivia, 193, 281–282

Borden, Sir Robert, 296

Bourgeois, Léon, 191

Bowman, Isaiah, 128, 181 n., 233; quoted, 127–128

Branting, Hjalmar, 210, 257

Brazil, 169, 192, 193, 195, 199

Briand, Aristide, 125–126, 135, 156, 209, 280

British Empire, 226 n.

Bryce, James, 38

Buchanan, Sir George, 12

Bulgaria, 8, 18, 40, 125, 181, 184, 194; and peaceful settlement, 169, 226 n., 279–280; trade of, 100, 101; vital statistics of, 66

Calonder, F., 237, 238

Canada, 296

Cannes Conference, 125, 126

Capital, loans of, 77, 92, 99–100, 129

Carelia, Eastern, 276, 283
Caribbean America, 63, 64, 91
Cecil, Lord Robert, 191, 197, 205–
206, 210, 212–213, 234, 237,
238, 239, 243, 264, 265
Central America, 90
See also Caribbean America
Charles, Emperor, 22, 28, 29, 182
Chili, 169, 194
China, 88, 192, 226 n.
Clemenceau, Georges, 232
Coal, 83–87
Colombia, 194
Commercial treaties, 132, 140–146,
182
Conference of Ambassadors, 114–
116, 117, 182, 253, 278–279
Coolidge, Calvin, 128; quoted, 162
Coöperation, international, 5, 48–
50, 55, 56–57, and passim;
modes of, 107–110; types of,
under League, 265–271
See also Diplomacy
Corfu, 278–279
Costa Rica, 192, 193
Cuno, C. J. W., 154
Currencies, fluctuating, 142, 143
Czechoslovakia, 30, 31, 40, 66;
alliances of, 178–181, 183;
economic state of, 85, 98, 101;
and pacific settlement, 169,
179, 277

Dandurand, Raoul, 257
Danzig, 3, 113, 115
Daszynski, I., 33
David, Edward, quoted, 23
Davis, Norman H., 278
Dawes Commission, 128, 129, 298
Democracy, 37, 55; crisis of, 36–
38, 43–44, 46–47; and diplo-
macy, 53–54
Denmark, 40, 66, 74, 169, 226 n.
Dictatorships, 36, 37–46; diplo-
macy of, 50–52, 54–55; eco-

nomic structure and, 39–44,
46; war and, 39, 43–44
Diplomacy, 207, 227; and democracy, 53–54; of dictators, 50–
52, 54–55; open, 52, 54, 55
Disarmament. See Armament,
limitation of
Drummond, Sir Eric, 215 n.
Durand, Dana, 195

Ebert, Friedrich, 23, 24
Economic Conference, World,
142–145
Economic interdependence, 4, 5,
47, 260–263, 271, 302
Economic interests, and foreign
affairs, 56–57
See also Prosperity
Economic self-sufficiency, 5, 94,
132, 141–142, 147, 260
Economic structure, 73–75; and
dictatorships, 39–44, 46
Ecuador, 192, 193
England and Wales, occupational
distribution in, 74; vital sta-
tistics of, 66, 68, 70
See also Great Britain
Erkelenz, A., 24 n.
Erzberger, Matthias, 18
Esthonia, 30, 40, 66, 169, 183,
226 n.
Ethiopia, 169
Europe, foreign trade of, 95, 98,
100, 102, 103; population of,
60–72, 76, 77–78; production
in, 78, 80–82, 84, 88–92
Experts' Committee of 1929, 130

Finland, 30, 34, 98, 183; occupational distribution in, 40, 74;
and peaceful settlement, 169,
226 n., 275, 276; vital statistics of, 66
Fisher, H. A. L., 9 n.; quoted, 9 n.
Foodstuffs, 79–83, 87–89, 96

Foreign affairs, and domestic policy, 50, 52–53, 55; economic interests and, 56–57

France, 32, 38, 85, 151, 201; occupational distribution in, 40, 74; and peaceful settlement, 155, 169, 226 n.; relations of, with Germany, 118, 123–124, 126, 127, 155, 190; relations of, with Great Britain, 118, 124, 126–127, 128, 135, 136, 175–176, 178, 180, 277; and security, 150, 175–176, 177–180, 295; trade of, 98, 101; and treaty execution, 118, 123–124; vital statistics of, 62, 66, 68, 69, 70

Geneva, seat of League, 229–244
Geneva Protocol, 72, 159, 286–287, 291–292, 297
Genoa Conference, 125–126, 132–137, 145, 153
Germany, 85, 113, 134, 169, 180, 276, 278; and Belgium, 118, 155; and coöperation, 130, 154–156, 179, 198, 201, 221, 244, 298; foreign trade of, 100–102; occupational distribution in, 40, 74; occupied territory of, 118, 123–124, 126, 127–128, 130; relations of, with France, 118, 123–124, 126, 127, 155, 190; republicanization of, 8, 9–10, 16–27, 16 n.; and Russia, 100, 101, 126, 136; vital statistics of, 66, 68, 69, 70
Gilbert, S. Parker, 129
Graham, M. W., 12
Great Britain, 40, 201, 220; and coal, 83, 85; democracy in, 37, 38; foreign trade of, 100–102, 147; and pacific settlement, 155, 169, 226 n., 279; relations of, with France, 118, 124, 126–127, 128, 135, 136, 175–176, 178, 180, 277; and treaty execution, 118, 124
Great Powers, power of, in League Council, 197–200
Greece, 8, 40, 101, 183, 184, 276; and pacific settlement, 169, 278–279, 279–280; vital statistics of, 66, 69
Guarantee, Draft Treaty of Mutual, 286, 287, 297; treaties of: see Alliances
Guatemala, 169

Haase, Hugo, quoted, 21–22
Haiti, 169, 226 n.
Haussmann, Konrad, 21
Hedjaz, 192
Hindenburg, Paul von, 26; quoted, 26
Holland. See Netherlands
Hoover, Herbert, quoted, 161
House, E. M., 190, 205, 232, 233, 236, 237, 238, 243, 263, 265
Hudson, Manley O., 294
Hughes, Charles E., 128, 154
Hungary, 40, 81, 85, 101, 125, 184, 194; dictatorship in, 38, 42; Little Entente and, 180–181, 182; and pacific settlement, 169, 280–281; republicanization of, 7, 8, 28, 29; vital statistics of, 66
See also Austria-Hungary
Hymans, Paul, 173, 191, 234, 238, 239

Industry, 74–75, 97; and birth rate, 67–68, 76
Interdependence, economic, 4, 5, 47, 260–263, 271, 302
International bureaux, 137–140
International law, 292–294

Iraq, 279
Ireland, 3, 7, 40, 66, 69, 95, 101, 169, 193
Italy, 38, 42, 55, 101, 118, 151, 180, 183, 184; occupational distribution in, 40, 74; and peaceful settlement, 155, 169, 226 n., 278–279; vital statistics of, 66

Japan, 151, 156, 169
Jusserand, J., 154

Karolyi, M., Count, 28
Kellogg Pact, 156–165, 169, 288
Kerensky, Alexander F., 8; quoted, 10–11, 13–15, 15–16
Kramar, Karel, 31, 239
Kuczynski, R. R., 68, 69; quoted, 69–70

Labor Organization, International, 223–224
Landsberg, Otto, quoted, 24
Larnaude, 238
Latvia, 30, 40, 66, 169, 183
Lausanne, Treaty of, 279
League of Nations, 110, 125, 130, 301; advisory commissions of, 219, 221–223; and alliances, 170, 171, 172–174, 175–177, 179, 185; Assembly of, 202, 205–211; coöperation of non-member states with, 195, 223, 272; Council of, 196–204, 208, 210, 214, 283, 289; defeated states in, 125, 130, 194, 198, 201, 221, 244, 258–259, 298; and disarmament, 296–297; and economic coöperation, 131, 137, 137–139, 142–146, 262–272; and execution of treaties, 247–260, 279; leading statesmen attending, 200–204, 218;

members of, 189–196; organ of public opinion, 205, 206–208, 209, 210, 256, 257; peace-maintaining machinery of, 284–285, 288–289, 294; and population growth, 72; and promotion of peace, 272–294; seat of, 229–244; Secretariat of, 211–221, 241; and security, 152, 187, 263, 290, 291, 295–299
Liberia, 169
Lippmann, Walter, 233
Lithuania, 30, 38, 40, 42, 66, 183; and peaceful settlement, 169, 226, 226 n., 275, 278; trade of, 98
Little Entente, 180–183, 184
Lloyd George, David, 126, 133–136, 158, 175, 178, 232; quoted, 133–134, 135, 136, 153–154
Locarno treaties, 130, 154–156, 179, 290, 298
London Conference, 128–129
Loveday, A., 62, 77, 78, 79, 87, 88, 90
Ludendorff, Erich, 18, 21, 22
Luxemburg, 40, 66, 193

MacDonald, Ramsay, 128, 129; quoted, 128–129
Makino, Baron, 238
Mandates, 255, 256
Marx, Wilhelm, quoted, 129
Masaryk, T. G., 31; quoted, 37
Max von Baden, Prince, 16–19, 20, 22, 23–24, 23 n.; quoted, 17, 19, 21
Memel, 113, 118, 278
Mexico, 191, 193, 195
Michael, Grand Duke, 11–12
Migration, 64, 70, 73
Miliukov, Paul, 12–13, 15; quoted, 13

Miller, David Hunter, quoted, 173–174, 237–238
Minorities, 49, 180–181, 181 n., 253, 255, 257
Mommsen, W., 24 n.
Monarchy, 8–9, 17, 22, 24, 27
Monnet, Jean, 241
Monroe Doctrine, 7, 174, 177, 281
Morrison, Charles Clayton, quoted, 160–161
Most-favored-nation treatment, 145–146
Mosul, 220
Motta, Giuseppe, quoted, 243–244
Mousset, A., 181 n.
Murray, Gilbert, 210

Nansen, Fridtjof, 210
Nationalism, 5, 10, 29, 34, 35, 51, 262
    See also Self-determination
Netherlands, 38, 40, 66, 74, 85, 169, 194, 226 n.
Neutrality, 236, 237–238, 240; treaties of, 152
Nicholas II, 10, 11
Non-aggression treaties, 150, 152–157, 159, 179, 288
North America, foreign trade of, 95, 97, 98, 99; population of, 63–64, 77–78; production in, 78, 80, 81, 82, 84, 88–92
Norway, 40, 66, 68, 74, 169, 226 n.

Occupational groups, population by, 40, 73–74
Oceania, 63, 88, 91
Orlando, V. E., 232, 238

Paderewski, Ignace, 33
Pan-American Conference, 282
Paraguay, 169, 281–282
Patterson, E. M., 57

Payments, international, balance of, 77, 99
Peaceful settlement of disputes, 150, 152, 155, 157, 162, 165–169, 179, 182, 186, 285, 285–292; compulsory, 226–227, 226 n.
Peace treaties, 112, 113, 115, 123, 247, 251–253; execution of, 108, 112–120, 247–260, 279
Permanent Court of International Justice, 166, 224–229, 285, 289
Persia, 194, 296
Peru, 169, 193
Pessoa, Epitacio da Silva, 197
Phillimore Plan, 172, 190, 205, 263, 265, 294
Pilsudski, Joseph, 33
Poincaré, Raymond, 126, 127, 128, 135, 154, 178
Poland, 30, 184, 199; alliances of, 178, 179, 180, 183; economic state of, 40, 81, 85, 98, 101; form of government of, 32–34, 38, 42; and pacific settlement, 169, 275, 276, 277, 278
Politis, Nicholas, 210
Population, 60–76, 77–78; migration of, 64, 70, 73
Portugal, 38, 40, 66, 69, 101, 169, 226 n.
Procopé, H. J., 257
Producers' associations, 141
Production, 76–93; of coal, 83–87; of foodstuffs, 79–83, 87–89; of raw materials, 83–87, 89–91
Prosperity, 107, 131–147; League and, 262–272; subordinated to security, 5, 94, 132, 141–142, 147
    See also Economic interests
Public opinion, 224; expressed by

League, 205, 206–208, 209, 210, 256, 257

Rapallo agreement, 126
Raw materials, 83–87, 89–91
Reparation, 122, 128–130, 150
Republican institutions, 5–10, 35–36, 37, 50; in Austria, 8, 9–10, 16, 22–23, 27–30; in Eastern Europe, 31–35; in Germany, 8, 9–10, 16–27; in Russia, 8, 9–16; War and, 8–9, 25, 29, 35; Wilson and, 19, 20, 21, 22, 23, 25, 29, 30
Rhineland, 115 n.; occupation of, 123–124
Ruhr, occupation of, 118, 126, 127–128, 130
Rumania, 66, 181 n., 184; alliances of, 179, 180, 181, 183; economic state of, 40, 81, 85, 100; and pacific settlement, 169, 179, 280–281
Russia, 61, 183, 193, 276; and coöperation, 120–121, 126, 132, 135–136, 147, 153, 195; economic state of, 40, 81, 85, 88, 91, 92, 98, 100, 101; form of government of, 8, 9–16, 34, 35, 38, 43, 47; vital statistics of, 62, 63, 66

Saar territory, 3, 255, 257
Salter, Sir Arthur, 57 n.; quoted, 143
Salvador, 194
Sanctions, 162, 285, 294–298
San Domingo, 193
Scheidemann, P., 18, 19, 21, 23 n.
Scotland, 66, 74
    See also Great Britain
Security, 53, 72, 107, 134, 148–186; League and, 152, 187, 263, 290, 291, 295–299; pros-

perity subordinated to, 5, 94, 132, 141–142, 147
    See also Alliances; Non-aggression treaties; Peaceful settlement of disputes
Self-determination, 28, 29, 49
    See also Nationalism
Serbia, 28
Shotwell, James T., 163–164; quoted, 163
Siam, 169
Simonds, Frank, 126 n., 300
Smuts, J. C., 197, 200, 205–206, 207, 210, 238, 250, 256, 264; quoted, 200, 206, 250, 264
Social forces, control of, 46–48
South America, 63, 91
Spa Conference, 124
Spain, 38, 40, 55, 66, 85, 101, 169, 194, 199
Stefanik, M. R., 31
Stresemann, Gustav, 257
Supreme Council, 115–116, 117, 124, 253
Sweden, 40, 66, 68, 74, 194; and pacific settlement, 169, 226 n., 275
Swierzynski, Josef, 32–33
Switzerland, 38, 40, 66, 68, 74; and League, 235–238, 239–240, 242; and pacific settlement, 169, 226 n.

Tardieu, André, 175
Tariff and customs, 86, 97, 141–147, 186, 266
Theunis, George, quoted, 57
Toynbee, Arnold J., 113; quoted, 113–115
Trade, international, 4, 93–104; treaties concerning, 132, 140–146, 182
Treaties, commercial, 132, 140–146, 182; revision of, 72, 248–249, 249, 285

Trianon, Treaty of the, 181, 280
Turkey, 8, 184, 195, 220, 279

United States of America, 169,
229, 295, 296; and coöperation with Europe, 126, 132,
156, 163, 192, 193, 195, 198,
272, 298, 301–302; trade of,
99, 100–103; vital statistics
of, 66, 78
Upper Silesia, 275–276
Uruguay, 169, 226 n.
U.S.S.R. *See* Russia

Venezuela, 194
Venizelos, Eleutherios, 239
Versailles, Treaty of, 123
See also Peace treaties
Vesnitch, Milenko, 239

Warburg, Max, 18
War of 1914–18, 121–122; and
dictatorships, 39, 43–44; and
population, 64, 69; and republicanization, 8–9, 25, 29,
35
Washington Conference, 125–126,
151
William II, 17, 18, 22, 23, 24, 25;
quoted, 25 n.
Wilson, Woodrow, 174, 190, 191,
205, 294, 301, 302; quoted,
171, 172, 191, 243, 248–249,
302; on alliances, 170–173,
175–177, 185; Fourteen
Points of, 18; on purpose of
League, 248–250, 263, 265;
and republicanism, 19, 20, 21,
22, 23, 25, 29, 30; and seat
of League, 232–235, 237, 239,
242–244

Yugoslavia, 181 n., 184; alliances
of, 179, 180, 181, 183; economic state of, 40, 98; form
of government in, 7, 38, 42;
and pacific settlement, 169,
179, 276